Why the Haves Come Out Ahead

Why the Haves
Come Out Ahead

The Classic Essay and New Observations

Marc Galanter

with commentary by Shauhin A. Talesh and Robert W. Gordon

QUID PRO BOOKS
New Orleans, Louisiana

Portions originally published in 1974 by the *Law & Society Review* and in 2006 by the *Buffalo Law Review*. For the 1974 article, originally published as "Why the 'Haves' Come Out Ahead: Speculations on the Limits of Legal Change," permission to reprint has been granted by the Law and Society Association; for the 2006 article, originally published as "Planet of the APs: Reflections on the Scale of Law and its Users," permission to reprint has been granted by the *Buffalo Law Review*.

Published in 2014 by Quid Pro Books, as part of the *Classics of Law & Society* Series.

ISBN 978-1-61027-241-4 (pbk)
ISBN 978-1-61027-240-7 (hbk)
ISBN 978-1-61027-242-1 (ebk)

QUID PRO BOOKS
5860 Citrus Blvd.
Suite D-101
New Orleans, Louisiana 70123
www.quidprobooks.com

Publisher's Cataloging in Publication

Galanter, Marc.
 Why the Haves Come Out Ahead: The Classic Essay and New Observations / Marc Galanter.
  p. cm. — (Classics of law and society)
 Includes bibliographical references and index.
 ISBN 978-1-61027-241-4 (pbk)
1. Courts—United States. 2. Justice, Administration of—Social aspects—United States. 3. Lawyers—United States. I. Talesh, Shauhin A. II. Gordon, Robert W. III. Title. IV. Series.

KF8700 .G81 2014   357.38'1.543—dc22
                                                     2014622784

Frontispiece drawing, "The Fool Blindfolding Justice," is attributed to Albrecht Dürer, 1494, as a woodcut illustrating Sebastian Brant's *The Ship of Fools*, printed 1497 in Basel, Switzerland. Image courtesy of the Beinecke Rare Book and Manuscript Library, Yale University. Author photograph on back cover inset is © 2014 by Eve Galanter, used by permission.

Second paperback printing, September 2014.

CONTENTS

Acknowledgments

I am grateful to the Law and Society Association and to the *Buffalo Law Review* for permission to reprint the "Haves" essay and its "APs" sequel. I would like to acknowledge again the many colleagues who generously provided helpful and stimulating responses to the early versions of this material.

New translations of the "Haves" into Portuguese by Ana Catalina Chasin and into French by Liora Israel and Liliane Umubyeyi stirred me to consider its applicability in different cultural settings as well as to a different time. Paolo Alves da Silva helped by spotting difficulties for someone coming to the "Haves" from an unfamiliar setting. In preparing the new Introduction, I was advised by my longtime colleague Stewart Macaulay, who provided a transfusion of current American developments. I am reassured by Shauhin Talesh's confidence in its continuing relevance and I salute with gratitude Robert Gordon for extending the analysis into the present and beyond. Alan Childress of Quid Pro Books came up with the idea of putting the "Haves" into a little book and patiently and creatively guided me through the production process.

The continued appreciation of the "Haves" essay is a source of great satisfaction; 2014 America is in some ways quite remote from the early 1970s America in which it took shape. As time went on I became aware that the typical contemporary occupant of the repeat player role was a very different sort of entity than the typical one-shotter—and perhaps quite different from the repeat player of earlier times and other places. The most significant haves and repeat players on the current American scene are not persons at all except to minds overly susceptible to legal fiction. "Planet of the APs," the companion piece reprinted here, revisits the judicial/policy arena with an emphasis on artificial persons as the current incarnation of haves and repeat players in the legal game. These categories are not exactly the same but in contemporary society they display a deep connection.

M.G.

Madison, Wisconsin
July, 2014

i

FOREWORD

Why Marc Galanter's "Haves" Article is One of the Most Influential Pieces of Legal Scholarship Ever Written

Shauhin A. Talesh

A few of the adjectives that I use when describing Marc Galanter's article published in 1974, entitled *Why the "Haves" Come Out Ahead: Speculations on the Limits of Legal Change*, include seminal, blockbuster, canonical, game-changing, extraordinary, pivotal, and noteworthy. But do not take my word for it. Consider for a moment the article's place in the history of legal scholarship. In 1996, an empirical study of the most-cited law review articles of all time revealed that Galanter's article placed thirteenth (Shapiro 1996).[1] The Social Science Citation Index has named the article "a citation classic." Galanter's article was included in the 2006 volume entitled "The Canon of American Legal Thought" (Kennedy & Fisher 2006). Notably, the introduction to that volume considered the article's place in the development of American legal thought in the 20th century. For the article's 25th anniversary, the *Law & Society Review* published a symposium volume of articles dedicated to highlighting extensions and elaborations of the original article. In addition to being cited by numerous courts in the United States, Galanter's article has been translated into Italian, Dutch, Spanish, Chinese, French, and Portuguese, among other languages.

Aside from the article's impact on scholarly and policy discourse, the article impacts the training and education of students interested in studying law. Galanter's article is assigned in virtually every law and society or sociology of law undergraduate and graduate course in the United States. The article is cited in dozens of Civil Procedure casebooks that law professors use to teach first year law students. As we reach the forty year anniversary of this article's publication, I reach one uncontroverted conclusion: this article is one of the most influential pieces of legal scholarship ever written.

In *Why the "Haves" Come Out Ahead*, Marc Galanter explained how "repeat players," i.e., those persons and organizations that anticipate having repeat litigation and have resources to pursue long-term interests, shape the development of law and engage in a litigation game quite differently than do "one-shotters," i.e., those persons and organizations that deal with the legal system infrequently. Moving beyond legal formalism, Galanter's article provides a typology that highlights the various litigation configurations among one-shotters and repeat players: one-

---

[1] An updated version of this study revealed it is currently the 37th most-cited law review article (Shapiro & Pearse 2012). Over the years, it has often been regarded as one of the most-cited law review articles not involving constitutional law.

shotters versus repeat players, repeat players versus one-shotters, one-shotters versus one-shotters, and repeat players versus repeat players.

Galanter noted that repeat players (often large bureaucratic organizations) have long-term strategic interests beyond the immediate monetary stakes of an individual dispute. Specifically, repeat players play the odds in their repetitive interactions and engagements by settling cases that are likely to produce adverse precedent and litigating cases that are likely to produce rules that promote their interests. Factors that influence party decisions whether to litigate or settle include assessments of the likelihood of success, the resources available, and the costs of continuing litigation. By filtering cases in which courts develop law, repeat players secure legal interpretations that favor their interests and impede the ability for one-shotters to achieve significant social reforms through the legal system. Galanter's framework is significant because it highlights how unequal resources and incentives of parties may allow repeat players to control and determine the content of law. As a result, repeat players are able to influence the content and meaning of law.

By analyzing situations in which repeat players gain advantages in the legal system, Galanter set out an important agenda for legal scholars, sociologists, political scientists, and economists interested in examining (1) the law's capacity to produce social change, (2) the limits of the legal system to achieve redistributive outcomes, (3) the advantages and disadvantages of alternative and conventional legal procedures, (4) law and inequality, and (5) the gap between the law on the books and the law in action. Scholars have been exploring these and other questions for the past forty years in a variety of areas (Glenn 2003; Kritzer & Silbey 2003; Talesh 2013). Let me briefly highlight the multifaceted directions several generations of scholars and legal actors have taken the article.

Scholars empirically study and analyze the one-shotter v. repeat player framework in relation to courts. In particular, the various structural advantages repeat players enjoy in the legal system that Galanter emphasizes—namely, greater access to resources, information, specialists, reduced start-up costs, long-run strategic interests, and development of informal facilitative relationships with institutional incumbents—provide a valuable set of variables to explore. Empirical studies demonstrate that repeat player litigants with substantial organizational resources and strength are much more likely to win in the federal courts of appeals than one-shot litigants that have fewer resources (Songer et al. 1999). Another empirical study demonstrates that litigation resources are much more strongly related to success in the courts of appeals than in either the United State Supreme Court or state supreme courts (Songer & Sheehan 1992). With regard to state supreme courts, stronger parties, especially larger governmental units, achieve an advantage over weaker parties, though the advantage generally is rather small (Wheeler et al. 1987).

Research generated from Galanter's article is not limited to the United States, but shapes how scholars examine courts in other countries. For example, Szmer and colleagues examined the impact of lawyer capability on the decision making of the Supreme Court of Canada and found that litigation experience and litigation team size influenced Canadian court decision making (Szmer et al. 2007). A comparative analysis of 14,000 civil cases in the United States and United

Kingdom across a variety of disputing forums reveals that one important effect of lawyer representation is increased formality, which sometimes works to disadvantage people who attempt to represent themselves (Sandefur 2005). Studies of the Philippine Supreme Court (Haynie 1994, 1995; Haynie et al. 2001), the High Court of Australia (Willis & Sheehan 1999; Smyth 2000), the Court of Appeal of England and Wales (Atkins 1991), the Indian Supreme Court (Haynie et al. 2001), the South African Supreme Court (Haynie et al. 2001), and the Tanzanian Court of Appeals (Haynie et al. 2001) all examine outcomes under the "party capability theory" that Galanter set forth years ago. These studies provide general support for the proposition that in the context of appellate litigation, the "Haves" come out ahead against weaker parties because they have tangible and intangible resource advantages.

Party resource advantages, however, need not lie only with private actors. Other research demonstrates how that advantage lies even more with governments than business parties (Kritzer 2003). Kritzer's study highlights how the government does not merely have greater resources and experience, but has a fundamental advantage since it sets the rules by which cases are brought and decisions are made. Moreover, it is government officials such as judges who make the decisions. Other empirical studies focus on the pivotal role that lawyers play among Haves and Have-nots. A randomized experimental evaluation of a legal assistance program for low-income tenants shows that the provision of legal counsel produces large differences in outcomes for low-income tenants in housing court, independent of the merits of the case (Seron et al. 2001). Quite apart from examining the state of and resource capacity of different litigants, one study demonstrates that lawyers can be viewed as repeat players who affect judicial outcomes (McGuire 1995). While Galanter's article and its progeny mapped the dilemmas of judicially created common law rules, others have expanded the analysis to social reform legislation designed to address a specific social problem or protect disadvantaged interests (Albiston 1999). Thus, aside from traditional theories of lobbying, campaign contributions and agency capture, ongoing research using Galanter's typology over the past forty years reveals how repeat players are able to influence judicial decisions and social reform legislation.

Scholars also adopt Galanter's framework, however, when studying "court-appended systems," Galanter's term for referring to state and federal court-connected alternative dispute resolution (ADR) programs and private voluntary or mandatory ADR programs (see Talesh 2013 for summary). Amidst the challenges of using the formal court system to resolve conflicts, internal grievance and alternative dispute resolution are increasingly the forums for resolving potential legal disputes (Galanter & Lande 1992; Sutton et al. 1994; Edelman & Suchman 1999; Menkel-Meadow 1999). The increasing privatization of dispute resolution by organizations is supported and approved by legislatures (Talesh 2009, 2013, 2015) and courts across the United States (Edelman & Talesh 2011). Empirical studies in these forums that specifically use Galanter's framework focus on variation in complainants' success rates (Hanningan 1977; Bingham 1998; Bingham and Sarraf 2000; Eisenberg & Hill 2003; Hirsh 2008; Colvin 2011), the influence of occupational prestige and experience (Kinsey & Stalans 1999; Hirsh 2008), lawyer representation (Bingham 1997), legal resources (Steele 1974; Burstein 1989;

Bingham 1997; Hirsh 2008) and complaint handlers' decision making (Edelman, Erlanger & Lande 1993; Gilad 2010).

In addition to analyzing these mechanisms, scholars debate whether outcomes are better for one-shotters or repeat players in alternative forums. Moreover, policy debates concerning reforming alternative dispute resolution structures are often framed using Galanter's framework (Stone 1996; Menkel-Meadow 1999; Cole 2001; Talesh 2012, 2013). In sum, in addition to using Galanter's framework when evaluating party interaction with public legal institutions, scholars use his framework when examining private disputing forums.

But what about in the 21st century? How has the relationship between one-shotters and repeat players changed, if at all, amidst the move toward public-private partnerships and the contracting out of rights to private and quasi-private adjudicatory regimes? Surprisingly, although it is well-established that consumers and other aggrieved parties such as employees and shareholders are adjudicating public legal rights through internal grievance and alternative dispute resolution forums operated by private actors with the blessing of courts and legislatures, little empirical research addresses *how* these disputing forums are created, how do they operate, and in particular, what is the process through which the meaning of law is constructed through different organizational dispute resolution structures. Galanter on occasion has urged for more research on these very issues (Galanter & Lande 1992).

My own work attempts to synthesize these two strands of research that spawned from Galanter's seminal article concerning repeat player influence among public and private legal institutions. Rather than examining repeat player influence over public legal institutions and private dispute resolution structures separately, my research for the past decade tries to articulate a framework for understanding how the Haves come out ahead in the 21st century. As the boundaries between public and private become increasingly blurred, my empirical research suggests that the Haves create a private legal order, then influence the public legal order, in order to utilize and maintain a private legal order (Talesh 2009, 2012, 2013).

In response to powerful consumer protection laws aimed at manufacturers standing behind their warranties issued to consumers, my research shows how automobile manufacturers first created internal dispute resolution structures to adjudicate public legal rights outside the judicial process and then ceded control of these structures to third-party dispute resolution organizations for legitimacy purposes (Talesh 2009, 2013). The legislature ultimately codified these privatized adjudicatory systems into law and afforded considerable deference to these quasi-private and quasi-public regimes. Thus, I demonstrate a connection between the Haves creating a private disputing regime and influencing public legal institutions such as courts and legislatures. By analyzing how the quintessential repeat player—organizations—legalize their disputes themselves while also interacting with legislatures and courts, I offer a unique view into the processes and mechanisms through which law codified in public legal institutions is flowing from law that is created among and within organizations. Understanding how organizational repeat player influence converges in both spaces simultaneously is particularly important given the turn toward public-private partnerships in society.

Through participant observation and interviews, I continued my analysis by comparing how two different alternative dispute resolution forums (one created and administered by private organizations in California, and the other administered and run by the state of Vermont) operating outside the court system resolve consumer disputes. Unlike the single-arbitrator system in the private dispute resolution programs, Vermont uses an arbitration board consisting of a five-person panel of arbitrators (three citizens, an automotive dealer representative, and a technical expert). I find that the institutional design of dispute resolution, and how business and consumer values and perspectives are translated by field actors in different dispute resolution systems, leads to two different meanings of law operating in California and Vermont. Managerial and business values of rationality, efficiency, and discretion flow into law operating in California's private dispute resolution structures primarily through an arbitration training and socialization process conducted by third-party administrators hired by automobile manufacturers to run their lemon law arbitration program (Talesh 2012). The institutional context socializes arbitrators to ignore consumer emotion and narrows the fact-finding role of arbitrators to a passive arbiter reliant on parties to present facts. As a result, arbitrators are taught to adjudicate cases not in the shadow of the formal lemon law on the books, but in the shadow of a managerialized lemon law replete with its *own* rules, procedures, and construction of law that changes the meaning of consumer protection. Moreover, as business values flow through the disputing structure, organizational repeat players gain subtle opportunities for advantages through the operation of California dispute resolution structures.

Vermont's vastly different dispute resolution system has far less tendency than the process in California to introduce business values into the meaning and operation of lemon laws. To the extent business values are introduced into the process by the presence of dealer and technical expert board members, they are balanced with competing consumer logics by the presence of citizen panel members and a state administrator. Rather than emphasizing professional training and socialization, Vermont's structure illustrates how participatory representation, an inquisitorial fact-finding approach, and balancing consumer and business perspectives in the decision-making process can help curb repeat player advantages. In terms of consumer outcomes in these hearings, consumers do far worse in private than state-run disputing structures (Talesh 2012).

Thus, my own work builds upon and elaborates Galanter's work and offers an updated account of the relationship between repeat players and one-shotters in the 21st century. In a world where private actors are increasingly involved in handling functions traditionally run by the government, the Haves no longer simply play for favorable rules in the public arena, but rather play for removing the entire disputing game from the public arena into the private arena, actively create the terms of legal compliance, and reshape the meaning of consumer rights and remedies. This is a critical and as yet unrecognized way in which the Haves come out ahead. However, contrary to most studies that demonstrate how repeat players gain advantages in disputing structures, my comparative research design also allows me to explore how dispute resolution structures can also inhibit repeat player advantages. Simply stated, the institutional design can facilitate and inhibit repeat player advantages.

Galanter's article did not just provide us with a typology and vocabulary that has become part of the lexicon of law, it set forth a wide-reaching research agenda that has shaped the thinking of scholars and policymakers. More research is needed to explore how different dispute resolution systems with varying degrees of business and state involvement operate on the ground and interpret and implement law. If studies building upon Galanter's work have shown us anything, it is that there is great variation in when, whether, and how the Haves come out ahead. While much work has been done, scholars should continue to learn more about what is happening on the ground when Haves and Have-nots interact in legal settings.

In addition to spurring several decades of exciting and important research, *Why the "Haves" Come Out Ahead* has achieved canonical stature within college and university courses. I had the pleasure of being assigned the article as part of my undergraduate coursework, in law school, and during my doctoral studies. Having moved into academia, I now assign the article to my first-year law students every year when I teach Procedural Analysis.[2] Why? In most procedure courses, students learn the language, structure, and interpretation of the complex rules governing the operation of the American federal civil justice system. Students analyze cases and problems concerning when, where, and whether to bring a lawsuit, against whom to bring the action, and what procedural options are available to respond strategically to the changing circumstances as the lawsuit proceeds. At its core, the course is concerned with the lawyer's vast array of procedural options and maneuvers in bringing or defending a lawsuit. Certain themes generally prevail throughout a procedure course, including how should procedural systems balance justice and efficiency, what does procedural fairness mean in different contexts, and how does procedural fairness impact substantive fairness.

I assign Galanter's article because it succinctly conveys what procedure professors have emphasized to students for decades: procedure is not merely about "the rules," but rather how the rules are used and mobilized by the players in the litigation game. To the extent procedure affects and at times even trumps substantive fairness, Galanter's article provides a wonderful lens into *how* this occurs. Galanter does this by explaining how the actors who use the litigation system vary in resources and power. While procedure professors take a semester to unpack the distinction between procedure and substance, Galanter unpacks this issue in a few pages by highlighting the advantages that repeat players maintain in the civil litigation system. These repeat player advantages include but are not limited to (1) advanced intelligence and the ability to preplan transactions, (2) ongoing access to specialists and lawyers, reduced start-up costs and economies of scale, (3) informal facilitative relationships with institutional actors, (4) long-run strategic interests and the ability to play for favorable rules, and (5) experience in discerning which rule-changes are likely to "penetrate" into the law in action.

While Galanter's focus is on the configuration of power and the systematic structural advantages and disadvantages in litigation, the article does not offer a class or power elite analysis. He does not conclude that members of the dominant class or large wealthy organizations always win in litigation. Rather, he focuses

---

[2] UC Irvine's version of Civil Procedure is called Procedural Analysis.

on the way that the litigation system—and the procedural rules within it—create structural advantages for repeat players. In sum, I believe every law and legal studies student should be required to read his article because it contextualizes the procedural system as something more than a set of rules that should be memorized and mechanically applied. Galanter's gift is that his article reflects a sophisticated set of ideas, yet he still manages to convey the ideas in simple ways. Consequently, students benefit from reading this article because it illuminates how efficiency, justice, equality, and procedural and substantive fairness impact litigants in real and tangible ways. The article captures the real and lived experience of those who encounter law in society, and provides context for talking about rules that are too often thought of as "given" to society by formal legal institutions.

As we celebrate the 40th anniversary of this article, I do not think anyone—scholars, students, policymakers, judges, or individual citizens—can credibly dispute that this article continues to impact those who interact with the law. I hope that those interested in understanding the social and political dynamics of the law and law's capacity to produce social change will continue to draw from one of the most influential pieces of legal scholarship ever written. I certainly will.

SHAUHIN A. TALESH
Assistant Professor of Law,
Sociology, and
Criminology, Law & Society
University of California, Irvine
School of Law

Irvine, California
May, 2014

REFERENCES

ALBISTON, Catherine (1999) "The Rule of Law and the Litigation Process: The Paradox of Losing by Winning," 33 *Law & Society Rev.* 869-910.

ATKINS, Burton M. (1991) "Party Capability Theory as an Explanation for Intervention Behavior in the English Court of Appeal," 35 *American Journal of Political Science* 881-903.

BINGHAM, Lisa (1997) "Employment Arbitration: The Repeat Player Effect," 1 *Emp. Rts. & Emp. Pol'y J.* 189-99.

——— (1998) "On Repeat Players, Adhesive Contracts, and the Use of Statistics in Judicial Review of Employment Arbitration Awards," 29 *McGeorge L. Rev.* 223-59.

BINGHAM, Lisa B., and Simon SARRAF (2000) "Employment Arbitration Before and After the Due Process Protocol for Mediation and Arbitration of Statutory Disputes Arising Out of Employment: Preliminary Evidence that Self-Regulation Makes a Difference," presented at the Proceedings of the N.Y.U. 50th Annual Conference on Labor. New York.

BURSTEIN, Paul (1989) "Attacking Sex Discrimination intheLabor Market: A Study in Law and Politics," 67 *Social Forces* 641-65.

COLE, Sarah R. (2001) "Uniform Arbitration: 'One Size Fits All' Does Not Fit," 16 *Ohio St. J. on Disp. Resol.* 759.

COLVIN, Alexander J. S. (2011) "An Empirical Study of Employment Arbitration: Case Outcomes and Processes," 8 *J. of Empirical Legal Studies* 1-23.

EDELMAN, Lauren B., and Mark C. SUCHMAN (1999) "When the 'Haves' Hold Court: Speculations on the Organizational Internalization of Law," 33 *Law & Society Rev.* 941-92.

EDELMAN, Lauren B., Howard S. ERLANGER and John LANDE (1993) "Employers' Handling of Discrimination Complaints: The Transformation of Rights in the Workplace," 27 *Law & Society Rev.* 497-534.

EDELMAN, Lauren B. and Shauhin A. TALESH (2011) "To comply or not to comply—that isn't the question: how organizations construct the meaning of compliance," in C. PARKER and V. NIELSEN, eds., *Explaining Compliance.* Edward Elgar, Cheltenham, UK.

EISENBERG, Theodore, and Elizabeth HILL (2003) "Arbitration and Litigation of Employment Claims: An Empirical Comparison," 58 *Dispute Resolution J.* 44-55.

GALANTER, Marc, and John LANDE (1992) "Private Courts and Public Authority," 12 *Studies in Law, Politics, & Society* 393-415.

GILAD, Sharon (2010) "Why the 'Haves' Do Not Necessarily Come out Ahead in Informal Dispute Resolution," 32 *Law & Policy* 283-312.

GLENN, Brian J. (2003) "The Varied and Abundant Progeny," in H. KRITZER and S. SILBEY, eds., *In Litigation: Do the "Haves" Still Come Out Ahead?* 371-81.

HANNINGAN, John A. (1977) "The Newspapers Ombudsman and Consumer Complaints: An Empirical Assessment," 11 *Law & Society Rev.* 679-99.

HAYNIE, Stacia L. (1994) "Resource Inequalities and Litigation Outcomes in the Philippine Supreme Court," 56 *Journal of Politics* 752-72.

——— (1995) "Resource Inequalities and Regional Variation in Litigation Outcomes in the Philippine Supreme Court, 1961-1986," 48 *Political Research Quarterly* 371-80.

HAYNIE, Stacia L., C. Neal TATE, Reginald S. SHEEHAN, and Donald R. SONGER (2001) "Winners and Losers: A Comparative Analysis of Appellate Courts and Litigation Outcomes." Paper presented at the annual meeting of the American Political Science Association, San Francisco, August 30-September 2.

HIRSH, Elizabeth (2008) "Settling for Less? Organizational Determinants of Discrimination-Charge Outcomes," 42 *Law & Society Rev.* 239-74.

KENNEDY, David, and William W. FISHER, eds. (2006) *The Canon of American Legal Thought.* Princeton: Princeton University Press.

KINSEY, Karyl, and Loretta J. STALANS (1999) "Which 'Haves' Come Out Ahead and Why? Cultural Capital and Legal Mobilization in Frontline Law Enforcement," 33 *Law & Society Rev.* 993-1023.

KRITZER, Herbert M. (2003) "The Government Gorilla: Why Does Government Come Out Ahead in Appellate Courts?," in H. KRITZER and S. SILBEY, eds., *In Litigation: Do the "Haves" Still Come Out Ahead?* 342-70.

KRITZER, Herbert, and Susan S. SILBEY, eds. (2003) *In Litigation*. Stanford: Stanford University Press.

McGUIRE, Kevin T. (1995) "Repeat Players in the Supreme Court: The Role of Experienced Lawyers in Litigation Success," 57 *Journal of Politics* 187-96.

MENKEL-MEADOW, Carrie (1999) "Do the 'Haves' Come out Ahead in Alternative Judicial Systems?: Repeat Players in ADR," 15 *Ohio State J. on Dispute Resolution* 19-61, 19, 22, 43, 46-48.

SANDEFUR, Rebecca L. (2005) "Effects of representation on Trial and Hearing Outcomes in Two Common Law Countries," http://www.reds.msh-paris.fr/communication/docs/sandefur.pdf (accessed April 3, 2014).

SERON, Carroll, et al. (2001) "The Impact of Legal Counsel on Outcomes for Poor Tenants in New York City's Housing Court: Results of Randomized Experiment," 35 *Law & Society Rev.* 419-34.

SHAPIRO, Fred (1996) "The Most-Cited Law Review Articles Revisited," 71 *Chicago-Kent L. Rev.* 751-79.

SHAPIRO, Fred, and Michelle PEARSE (2012) "The Most-Cited Law Review Articles of All Time," 110 *Michigan L. Rev.* 1483-1520.

SMYTH, Russell (2000) "The 'Haves' and the 'Have Nots': An Empirical Study of the Rational Actor and Party Capability Hypothesis in the High Court 1948-99," 35 *Australian Journal of Pol. Sci.* 255-74.

SONGER, Donald R., and Reginald S. SHEEHAN (1992) "Who Wins on Appeal? Upperdogs and Underdogs in the United States Courts of Appeals," 36 *Am. J. Pol. Sci.* 235-58.

SONGER, Donald R., Reginald S. SHEEHAN, and Susan B. HAIR (1999) "Do the 'Haves' Come out Ahead over Time? Applying Galanter's Framework to Decisions of the U.S. Courts of Appeals, 1925-1988," 33 *Law & Society Rev.* 811-32.

STEELE, Eric H. (1974) "Fraud, Dispute, and the Consumer: Responding to Consumer Complaints," 123 *Univ. of Penn. L. Rev.* 1107-86.

STONE, Katherine V. W. (1996) "Mandatory Arbitration of Individual Employment Rights: The Yellow Dog Contract of the 1900s," 73 *Denver U. L. Rev.* 1017.

SUTTON, John, et al. (1994) "The Legalization of the Workplace," 99 *American J. of Sociology* 944-71.

SZMER, John, Susan W. JOHNSON, and Tammy A. SARVER (2007) "Does the Lawyer Matter? Influencing Outcomes on the Supreme Court of Canada," 41 *Law & Society Rev.* 279-303.

TALESH, Shauhin A. (2009) "The Privatization of Public Legal Rights: How Manufacturers Construct the Meaning of Consumer Law," 43 *Law & Society Rev.* 527-62.

——— (2012) "How Dispute Resolution System Design Matters: An Organizational Analysis of Dispute Resolution Structures and Consumer Lemon Laws," 46 *Law & Society Rev.* 463-92.

——— (2013) "How the 'Haves' Come Out Ahead in the Twenty-First Century," *62 DePaul Law Rev.* 529-54.

——— (2015) "Institutional and Political Sources of Institutional Change: Explaining How Private Organizations Influence the Form and Content of Consumer Protection Legislation," 40 *Law & Social Inquiry* (forthcoming 2015).

WHEELER, Stanton et al. (1987) "Do the 'Haves' Come out Ahead? Winning and Losing in State Supreme Courts, 1870-1970," 21 *Law & Society Rev.* 403-45.

WILLIS, Joy, and Reginald S. SHEEHAN (1999) "Success in the Australian High Court: Resource Inequality and Outcome." Paper presented at the annual meeting of the Southern Political Science Association, Savannah, Georgia, November 6-9.

Why the Haves Come Out Ahead

INTRODUCTION

Haves Ascendant

Marc Galanter

The universal spirit of Laws, in all countries is to favor the strong in opposition to the weak, and to assist those who have possessions against those who have none. This inconveniency is inevitable, and without exception.

Jean Jacques Rousseau (1762)

A Different Age

The "Haves" paper was written in a different age.[1] Its core was composed in the fall of 1970 when I was a fellow at the Yale Law School's remarkably fruitful but short-lived Program in Law and Modernization. This was before the ascent of law and economics, before the emergence of critical legal studies and its progeny, before the beatification of alternative dispute resolution, before the intensified exposure of the legal world by journalism, scholarship, and the internet.[2]

The "Haves" was conceived in an age of hopefulness that saw the triumph of civil rights movements, the proliferation of public interest law, and many initiatives in access to justice. It was the high point of assertive legal services in behalf of

---

[1] The colloquial term "have-nots," referring to those lacking wealth and/or other advantages, has been familiar to me as far back as I can remember. I can't recall encountering the less-familiar term "haves," which seems to be a back-formation from "have-nots," before it commended itself in the course of writing this paper. But it seems that my teacher Karl Llewellyn used it as long ago as 1930. In his famous introductory lectures to law students he told them, "[I]t is clear that the activity of the most skillful lawyers will be upon the side of the Haves and not upon the side of the Have-nots.... While in theory legal contests may be equal, the man with the longer purse who can hire the better, the more skillful man, has his advantage and will have it in the time to come." Karl Llewellyn, *The Bramble Bush: On Our Law and its Study* (1930), 144-45. Llewellyn was not the first; the *Oxford English Dictionary* traces the term to 1836.

[2] It was also before the institutionalization of law and society scholarship. The Law and Society Association, founded in 1964, was at first largely a support group dedicated to publishing the *Law & Society Review* (which was at volume 5 in 1970); its first national membership meeting took place in 1975.

the poor,[3] the time of California Rural Legal Assistance[4] and Nader's Raiders.[5] The number of women attending law school accelerated dramatically.[6] Although establishment lawyers found the ferment worrisome, it was a heady time for those who ardently wished to transform law from a buttress of the status quo and an instrument of oppression into a tool of liberation.[7] The world seemed to be opening up; dynamic judges like J. Skelly Wright and Frank Johnson were leading the way,[8] prodded by dedicated lawyers who devised arguments to show judges how they might dismantle oppressive structures and find new paths to substantive justice.

I was very much a newcomer to American law. Since my graduation from law school fourteen years earlier, I had been occupied with research on Indian law and with teaching general social science courses at the College of the University of Chicago.[9] When I arrived at Yale in 1970, it was the first time in a dozen years that I had been around an American law school.

[3] The "War on Poverty" launched by President Lyndon Johnson in 1965 was administered by the Office of Economic Opportunity [OEO]. OEO established a program of aggressive and proactive legal services in contrast to traditional "legal aid." Earl Johnson, *Justice and Reform: The Formative Years of the OEO Legal Services Program* (New York: Russell Sage Foundation, 1974). The Legal Services Corporation, the semi-governmental body that oversees federally-funded legal services for the poor, is descended from the OEO's Legal Services Program.

[4] California Rural Legal Assistance, a legal services program funded by the federal government, was founded in 1965 and achieved notable success in aggressive advocacy for migrant farmworkers and engendered bitter opposition from, among others, then-governor of California, Ronald Reagan.

[5] Ralph Nader (1934-), a dedicated consumer activist, gained national prominence in 1963 when it was revealed that the General Motors Corporation hired private detectives to discredit him, leading to Congressional committee hearings and a successful lawsuit for invasion of privacy. The proceeds of the lawsuit were used to fund campaigns to expose the deficiencies of administrative regulation, campaigns involving groups of students who gained the appellation "Nader's Raiders." After decades of persistent and creative advocacy on behalf of consumers, Nader mounted several unsuccessful runs for President; as Green Party candidate for president in 2000 he inadvertently helped George Bush (with the assistance of the U.S. Supreme Court) to wrest the Presidency from Al Gore, who received the majority of the popular vote.

[6] Enrollment of women students in American Bar Association-approved law schools increased from 1,364 (3.1%) in 1950 and 1,429 (3.5%) in 1960, to 8,914 (9.4%) in 1971 when the "Haves" paper was begun, and 21,788 (19.7%) in 1974, when it was published. Richard Abel, *American Lawyers* (New York: Oxford University Press, 1989), 285.

[7] As a visitor at Yale Law School, I received a complimentary copy of the new issue of the *Yale Law Journal* (May 1970), which included Edgar and Jean Cahn's "Power to People or the Profession?"; Stephen Wexler's "Practicing Law for Poor People"; a 90-page student survey of "The New Public Interest Lawyers"; and assessments of "Legal Theory and Legal Education" and "Legal Ethics and Professionalism" in the light of "the current call for a legal profession and a legal education dedicated to such values as the public interest and social justice."

[8] J. Skelly Wright (1911-1988), judge in the U.S. District Court for the Eastern District of Louisiana (1949-1962) and then in the U.S. Court of Appeals for the District of Columbia Circuit (1962-88), and Frank M. Johnson, Jr. (1918-1999), judge in the U.S. District Court in Alabama (1955-1979) and then in the U.S. Court of Appeals for the Fifth [later, Eleventh] Circuit (1979-1999), resolute and courageous judges in the struggle for desegregation and imaginative innovators of remedies to implement institutional reforms, were the inspiration for several generations of progressive legal activists. See, e.g., Jack Bass, *Unlikely Heroes* (New York: Simon & Schuster, 1981).

[9] On the carryover from the mindset of the Chicago social science curriculum to law and society, see Marc Galanter, "The Portable Soc 2; Or, What to Do Until the Doctrine Comes," in J. MacAloon, ed., *General Education in the Social Sciences: Centennial Reflections on the College of the University of Chicago* (Chicago: University of Chicago Press, 1992).

At that point, the legal system I knew best was India. In the late 1960s, I had rediscovered U.S. law, connecting with the nascent law and society movement. I shifted my teaching in this direction and eagerly consumed everything "social sciency" I could find about the U.S. legal system. The bookshelf of "law and society" work was not empty, but was quite sparse compared with more recent times.[10] The real foundation of the "Haves" paper, however, was my work in India, particularly my analysis of the Untouchability Offences Act (1955), India's national civil rights statute, which I had published in 1969.[11] India is not mentioned in the "Haves" paper and I do not recall thinking about India at all while I was writing it. Dissecting the accomplishments and limitations of the Indian attack on the practice of untouchability had honed the perspective that informed my new attention to the United States. Looking at the U.S. through the lens of my Indian experience, it seemed evident that the rules were only one aspect of legal reality and that pronouncement of new rules was only a small part of legal change.

The "Haves" begins with a familiar "man from Mars" conceit. If I was not a genuine Martian, I was a genuine outsider to the U.S. legal system in both my innocence of detail and my relative detachment. The "Haves" paper was a challenge to the judicial triumphalism that was the received wisdom of the progressive wing of the U.S. legal academy, which may help to account for the great difficulty in getting it published.[12] In effect, it attempted to show that, examined from the bottom-up, the U.S. displayed in a subtle form many of the contradictions that rendered grand programs of reform largely symbolic in their results. In the Indian setting these contradictions were glaringly evident to an outsider with the benefit

---

[10] Leading works included Jerome Carlin's *Lawyers on Their Own: A Study of Individual Practitioners in Chicago* (1962) and *Legal Ethics: A Survey of the New York City Bar* (1966); Harry Kalven and Hans Zeisel's *The American Jury* (1966); Stewart Macaulay's *Law and the Balance of Power: The Automobile Manufacturers and Their Dealers* (1966); Jerome Skolnick's *Justice without Trial: Law Enforcement in Democratic Society* (1966); Kenneth M. Dolbeare's *Trial Courts in Urban Politics: State Court Policy Impact and Functions in a Local Political System* (1967); James Q. Wilson's *Varieties of Police Behavior: The Management of Law and Order in Eight Communities* (1968); Richard F. Babcock's *The Zoning Game: Municipal Practices and Policies* (1969); and H. Laurence Ross's *Settled Out of Court* (1970). A pertinent work that I did not encounter until some years later was Erwin Smigel's *The Wall Street Lawyer: Professional Organization Man?* (1964).

[11] Marc Galanter, "Untouchability and the Law," 4 *Economic & Political Weekly* 131-70 (1969) (later published in J. Michael Mahar, ed., *The Untouchables in Contemporary India* (Tucson: University of Arizona Press, 1972)).

[12] It was rejected by a dozen or so law reviews and a couple of political science journals as well. In the mid-1980s, I met a prominent scholar who told me appreciatively how he assigned this paper to his students every year. He was disbelieving when I reminded him that as articles editor of a renowned law review, he had rejected it. Most law review rejections are quite cursory, but this one was memorable because it gave reasons: the paper was "fascinating and well written" but it controverted "what we can observe" about the legal system, in which have-nots "increasingly come to look to courts for the protection and articulation of their goals."

In 1973 I was about to take over as editor of the *Law & Society Review*. Although I would have preferred that the paper appear independently of my editorship, I knew the *Review* would be a good place for it and wondered how I might include it. My friend and then-dean, Richard Schwartz, solved the puzzle by suggesting that I invite a guest editor to organize a symposium into which this paper would fit. The symposium on litigation and dispute processing that resulted (*Law & Society Review*, vol. 9, nos. 1 and 2) turned out to be pathbreaking and influential in focusing research in that area.

of no allegiance to the prevailing myths. My passage to India was also a passage outside the perspective and assumptions of my American legal training, revealing that rules were only the surface of legal reality.[13] Writing the "Haves" was the return voyage from this "Journey to the East,"[14] a return greatly facilitated by the presence of the new law and society literature. I found my intuitions of India mirrored, enlarged, and refined by the pioneering observational research on American legal institutions, including especially the work of Stewart Macaulay, Lawrence Friedman, Joel Handler, and H. Laurence Ross, work with a bottom-up focus on the predicaments and strategies of litigants.

I came away from this collision of Indian and American experience with the abiding conviction that notwithstanding the law's aspiration (and pretension) to neutrality and equal treatment, we can never get away from the identity and resources of the parties. As Lynn LoPucki and Walter Weyrauch neatly put it many years later,

> [O]ne can no more predict the outcome of a case from the facts and the law than one can predict the outcome of a game of chess from the positions of the pieces and the rules of the game. In either case, one needs to know who is playing.[15]

Although the surprise has worn off, I am still immensely gratified that my attempt to grapple with this dismaying revelation has been found insightful and provocative by several generations of scholars and legal actors.[16] A literature review published in 2003 summarizes hundreds of its "varied and abundant progeny."[17] And in what is surely an ironic turn, the "Haves" paper was included in a 2006 volume entitled *The Canon of American Legal Thought*,[18] where it is accompanied by further references and an introduction that considers its place in the development of American legal thought in the 20th century.

---

[13] My self-dramatization here relies on the familiar trope of using the departure from the familiar as a prerequisite for penetrating beyond the surface of the one's taken-for-granted surroundings. Looking at India with American eyes became the basis for re-examining American law with eyes informed by Indian experience.

[14] I refer here to two books that famously engage the experience of encountering India: E.M. Forster's *A Passage to India* (1924) and Herman Hesse's *Die Morgenlandfahrt* (1932), translated into English by Hilda Rosner and published as *The Journey to the East* (1957).

[15] Lynn M. LoPucki and Walter O. Weyrauch, "A Theory of Legal Strategy," 49 *Duke Law Journal* 1405, 1472 (2000).

[16] A symposium on the 25th anniversary of the article, "Do the 'Haves' Still Come Out Ahead?" is found at *Law & Society Review* 33(4): 793-1131 (1999). In Herbert Kritzer and Susan S. Silbey, eds., *In Litigation: Do the "Haves" Still Come Out Ahead?* (Stanford: Stanford University Press, 2003), the article is accompanied by a collection of related studies. Articles relating to the "Haves" appear in two symposia concerned with my work: *Law and Contemporary Problems*, Vol. 71, No. 2 (Spring 2008), and *DePaul Law Review*, Vol. 62, No. 2 (Winter 2013). It was reported to be among "the most cited law review articles of all time," as Shauhin Talesh recounts in the Foreword; he further notes that the article has been translated into several languages. And it has been cited in a number of judicial opinions.

[17] Brian J. Glenn, "The Varied and Abundant Progeny," in Kritzer and Silbey, note 16 above, pp. 371-419.

[18] David Kennedy and William W. Fisher III, eds. (Princeton: Princeton University Press, 2006). The article is at pages 495-545, and the editors' introductory essay, at pages 483-94.

The Turn Against Law

The surging faith in law that the "Haves" challenged was soon attacked from a very different quarter. Starting in the mid-1970s, important sections of American elites, including its legal establishment, were overtaken by a sense of surfeit. Instead of "too little justice," it was "too much law" that was bothersome and disturbing.[19] If this "turning away from law"[20] began with prominent judges and lawyers,[21] it was soon taken up by business and political elites, who were offended and outraged by the shrinking of the leeways and immunities that the system had always afforded them and who now found themselves the targets of an onerous new accountability.

An emblematic moment in the turn against the expansion of justice for ordinary citizens was a 1971 "Confidential Memorandum" prepared, at the invitation of the Chairman of the Education Committee of the United States Chamber of Commerce, by Lewis Powell, then a lawyer in private practice but soon to become a Justice of the U.S. Supreme Court. Powell described a "broad-based and consistently pursued" assault on the American free enterprise system that was "gaining momentum and converts." He bemoaned the "impotency of business" in policy arenas and its default in intellectual and scholarly forums. He advised the Chamber to mount an aggressive campaign of intervention in intellectual, scholarly, and judicial realms to support the system, to cultivate and support scholars "who do believe in the system" to critique textbooks, to promote a "steady flow" of scholarly and popular articles, and to intervene before the courts.[22] This document foreshadows the development of "New Right" think tanks, institutes, and foundations, the pronounced increase in business spending on politics, and the judicial encouragement of corporate campaign contributions as protected free speech. The campaign that Powell advocated was facilitated by the intensified politicization of judicial appointments.[23]

The recoil by society's managers and authorities against the enlargement of accountability and of remedy for "have-nots" is an important component of the movements for deregulation and "tort reform."[24] Although the rhetoric is often

---

[19] Marc Galanter, "Predators and Parasites: Lawyer-Bashing and Civil Justice," *Georgia Law Review* 28: 633-81 (1994).

[20] David M. Trubek, "Turning Away from Law," *Michigan Law Review* 82: 824-35, at 824 (1984).

[21] An important marker of the recoil of the legal establishment is the 1976 Pound Conference organized by Chief Justice Warren Burger. See A. Leo Levin and Russell R. Wheeler, eds., *The Pound Conference: Perspectives on Justice in the Future: Proceedings of the National Conference on the Causes of the Popular Dissatisfaction with the Administration of Justice* (St. Paul: West Publishing Co., 1979).

[22] Lewis F. Powell, Jr. (1971), Confidential Memorandum/Attack on American Free Enterprise System, addressed to Mr. Eugene B. Sydnor, Jr., Chairman, Education Committee, U.S. Chamber of Commerce, dated Aug. 23, 1971. Available at http://reclaimdemocracy.org/powell_memo_lewis/

[23] The literature is vast. For a start, see Sheldon Goldman, Elliot Slotnick, Gerard Gryski and Sara Schiavoni, "W. Bush's Judiciary: The First Term Record," *Judicature* 84: 244 (May-June 2005); Cass R. Sunstein, David Schkade and Lisa Michelle Ellman, "Ideological Voting on Federal Courts of Appeals: A Preliminary Investigation," *Virginia Law Review* 90: 301 (2004).

[24] Marc Galanter, "The Turn Against Law: the Recoil Against Expanding Accountability," *Texas*

expansive, indicting all lawyers and the entire legal system, the proposals that emerge from this recoil are more patterned: the features of the system under attack are legal services for the poor, contingency fees,[25] the "American rule" on costs (i.e., no "loser pays"),[26] "trial lawyers,"[27] class actions, punitive damages, awards for pain and suffering, and the civil jury. We have seen a thirty-year barrage of attacks on rules and devices that give some leverage and protection to "have nots" while leaving undisturbed the capacity of corporate actors to use the legal system to advantage.

This campaign (really a set of discrete but overlapping campaigns) can claim considerable success. For example, it has succeeded, with the enthusiastic support of the United States Supreme Court, in institutionalizing the use of arbitration clauses (even ones hidden in sealed packages) to circumvent legislative and judicial protection of consumers.[28] The quest for inexpensive and accessible "alternative" forums that emerged from the access to justice movement has morphed into a playbook for constricting access to forums capable of inducing consequential change[29]—a transition facilitated and promoted by the Supreme Court's fervid embrace of arbitration clauses.[30]

The enlargement of rights and the heightened expectation of protection and remedy, now under sustained attack, is one of the master trends of legal development in the 20th century.[31] Another equally important, but less celebrated, master

---

Law Review 81: 285-304 (2002).

[25] The contingency (or contingent) fee is an agreement that the client will pay a specified percentage of the amount recovered, but no payment is to be made in cases where the claimant loses. On the advantages and disadvantages of the contingency fee, see Marc Galanter, "Anyone Can Fall Down a Manhole: The Contingency Fee and Its Discontents," *DePaul Law Review* 47: 457-77 (1997).

[26] As a general practice American courts follow the so-called "American rule" on costs under which the losing side in litigation is not obliged to pay the litigation expenses of the winner. This contrasts with the "English rule" of "loser pays" (frequently summed up in the less-than-clear maxim "costs follow the event"), in which at least some part of the winner's costs are taxed against the loser. American law does, however, contain legislative provisions in specific types of cases for a winning plaintiff to collect his costs, while a winning defendant cannot collect. This goes by the name of "one way fee shifting."

[27] Although the term literally includes lawyers for both plaintiffs and defendants, in American usage "trial lawyer" typically refers to lawyers who specialize in representing claimants in personal injury and other types of cases, typically on a contingency fee arrangement. The success of the campaign to demonize "trial lawyers" as the bad guys in the litigation explosion may be gauged by the national association of plaintiffs' lawyers changing its name in 2006 from the Association of Trial Lawyers of America to the American Association for Justice.

[28] See Stewart Macaulay, "Freedom From Contract: Solutions in Search of a Problem," *Wisconsin Law Review* 2004: 777 (2004); Cheryl B. Preston and Eli W. McCann, "Unwrapping Shrinkwraps, Clickwraps, and Browsewraps: How the Law Went Wrong from Horse Traders to the Law of the Horse," *BYU Journal of Public Law* 26: 1 (2012).

[29] On the original connection of the movement for Alternative Dispute Resolution with the movement for access to justice and the subsequent realignment, see Marc Galanter, "Access to Justice in a World of Expanding Social Capability," *Fordham Urban Law Journal* 37: 115-128, at 120-21 (2010).

[30] Jean Sternlight, "Creeping Mandatory Arbitration: Is It Just?," *Stanford Law Review* 57: 1631-1675 (2005); *Law and Contemporary Problems*, Vol. 67, Nos. 1-2 ("Mandatory Arbitration") (2004).

[31] Lawrence M. Friedman, *Total Justice* (New York: Russell Sage Foundation, 1975); Galanter,

trend is implicated in the recoil against the expansion of remedies for ordinary persons—the increasing corporatization of legal life and the related legalization of organizational life.[32] Increasingly, the legal actors that play the repeat-player role are organizations—corporations, associations, or governmental bodies. They are the carriers of the advantages typically enjoyed by repeat-players.[33]

More and more of our encounters and relations are with corporate entities rather than natural persons. More and more of our common life is pursued under the auspices of "artificial persons." With their ascent has come a pervasive legalization of life. The sheer amount of law in American society has increased enormously since 1970 and with it the total amount of legal services provided by a much larger and more proficient body of lawyers. To take just a single summary indicator, the portion of the gross domestic product consisting of legal services rose from 0.6% in 1967 to 1.6% in 1993.[34] As the size of the legal services "pie" has increased, a greater and greater share of that pie has been consumed by business and government organizations and a shrinking share by individuals. In 1967, individuals bought fifty-five percent of the product of the legal services industry and businesses bought thirty-nine percent. With each subsequent five-year period, the business portion has increased and the share consumed by individuals has declined. By 1992, the share bought by businesses had risen (from thirty-nine percent) to fifty-one percent and the share bought by individuals had fallen to forty percent (from fifty-five percent).[35]

The increasing predominance of organizations as users of law is displayed from another angle in the magisterial study of the Chicago bar, initially conducted in 1975 and splendidly replicated twenty years later.[36] In 1975 Heinz and Laumann found that law practice in Chicago was divided into

> lawyers who represent large organizations (corporations, labor unions, or government) and those who represent individuals. The two kinds of law practice are two hemispheres of the profession. Most lawyers reside exclusively in one,

---

"The Travails of Total Justice," in R. W. Gordon and M. J. Horwitz, eds., *Law, Society and History: Themes in the Legal Sociology and Legal History of Lawrence M. Friedman* (Cambridge University Press, 2011), pp. 103-117.

[32] Lauren B. Edelman and Mark C. Suchman, "When the 'Haves' Hold Court: Speculations on the Organizational Internalization of Law," *Law & Society Review* 33: 941-91 (1999); Galanter, "Planet of the APs: Reflections on the Scale of Law and Its Users," *Buffalo Law Review* 53: 1369-1417 (2006), reprinted in this volume at pages 77-110.

[33] Galanter, "Planet of the APs," cited at note 32 above and reprinted in this volume.

[34] In U.S. Bureau of the Census, *Census of Service Industries: Legal Services*, the legal services category includes all law practices that have a payroll, which means virtually all lawyers in private practice.

[35] U.S. Bureau of the Census, *Census of Service Industries,* 1972, 1977, 1982, 1987, 1992 (Washington, DC: Government Printing Office). (U.S. Department of the Census 1972: Table 4; 1977: Table 9; 1982: Table 30; 1987: Table 42; 1992: Table 49.) For 1967, only total receipts are available from the U.S. Census. Percentages for classes of clients in 1967 are estimates taken from Richard H. Sander and E. Douglass Williams, "Why Are There So Many Lawyers? Perspectives on a Turbulent Market," *Law & Social Inquiry* 14: 432-79, at 141 (1989).

[36] John P. Heinz and Edward O. Laumann, *Chicago Lawyers: The Social Structure of the Bar* (New York: Russell Sage Foundation, 1982), 319; John P. Heinz, Robert L. Nelson, Rebecca L. Sandefur, and Edward O. Laumann, *Urban Lawyers: The New Social Structure of the Bar* (Chicago: University of Chicago Press, 2005).

hemisphere or the other and seldom, if ever, cross the equator.[37]

They estimated that in 1975, "more than half (53%) of the total effort of Chicago's bar was devoted to the corporate client sector, and a smaller but still substantial proportion (40%) is expended on the personal client sector."[38] When the study was replicated twenty years later, the researchers found that there were roughly twice as many lawyers working in Chicago.[39] In 1995, however, about sixty-one percent of the total effort of all Chicago lawyers was devoted to the corporate client sector and only twenty-nine percent to the personal/small business sector.[40] Because the number of lawyers in Chicago had doubled, the total effort devoted to the personal sector had increased by forty-five percent, while the effort devoted to the corporate sector grew by 126%. (To the extent that lawyers serving the corporate sector were able to combine more staff and support services with their efforts, these figures understate the disparity in services delivered.)

The increasing presence of these organizational players—and I include governments and associations as well as corporations—means more occasions to deploy the structural advantages that are discussed in the "Haves" paper. To clarify, when I say corporations and other artificial persons are on the whole more capable players of the law game, I am not attributing to them a preternatural competence and freedom from error (as I elaborate in this volume's chapter on such artificial persons—"APs"). Corporations blunder just as do individuals, and the level of blundering is a reflection of the internal organizational features of corporations—i.e., their problems of coordination and the necessity of acting through agents with their own limited perspectives and separate ambitions. I would argue, however, that on the whole, the corporate entity's incremental increase in capability as a legal actor outweighs these distractions.[41]

In addition to their structural advantages, artificial persons enjoy "cultural" advantages in the American legal forum. U.S. courts have been very receptive to the notion that corporate actors are persons with rights of their own rather than merely instruments of natural persons. In a string of Supreme Court opinions, corporations have won significant Bill of Rights protections involving double jeopardy, search and seizure, and free speech protection on corporate political spending and advertising. One commentator characterized these opinions as symbolic of "the transformation of our constitutional system from one of individual freedoms to one of organizational prerogatives."[42] This transformation has proceeded apace with the 2010 Supreme Court decision in *Citizens United v. Federal Election Commission*.[43] That case struck down restraints on corporate spending in elec-

---

[37] Heinz and Laumann, note 16 above, at 319.

[38] Ibid., p. 42.

[39] John P. Heinz, Robert L. Nelson, Edward O. Laumann, & Ethan Michelson, "The Changing Character of Lawyers' Work: Chicago in 1975 and 1995," *Law & Society Review* 32: 751-75 (1998).

[40] Ibid., Table 3.

[41] Marc Galanter, "Planet of the APs: Reflections on the Scale of Law and Its Users," *Buffalo Law Review* 53: 1369-1417 (2006), reproduced in this volume.

[42] Carl J. Mayer, "Personalizing the Impersonal: Corporations and the Bill of Rights," *Hastings Law Journal* 41: 577-667, at 578 (1990).

[43] 558 U.S. 50 (2010).

tions, combining the proposition that corporations are persons who enjoy free speech rights under the First Amendment of the United States Constitution with the proposition that spending money is a form of speech entitled to constitutional protection.

Corporations also enjoy additional prerogatives. In effect, they are largely immune from criminal punishment.[44] They cannot be imprisoned, fines are typically minimal from a corporate vantage because they are usually designed with natural persons in mind, and in any case fines penalize shareholders rather than the actors who designed, directed, and performed the criminal acts. On the other hand, corporate actors frequently and successfully use the criminal justice system to punish and deter offenses against themselves.[45]

We tend to be forgiving of corporate folly. Rather than chastening, many of the blunders of corporations are deemed worthy of solace in the form of tax deductions.[46] Corporations enjoy a relative impunity to moral condemnation for single-minded pursuit of advantage that would be condemned as unworthy if not felonious when undertaken by natural persons (for example, abandoning vulnerable dependents, changing residence or status to secure tax advantages, relocating assets to avoid liability, and so forth).

While individuals who invoke the legal system arouse suspicion and reproach,[47] corporate actors are rarely condemned for aggressively using litigation in pursuit of their interests.[48] A few years ago, I found that about ninety-five percent of a very skeptical class of Wisconsin undergraduates was outraged by the award in the famous McDonald's coffee case.[49] After my eloquent and persuasive briefing about

[44] John C. Coffee, Jr., "'No Soul to Damn: No Body to Kick': An Unscandalized Inquiry into the Problem of Corporate Punishment," *Michigan Law Review* 79: 386-459 (1981).

[45] John Hagan, "The Corporate Advantage: A Study of the Involvement of Corporate and Individual Victims in a Criminal Justice System," *Social Forces* 60: 993-1022 (1982).

[46] Reed Abelson, "Tax Reformers, Take Your Mark," *New York Times*, Feb. 11, 2011, 1996, Sec. 3, pp. 1, 12.

[47] David Engel, "The Oven Bird's Song: Insiders, Outsiders, and Personal Injuries in an American Community," *Law & Society Review* 18: 551-82 (1984); Valerie Hans, "The Jury's Response to Business and Corporate Wrongdoing," *Law & Contemporary Problems* 52: 177-203 (1989); Valerie Hans, "The Contested Role of the Civil Jury in Business Litigation," *Judicature* 79: 242-48 (1996).

[48] Ross E. Cheit, "Corporate Ambulance Chasers: The Charmed Life of Business Litigation," *Studies in Law, Politics, & Society* 11: 119-40 (1991).

[49] The reference here is to the case of Stella Liebeck, who in 1994 sued McDonald's after spilling their coffee while opening the container. The coffee was considerably hotter than served by most vendors, causing third degree burns on her legs and groin, necessitating skin grafts. McDonald's refused her initial request for about $11,000 to cover her medical and attendant expenses, and countered with an offer of $800.

After she filed suit McDonald's rejected several settlement proposals by her lawyer and a court-appointed mediator's recommendation that the parties settle for $225,000. At the trial, it was revealed that McDonald's had encountered some seven hundred claims of this type, some of which it had settled, for a total outlay of more than $500,000. The jury awarded Ms. Liebeck compensatory damages of $160,000 and punitive damages of $2.7 million, supposedly an estimation of two days of McDonald's coffee sales.

The judge reduced the punitive award to $480,000 (three times the amount of the compensatory damages). Subsequently the parties settled for an undisclosed amount. McDonald's lowered the temperature of its coffee. See Marc Galanter, "An Oil Strike in Hell: Contemporary Legends

the facts and the context, the percentage that was outraged dropped to no more than ninety-two percent. At the same time, they were quite sanguine about the Texaco-Pennzoil award, which they saw as unexceptional protection of business interests.[50]

A similar cultural tilt is found within the legal profession itself. Heinz and Laumann report that the prestige ranking of legal fields mirrors the structural division of the profession, "with fields serving big business clients at the top and those serving individual clients (especially clients from lower socioeconomic groups) at the bottom."[51] In other words, "the higher a specialty stands in its reputation for being motivated by altruistic (as opposed to profitable) considerations, the lower it is likely to be in the prestige order."[52]

Just Joking

One of my preoccupations in recent years has been to examine lawyer jokes and their history.[53] From this source, I have a sense that several generations back, corporations attracted more moral condemnation for their misdeeds. Jokes about lawyers, as about many things, are usually long-lived, but some do drop out of the body of jokes in circulation. One cluster of such dropouts is jokes about corporate manipulation of law. These jokes flourished from the early years of the 20th century and had faded from view by the end of World War II. Here are three examples, none of which is in circulation today.

1. *The big business magnate entered the famous lawyer's office wearing a worried frown. "That law I spoke to you about is stopping a big deal of mine," he said, "and I'd like to know if you can prove it unconstitutional?" "Very easily," declared the lawyer. "All right; then get busy and familiarize yourself with the law," he was instructed. "No need to," replied the lawyer. "It's that same law you had me prove constitutional a couple of years ago."*[54]

about the Civil Justice System," *Arizona Law Review* 40: 717-52, at 731-32 (1998); William Haltom and Michael McCann, *Distorting the Law: Politics, Media and the Litigation Crisis* (Chicago: University of Chicago Press, 2004), ch. 6.

[50] In 1984, Pennzoil Co. made a deal to purchase the Getty Oil Company. Before the formalities were consummated, oil giant Texaco inserted itself and effected a purchase of Getty, which led to a lawsuit by Pennzoil against Texaco for interference with their contract. A Texas jury returned a verdict of $10.5 billion (then the largest civil verdict ever)—$7.5 billion in compensatory damages and $3 billion punitive damages. On appeal to the U.S. Supreme Court, the compensatory award was upheld and the punitive award was reduced from $3 billion to $1 billion. Pennzoil v. Texaco, Inc., 481 U.S. 1 (1987). See Robert M. Lloyd, "*Pennzoil v. Texaco* Twenty Years After: Lessons for Business Lawyers," *Transactions: The Tennessee Journal of Business Law* 6: 320-59 (2005).

[51] John P. Heinz and Edward O. Laumann, *Chicago Lawyers: The Social Structure of the Bar* (New York: Russell Sage Foundation, 1982), 127.

[52] Edward O. Laumann and John P. Heinz, "Specialization and Prestige in the Legal Profession: The Structure of Deference," *American Bar Foundation Research Journal* 1977: 155-216, at 202 (1977).

[53] On the opportunities for using jokes to examine legal culture, see Galanter, *Lowering the Bar: Lawyer Jokes and Legal Culture* (Madison: University of Wisconsin Press, 2005).

[54] Evan Esar, *Esar's Joke Dictionary* (New York: Harvest House (1945), 260. For other citations, starting from 1915, see Galanter, *Lowering the Bar*, p. 351, note 22. This story evidently predates

2. *The eminent trust magnate was going over the books with his new system expert. "Whew!" Whistled the system expert "Your legal department costs you a heap. Still, I suppose you have to maintain it?"*

   "Well, I don't know. Sometimes I think it would be cheaper to obey the law."[55]

3. *A New York lawyer tells of a conversation that occurred in his presence between a bank president and his son who was about to leave for the West, there to engage in business on his own account. "Son," said the father, "on this, the threshold of your business life, I desire to impress one thought upon your mind. Honesty, ever and always is the policy that is best."*

   "Yes, father," said the young man.

   "And, by the way," added the gray beard, "I would advise you to read up a little on corporation law. It will amaze you to discover how many things you can do in a business way and still be honest."[56]

These stories express not only a generic suspicion of corporations, but distinct notions about law: (1) that despite its air of solidity and majesty, law is malleable; (2) that despite its avowed link to morality, law can be used to circumvent morality; and (3) that despite their pretensions to public virtue and communal service, lawyers are hired guns who manipulate the law for their clients. Does the demise of these jokes indicate that Americans no longer believe these things? I think there is solid evidence that they continue to believe these things, perhaps even more intensely than before.

These "justice" jokes have disappeared not because the underlying sentiments have departed, but because the stories no longer work as jokes. To function as a joke, a story has to have a punchline, a concluding twist that surprises us at the same time that it follows plausibly from what proceeded. But we are so suffused with cynical knowledge that the notions in these jokes (the malleability of law, its use for immoral purposes, lawyers as whores) are no longer sufficiently surprising (or difficult to acknowledge) to support a punchline. So these observations about law and lawyers no longer require the indirection of the joke form and have migrated to other forms of expression.

Although wide publics buy into much of the "litigation explosion" lore promulgated by corporate, media, and political elites, there is a widespread and abiding popular perception that the law's departure from justice is not random, but that it systematically favors the rich and powerful. That those with superior fiscal and organizational resources enjoy advantages in litigation has been appreciated by most

the era of lawyers charging for their services by the hour. On the transition to hourly billing from about 1960, see Marc Galanter and Thomas Palay, *Tournament of Lawyers: The Transformation of the Big Law Firm* (Chicago: University of Chicago, 1991), 34.

[55] William T. Johnston, ed., *Bill Johnston's Joy Book* (Cincinnati: Stewart, 1922), item 1136. See also Galanter, *Lowering the Bar*, p. 350, note 6.

[56] Marion Dix Mosher, ed., *More Toasts: Jokes, Stories and Quotations* (New York: H.W. Wilson, 1932 [first published 1922]), 72. For further citations see Galanter, *Lowering the Bar*, p. 352, note 41.

observers (not just on the left) for a long time.[57] Although survey researchers seem
to avoid asking questions about organizational potency, the responses to their
questions about treatment of rich and poor reveal a sanguine public estimation
that the legal system is biased in favor of the "haves." In the 1970s, fifty-nine percent of a national sample agreed that "the legal system favors the rich and powerful
over everyone else."[58] In a 1985 survey, when asked whether "the justice system
in the United States mainly favors the rich" or "treats all Americans as equally as
possible," fifty-seven percent of respondents chose the "favored the rich" response
and only thirty-nine percent the "equally" response.[59] Ten years later, in a survey
conducted by *U.S. News & World Report,* fully three-quarters of the respondents
thought that the U.S. legal system affords less access to justice to "average Americans" than to rich people, and four out of five of these thought "much less."[60] In
August 1998, only thirty-three percent of respondents to a national survey agreed
with the statement, "Courts try to treat poor people and wealthy people alike," but
ninety percent agreed that "wealthy people or companies often wear down their
opponents by dragging out the legal proceedings."[61] Half a year later in another
national survey, eighty percent of respondents thought that the "wealthy" receive
better treatment from the courts than do other people, and two-thirds agreed with
the statement, "When a person sues a corporation, the courts generally favor the
corporation over the person."[62]

There seems to be no shortage of cynical knowledge. It is no secret that the
"haves" come out ahead. (Were we, scholars of the legal system, the last to know?).
Although in the abstract this may be decried as a violation of norms of equality, in
actual social practice our beliefs in equality and justice may be reconciled with the
tilt toward the "haves." Psychologists have identified a repertoire of psychological
mechanisms for aligning unequal and unjust outcomes with a reassuring belief
that the world is a fundamentally just place.[63]

---

[57] Compare the observations of William Howard Taft, soon to be President and eventually Chief
Justice, on the advantages of rich parties flowing from the structure of litigation. "The Delays of
the Law," *Yale Law Journal* 18: 28-39, at 33, 35 (1908), quoted at length at Galanter, "Planet of
the APs," note 125 [p. 105 as reprinted here].

[58] Barbara Curran, *The Legal Needs of the Public: The Final Report of a National Survey* (Chicago: American Bar Foundation, 1977), 234.

[59] *ABC News/Washington Post* survey 1985 (USACWP.196.R24) (on file with author).

[60] *U.S. News & World Report,* news release, Jan. 21, 1995 (on file with author).The same survey
shows the public placing responsibility for this imbalance squarely on lawyers. Respondents were
asked: "Here are some things that people say about lawyers. Which one of the following comes
closest to your views? [1] Lawyers have an important role to play in holding wrongdoers accountable and helping the injured. [2] Lawyers use the legal system to protect the powerful and get
rich." Fifty-six percent affirmed the "protect the powerful and get rich" response; only 35% the
"helping" response.

[61] American Bar Association, *Perceptions of the U.S. Justice System* (Chicago: American Bar Association, 1999). This 90% response, quite uniform across demographic groups, is the closest to
unanimity of any response to any item in a lengthy survey, outranking complaints about delay,
expense, and leniency toward criminals.

[62] National Center for State Courts, *How the Public Views the State Courts: A 1999 National Survey* (Williamsburg, VA: National Center for State Courts, 1999), Figs. 23 and 24.

[63] Melvin J. Lerner, *The Belief in a Just World: A Fundamental Delusion* (1980); Carolyn L.
Hafter and Laurent Begue, "Experimental Research on Just-World Theory: Problems, Develop-

Optimism of the Will

We arrive at a tangle of questions concerning the relationship between our growing knowledge about the legal world, public perceptions of that world, and the course of action in that world. Does our knowledge affect the working of the legal world? Does the functioning of legal institutions require the support of myths about the law's moral grandeur? How much cynical knowledge can the public—or scholars—absorb or tolerate? How do we manage to combine that knowledge with the myths of legality?[64] One of the curiosities of the current American scene is that the more established and advantaged sections of the population, those who know more about the legal system and benefit most from its working, tend to be the most disconsolate and angry with it. While enjoying the comforts of its protections, the "haves" sponsor campaigns against the legal system, trying to persuade the wider public that it is "demented" and "spun out of control."[65]

In American law we seem to be at a moment when contraction of the rights of ordinary persons is juxtaposed with the elaboration of rights of rich persons and corporate actors.[66] Is this backlash against the equalization of rights and the expansion of access to justice just a blip, a temporary reversal in a long-term movement, or is it a regression to the historical mean, to the normal condition of elite dominance?

The legal realm provides exceptionally nutritious soil for illusion so it is unsurprising that our understanding of law's working is constantly deflected by wishful thinking. Notwithstanding my skepticism, I am recurrently seduced by the notion that law can not only order our affairs, but assist in transforming them closer to our dreams of justice. So I remain an adherent of the maxim "be a pessimist of the intellect, an optimist of the will," popularized by Antonio Gramsci.[67] Gramsci (1891-1937), it turns out, had it from Romain Rolland (1866-1944), a grand literary figure of the early 20th century,[68] who in turn reported drawing his inspiration from Indian philosophy (coming full circle?). For Rolland, penetrating to the truth requires the creative destruction of our illusions. He tells us:

> Never do I hesitate to look squarely at the unexpected face that every passing hour unveils to us, and to sacrifice the false images of it formed in advance, however dear they may be.[69]

---

ments and Future Challenges," *Psychological Bulletin* 131(1): 128-67 (2005).

[64] Patricia Ewick and Susan S. Silbey, *The Common Place of Law: Stories from Everyday Life* (Chicago: University of Chicago Press, 1998).

[65] Galanter, "The Turn Against Law," note 24 above, at 726.

[66] See discussion of the *Citizens United* case, above, note 43 and accompanying text.

[67] Antonio Gramsci, *Selections from the Prison Notebooks*, Q. Hoare and G. N. Smith, trans. & eds. (New York: International Publishers, 1971), 175.

[68] "Romain Rolland's maxim, 'Pessimism of the intelligence, optimism of the will' was made by Gramsci into something of a programmatic slogan as early as 1919, in the pages of Ordine Nuovo." Hoare and Smith, *Selections from the Prison Notebooks*, at 175.

[69] Romain Rolland, *Journey Within* (New York: Philosophical Library, 1947), p. xi. The phrase "creative destruction," taken from Marx *via* Sombart, was famously popularized by Joseph Schumpeter in his *Capitalism, Socialism and Democracy* (1942).

Two Final Thoughts

The two essays that follow, separated by more than thirty years, are linked by the overlap and convergence between the repeat players (RPs) of the "Haves" essay and the artificial persons of the APs essay. The idea that, in the American setting at least, the RP role would typically be played by an organization—an artificial person or AP—was there from the start. A collection of further evidence of the advantages of repeat players, presented shortly after the first publication of the "Haves," asked:

> Why treat the [repeat player/one-shotter] distinction as fundamental? Basically this distinction is between the casual participant for whom the game is an emergency and the party who is equipped to do it as part of his routine activity. The sailor overboard and the shark are both swimmers, but only one is in the swimming business.... It is generally organizations that can be repeat players—because law in America is a complex and expensive activity requiring employment of full-time specialists.[70]

Repeat players and artificial persons are different expressions of the same underlying phenomenon: the potency of the combination of scale and experience that transforms some actors into more sophisticated and formidable users of the legal system.

Beyond the relative advantages conferred on APs by the circumstances of repeat play, their characteristics and powers may be enlarged or constrained by features of the particular setting, including the ideological disposition of legal decision-makers. In the realm of law, unlike for example plumbing or pest-control, saying makes it so—not that the underlying 'facts' are changed, but a new 'operable fact' may be created that, just like a leaking pipe or a colony of termites, must be taken into account. So we recently learned that corporations, or some of them, can 'have' or 'exercise' religion for the purpose of gaining exemption from otherwise-binding legal obligations.[71] APs, many of whose characteristics are metaphoric reflections of the attributes of natural persons, continue to acquire more of the prerogatives of natural persons.

---

[70] Galanter, "Afterword: Explaining Litigation," *Law & Society Review* 10: 347, at 363 (1975). This essay contains further examples of the configuration of litigants and their relative success.
[71] *Burwell v. Hobby Lobby Stores, Inc.*, 573 U.S. ___, 134 S. Ct. 2751 (June 30, 2014).

Why the "Haves" Come Out Ahead: Speculations on the Limits of Legal Change

Marc Galanter

This essay attempts to discern some of the general features of a legal system like the American by drawing on (and rearranging) commonplaces and less than systematic gleanings from the literature. The speculative and tentative nature of the assertions here will be apparent and is acknowledged here wholesale to spare myself and the reader repeated disclaimers.

I would like to try to put forward some conjectures about the way in which the basic architecture of the legal system creates and limits the possibilities of using the system as a means of redistributive (that is, systemically equalizing) change. Our question, specifically, is, under what conditions can litigation[1] be redistributive, taking litigation in the broadest sense of the presentation of claims to be decided by courts (or court-like agencies) and the whole penumbra of threats, feints, and so forth, surrounding such presentation.

For purposes of this analysis, let us think of the legal system as comprised of these elements:

---

[1] "Litigation" is used here to refer to the pressing of claims oriented to official rules, either by actually invoking official machinery or threatening to do so. "Adjudication" refers to full-dress individualized and formal application of rules by officials in a particular litigation.

This essay grew out of a presentation to Robert Stevens' Seminar on the Legal Profession and Social Change at Yale Law School in the autumn of 1970, while the author was Senior Fellow in the School's Law and Modernization Program. It has gathered bulk and I hope substance in the course of a succession of presentations and revisions. It has accumulated a correspondingly heavy burden of obligation to my colleagues and students. I would like to acknowledge the helpful comments of Richard Abel, James Atleson, Guido Calabresi, Kenneth Davidson, Vernon Dibble, William L.F. Felstiner, Lawrence M. Friedman, Marjorie Girth, Paul Goldstein, Mark Haller, Stephen Halpern, Charles M. Hardin, Adolf Homberger, Geoffrey Hazard, Quintin Johnstone, Patrick L. Kelley, David Kirp, Arthur Leff, Stuart Nagel, Philippe Nonet, Saul Touster, David M. Trubek and Stephen Wasby on earlier drafts, and to confer on them the usual dispensation.

The development of this essay was linked in many places to a contemporaneous project on the Deployment Process in the Implementation of Legal Policy supported by the National Science Foundation. I am grateful to the Foundation for affording me the opportunity to pursue several lines of inquiry touched on here. The Foundation bears no responsibility for the views set forth here.

An earlier version was issued as a working paper of the Law and Modernization Program; yet another version of the first part is contained in the proceedings (edited by Lawrence Friedman and Manfred Rehbinder) of the Conference on the Sociology of the Judicial Process, held at Bielefeld, West Germany in September, 1973.

This article is cited as 9 Law & Society Review 95 (1974).

A body of authoritative normative learning—for short, RULES

A set of institutional facilities within which the normative learning is applied to specific cases—for short, COURTS

A body of persons with specialized skill in the above—for short, LAWYERS

Persons or groups with claims they might make to the courts in reference to the rules, etc.—for short, PARTIES

Let us also make the following assumptions about the society and the legal system:

It is a society in which actors with different amounts of wealth and power are constantly in competitive or partially cooperative relationships in which they have opposing interests.

This society has a legal system in which a wide range of disputes and conflicts are settled by court-like agencies which purport to apply pre-existing general norms impartially (that is, unaffected by the identity of the parties).

The rules and the procedures of these institutions are complex; wherever possible disputing units employ specialized intermediaries in dealing with them.

The rules applied by the courts are in part worked out in the process of adjudication (courts devise interstitial rules, combine diverse rules, and apply old rules to new situations). There is a living tradition of such rule-work and a system of communication such that the outcomes in some of the adjudicated cases affect the outcome in classes of future adjudicated cases.

Resources on the institutional side are insufficient for timely full-dress adjudication in every case, so that parties are permitted or even encouraged to forego bringing cases and to "settle" cases,—that is, to bargain to a mutually acceptable outcome.

There are several levels of agencies, with "higher" agencies announcing (making, interpreting) rules and other "lower" agencies assigned the responsibility of enforcing (implementing, applying) these rules. (Although there is some overlap of function in both theory and practice, I shall treat them as distinct and refer to them as "peak" and "field level" agencies.)

Not all the rules propounded by "peak" agencies are effective at the "field level," due to imperfections in communication, shortages of resources, skill, understanding, commitment and so forth. (Effectiveness at the field level will be referred to as "penetration."[2])

I. A TYPOLOGY OF PARTIES

Most analyses of the legal system start at the rules end and work down through institutional facilities to see what effect the rules have on the parties. I would like to reverse that procedure and look through the other end of the telescope. Let's think

---

[2] Cf. Friedman (1969:43) who defines penetration as "the number of actors and spheres of action that a particular rule . . . actually reaches."

about the different kinds of parties and the effect these differences might have on the way the system works.

Because of differences in their size, differences in the state of the law, and differences in their resources, some of the actors in the society have many occasions to utilize the courts (in the broad sense) to make (or defend) claims; others do so only rarely. We might divide our actors into those claimants who have only occasional recourse to the courts (one-shotters or OS) and repeat players (RP) who are engaged in many similar litigations over time.[3] The spouse in a divorce case, the auto-injury claimant, the criminal accused are OSs; the insurance company, the prosecutor, the finance company are RPs. Obviously this is an oversimplification; there are intermediate cases such as the professional criminal.[4] So we ought to think of OS-RP as a continuum rather than as a dichotomous pair. Typically, the RP is a larger unit and the stakes in any given case are smaller (relative to total worth). OSs are usually smaller units and the stakes represented by the tangible outcome of the case may be high relative to total worth, as in the case of injury victim or the criminal accused. Or, the OS may suffer from the opposite problem: his claims may be so small and unmanageable (the shortweighted consumer or the holder of performing rights) that the cost of enforcing them outruns any promise of benefit. See Finklestein (1954: 284-6).

Let us refine our notion of the RP into an "ideal type" if you will—a unit which has had and anticipates repeated litigation, which has low stakes in the outcome of any one case, and which has the resources to pursue its long-run interests.[5] (This does not include every real-world repeat player; that most common repeat player, the alcoholic derelict, enjoys few of the advantages that may accrue to the RP [see below]. His resources are too few to bargain in the short run or take heed of the

---

[3] The discussion here focuses on litigation, but I believe an analogous analysis might be applied to the regulatory and rule-making phases of legal process. OSs and RPs may be found in regulatory and legislative as well as adjudicative settings. The point is nicely epitomized by the observation of one women's movement lobbyist:

> By coming back week after week . . . we tell them not only that we're here, but that we're here to stay. We're not here to scare anybody. . . . The most threatening thing I can say is that we'll be back. *New York Times*, Jan. 29, 1974, p. 34, col. 7–8.

For an interesting example of this distinction in the regulatory arena, see Lobenthal's (1970:20 ff.) description of the regulation of parking near a pier, contrasting the "permanent" shipping company and longshoreman interests with the OS pier visitors, showing how regulation gravitates to the accommodation of the former. This is, of course, akin to the "capture by the regulated" that attends (or afflicts) a variety of administrative agencies. *See, e.g.*, Bernstein (1955); Edelman (1967).

[4] Even the taxpayer and the welfare client are not pure OSs, since there is next year's tax bill and next month's welfare check. Our concept of OS conceals the difference between pure OSs—persons such as the accident victim who get in the situation only once—and those who are in a continuing series of transactions (welfare clients or taxpayers) but whose resources permit at most a single crack at litigation.

[5] Of course a Repeat Player need not engage in adjudication (or even in litigation). The term includes a party who makes or resists claims which may occupy any sector of the entire range of dispute processing mechanisms discussed in section V below. Perhaps the most successful RPs are those whose antagonists opt for resignation.

long run.[5]) An OS, on the other hand, is a unit whose claims are too large (relative to his size) or too small (relative to the cost of remedies) to be managed routinely and rationally.

We would expect an RP to play the litigation game differently from an OS. Let us consider some of his advantages:

(1) RPs, having done it before, have advance intelligence; they are able to structure the next transaction and build a record. It is the RP who writes the form contract, requires the security deposit, and the like.

(2) RPs develop expertise and have ready access to specialists.[7] They enjoy economies of scale and have low startup costs for any case.[8]

(3) RPs have opportunities to develop facilitative informal relations with institutional incumbents.[9]

(4) The RP must establish and maintain credibility as a combatant. His interest in his "bargaining reputation" serves as a resource to establish "commitment"

---

[6] In the "processing" of these parties and their limited strategic options, see Foote (1956); Spradley (1970: Chap. 6).

[7] Ironically, RPs may enjoy access to competent paraprofessional help that is unavailable to OSs. Thus the insurance company can, by employing adjusters, obtain competent and experienced help in routine negotiations without having to resort to expensive professionally qualified personnel. See Ross (1970:25) on the importance of the insurance adjuster in automobile injury settlements.

[8] An intriguing example of an RP reaping advantage from a combination of large scale operations and knowledgeability is provided by Skolnick's (1966:174 ff.) account of professional burglars' ability to trade clearances for leniency

[9] See, for example, Jacob's (1969:100) description of creditor colonization of small claims courts:

> . . . the neutrality of the judicial process was substantially compromised by the routine relationships which developed between representatives of frequent users of garnishment and the clerk of the court. The clerk scheduled cases so that one or two of the heavy users appeared each day. This enabled the clerk to equalize the work flow of his office. It also consolidated the cases of large creditors and made it unnecessary for them to come to court every day. It appeared that these heavy users and the clerk got to know each other quite well in the course of several months. Although I observed no other evidence of favoritism toward these creditors, it was apparent that the clerk tended to be more receptive toward the version of the conflict told by the creditor than disclosed by the debtor, simply because one was told by a man he knew and the other by a stranger.

The opportunity for regular participants to establish relations of trust and reciprocity with courts is not confined to these lowly precincts. Scigliano (1971:183–84) observes that:

> The Government's success in the Supreme Court seems to owe something . . . to the credit which the Solicitor General's Office has built up with the Court . . . in the first place, by helping the Court manage its great and growing burden of casework. . . . He holds to a trickle what could be a deluge of Government appeals. . . . In the second place by ensuring that the Government's legal work is competently done. So much so that when the Justices or their clerks want to extract the key issues in a complicated case quickly, they turn, according to common report, to the Government's brief.

> [Third.] The Solicitor General gains further credit . . . by his demonstrations of impartiality and independence from the executive branch.

to his bargaining positions. With no bargaining reputation to maintain, the OS has more difficulty in convincingly committing himself in bargaining.[10]

(5) RPs can play the odds.[11] The larger the matter at issue looms for OS, the more likely he is to adopt a minimax strategy (minimize the probability of maximum loss). Assuming that the stakes are relatively smaller for RPs, they can adopt strategies calculated to maximize gain over a long series of cases, even where this involves the risk of maximum loss[12] in some cases.[13]

(6) RPs can play for rules as well as immediate gains. First, it pays an RP to expend resources in influencing the making of the relevant rules by such methods as lobbying.[14] (And his accumulated expertise enables him to do this persuasively.)

(7) RPs can also play for rules in litigation itself, whereas an OS is unlikely to. That is, there is a difference in what they regard as a favorable outcome. Because his stakes in the immediate outcome are high and because by definition OS is unconcerned with the outcome of similar litigation in the future, OS will have little interest in that element of the outcome, which might influence the disposition of the decision-maker next time around. For the RP, on the other hand, anything that will favorably influence the outcomes of future cases is a worthwhile result. The larger the stakes for any player and the lower the probability of repeat play, the less likely that he will be concerned with the rules which govern future cases of the same kind. Consider two parents contesting the custody of their only child, the prizefighter vs. the IRS for tax arrears, the convict facing the death penalty. On the

---

[10] See Ross (1970:156 ff.); Schelling (1963:22 ff., 41). An offsetting advantage enjoyed by some OSs deserves mention. Since he does not anticipate continued dealings with his opponent, an OS can do his damnedest without fear of reprisal next time around or on other issues. (The advantages of those who enjoy the luxury of singlemindedness are evidenced by some notorious examples in the legislative arena, for instance, the success of prohibitionists and of the gun lobby.) Thus there may be a bargaining advantage to the OS who (a) has resources to damage his opponent; (b) is convincingly able to threaten to use them. An OS can burn up his capital, but he has to convince the other side he is really likely to do so. Thus an image of irrationality may be a bargaining advantage. See Ross (1970:170n.); Schelling (1963:17). An OS may be able to sustain such an image in a way that an RP cannot. But cf. Leff (1970a:18) on the role of "spite" in collections and the externalization to specialists of "irrational" vengeance.

[11] Ross (1970:214) notes that in dealing with the injury claimant, the insurance adjuster enjoys the advantage of "relative indifference to the uncertainty of litigation . . . the insurance company as a whole in defending large numbers of claims is unaffected by the uncertainty with respect to any one claim. . . . [F]rom the claimant's viewpoint [litigation] involves a gamble that may be totally lost. By taking many such gambles in litigating large numbers of cases the insurance company is able to regard the choice between the certainty and the gamble with indifference."

[12] That is, not the whole of RPs' worth, but the whole matter at issue in a single claim.

[13] Cf. the overpayment of small claims and underpayment of large claims in automobile injury cases. Franklin, Chanin and Mark (1961); Conard, *et al.* (1964). If small claim overpayment can be thought of as the product of the transaction costs of the defendants (and, as Ross [1970:207] shows, organizational pressures to close cases), the large claim underpayment represents the discount for delay and risk on the part of the claimant. (Conard, *et al.* 1964:197–99).

[14] Olson's analysis (1965:36ff, 127) suggests that their relatively small number should enhance the capacity of RPs for coordinated action to further common interests. See note 127.

other hand, the player with small stakes in the present case and the prospect of a series of similar cases (the IRS, the adoption agency, the prosecutor) may be more interested in the state of the law.

Thus, if we analyze the outcomes of a case into a tangible component and a rule component,[15] we may expect that in case 1, OS will attempt to maximize tangible gain. But if RP is interested in maximizing his tangible gain in a series of cases 1 . . . n, he may be willing to trade off tangible gain in any one case for rule gain (or to minimize rule loss).[16] We assumed that the institutional facilities for litigation were overloaded and settlements were prevalent. We would then expect RPs to "settle" cases where they expected unfavorable rule outcomes.[17] Since they expect to litigate again, RPs can select to adjudicate (or appeal) those cases which they regard as most likely to produce favorable rules.[18] On the other hand,

---

[15] This can be done only where institutions are simultaneously engaged in rule-making and dispute-settling. The rule-making function, however, need not be avowed; all that is required is that the outcome in Case 1 influence the outcome in Case 2 in a way that RP can predict.

[16] This is not to imply that rule loss or gain is the main determinant of settlement policy. First, the RP must litigate selectively. He can't fight every case. Second, rules are themselves the subject of dispute relatively rarely. Only a small fraction of litigation involves some disagreement between the parties as to what the rules are or ought to be. Dibble (1973).

In addition, the very scale that bestows on RPs strategic advantages in settlement policy exposes them to deviations from their goals. Most RPs are organizations and operate through individual incumbents of particular roles (house counsel, claims adjuster, assistant prosecutor) who are subject to pressures which may lead them to deviate from the optimization of institutional goals. Thus Ross (1970:220–21) notes that insurance companies litigate large cases where, although settlement would be "rational" from the overall viewpoint of the company, it would create unacceptable career risk to incumbents. Newman (1966:72) makes a similar observation about prosecutors' offices. He finds that even where the probability of conviction is slim "in cases involving a serious offense which has received a good deal of publicity . . . a prosecutor may prefer to try the case and have the charge reduction or acquittal decision made by the judge or jury."

[17] The assumption here is that "settlement" does not have precedent value. Insofar as claimants or their lawyers form a community which shares such information, this factor is diminished—as it is, for example, in automobile injury litigation where, I am told, settlements have a kind of precedent value.

[18] Thus the Solicitor General sanctions appeal to the Supreme Court in one-tenth of the appealable defeats of the Government, while its opponents appeal nearly half of their appealable defeats. Scigliano points out that the Government is more selective because:

> In the first place, lower-court defeats usually mean much less to the United States than they do to other parties. In the second place, the government has, as private litigants do not, an independent source of restraint upon the desire to litigate further (1971:169).

Appellants tend to be winners in the Supreme Court—about two-thirds of cases are decided in their favor. The United States government wins about 70% of the appeals it brings.

> What sets the government apart from other litigants is that it wins a much higher percentage of cases in which it is the appellee (56% in 1964–66). (1971:178).

Scigliano assigns as reasons for the government's success in the Supreme Court not only the "government's agreement with the court on doctrinal position" but the "expertise of the Solicitor General's Office" and "the credit which the Solicitor General has developed with the Court." (1971:182).

More generally, as Rothstein (1974:501) observes:

OSs should be willing to trade off the possibility of making "good law" for tangible gain. Thus, we would expect the body of "precedent" cases— that is, cases capable of influencing the outcome of future cases—to be relatively skewed toward those favorable to RP.[19]

Of course it is not suggested that the strategic configuration of the parties is the sole or major determinant of rule-development. Rule-development is shaped by a relatively autonomous learned tradition, by the impingement of intellectual currents from outside, by the preferences and prudences of the decision-makers. But courts are passive and these factors operate only when the process is triggered by parties. The point here is merely to note the superior opportunities of the RP to trigger promising cases and prevent the triggering of unpromising ones. It is not incompatible with a course of rule-development favoring OSs (or, as indicated below, with OSs failing to get the benefit of those favorable new rules).

In stipulating that RPs can play for rules, I do not mean to imply that RPs pursue rule-gain as such. If we recall that not all rules penetrate (i.e., become effectively applied at the field level) we come to some additional advantages of RPs.

(8) RPs, by virtue of experience and expertise, are more likely to be able to

The large volume litigant is able to achieve the most favorable forum; emphasize different issues in different courts; take advantage of difference in procedure among courts at the state and federal level; drop or compromise unpromising cases without fear of heavy financial loss; stall some cases and push others; and create rule conflicts in lower courts to encourage assumption of jurisdiction in higher courts. Cf. Hazard (1965:68).

[19] Macaulay (1966:99–101) in his study of relations between the automobile manufacturers and their dealers recounts that the manufacturers:

. . . had an interest in having the [Good Faith Act] construed to provide standards for their field men's conduct. Moreover they had resources to devote to the battle. The amount of money involved might be major to a canceled dealer, but few, if any cases involved a risk of significant liability to the manufacturers even if the dealer won. Thus the manufacturers could afford to fight as long as necessary to get favorable interpretations to set guidelines for the future. While dealers' attorneys might have to work on a contingent fee, the manufacturers already had their own large and competent legal staffs and could afford to hire trial and appellate specialists. . . . [A]n attorney on a contingent fee can afford to invest only so much time in a particular case. Since the manufacturers were interested in guidelines for the future, they could afford to invest, for example, $40,000 worth of attorneys' time in a case they could have settled for $10,000. Moreover, there was the factor of experience. A dealer's attorney usually started without any background in arguing a case under the Good Faith Act. On the other hand, a manufacturer's legal staff became expert in arguing such a case as it faced a series of these suits. It could polish its basic brief in case after case and even influence the company's business practices—such as record keeping—so that it would be ready for any suit.

. . . While individual dealers decide whether or not to file a complaint, the manufacturer, as any fairly wealthy defendant facing a series of related cases, could control the kinds of cases coming before the courts in which the Good Faith Act could be construed. It could defend and bring appeals in those cases where the facts are unfavorable to the dealer, and it could settle any where the facts favor the dealer. Since individual dealers were more interested in money than establishing precedents . . . the manufacturers in this way were free to control the cases the court would see.

The net effect . . . was to prompt a sequence of cases favorable to the manufacturers.

discern which rules are likely to "penetrate" and which are likely to remain merely symbolic commitments. RPs may be able to concentrate their resources on rule-changes that are likely to make a tangible difference. They can trade off symbolic defeats for tangible gains.

(9) Since penetration depends in part on the resources of the parties (knowledge, attentiveness, expert services, money), RPs are more likely to be able to invest the matching resources necessary to secure the penetration of rules favorable to them.

It is not suggested that RPs are to be equated with "haves" (in terms of power, wealth and status) or OSs with "have-nots." In the American setting most RPs are larger, richer and more powerful than are most OSs, so these categories overlap, but there are obvious exceptions. RPs may be "have-nots" (alcoholic derelicts) or may act as champions of "have-nots" (as government does from time to time); OSs such as criminal defendants may be wealthy. What this analysis does is to define a position of advantage in the configuration of contending parties and indicate how those with other advantages tend to occupy this position of advantage and to have their other advantages reinforced and augmented thereby.[20] This position of advantage is one of the ways in which a legal system formally neutral as between "haves" and "have-nots" may perpetuate and augment the advantages of the former.[21]

* * *

---

[20] Of course, even within the constraints of their strategic position, parties may fare better or worse according to their several capacities to mobilize and utilize legal resources. Nonet (1969: Chap. IV) refers to this as "legal competence"—that is, the capacity for optimal use of the legal process to pursue one's interests, a capacity which includes information, access, judgment, psychic readiness, and so forth.

An interesting example of the effects of such competence is provided by Rosenthal (1970: Chap. 2) who notes the superior results obtained by "active" personal injury plaintiffs. ("Active" clients are defined as those who express special wants to their attorneys, make follow-up demands for attention, marshal information to aid the lawyer, seek quality medical attention, seek a second legal opinion, and bargain about the fee.) He finds such "active" clients drawn disproportionately from those of higher social status (which presumably provides both the confidence and experience to conduct themselves in this active manner).

The thrust of the argument here is that the distribution of capacity to use the law beneficially cannot be attributed solely or primarily to personal characteristics of parties. The personal qualities that make up competence are themselves systematically related to social structure, both to general systems of stratification and to the degree of specialization of the parties. The emphasis here differs somewhat from that of Nonet, who makes competence central and for whom, for example, organization is one means of enhancing competence. This analysis views personal competence as operating marginally within the framework of the parties' relations to each other and to the litigation process. It is submitted that this reversal permits us to account for systematic differentials of competence and for the differences in the structure of opportunities which face various kinds of parties when personal competence is held constant.

[21] The tendency for formal equality to be compatible with domination has been noted by Weber (1954:188–91) and Ehrlich (1936:238), who noted: "The more the rich and the poor are dealt with according to the same legal propositions, the more the advantage of the rich is increased."

Digression on Litigation-Mindedness

We have postulated that OSs will be relatively indifferent to the rule-outcomes of particular cases. But one might expect the absolute level of interest in rule-outcomes to vary in different populations: in some there may be widespread and intense concern with securing vindication according to official rules that overshadows interest in the tangible outcomes of disputes; in others rule outcomes may be a matter of relative indifference when compared to tangible outcomes. The level and distribution of such "rule mindedness" may affect the relative strategic position of OSs and RPs. For example, the more rule minded a population, the less we would expect an RP advantage in managing settlement policy.

But such rule mindedness or appetite for official vindication should be distinguished from both (1) readiness to resort to official remedy systems in the first place and (2) high valuation of official rules as symbolic objects. Quite apart from relative concern with rule-outcomes, we might expect populations to differ in their estimates of the propriety and gratification of litigating in the first place.[22] Such

---

[22] Cf. Hahm (1969); Kawashima (1963) for descriptions of cultural settings in which litigation carries high psychic costs. (For the coexistence of anti-litigation attitudes with high rates of litigation, see Kidder [1971].) For a population with a greater propensity to litigate consider the following account (*New York Times*, Oct. 16, 1966) of contemporary Yugoslavia:

> Yugoslavs often complain of a personality characteristic in their neighbors that they call inat, which translates roughly as "spite." . . . One finds countless examples of it chronicled in the press . . . the case of two neighbors in the village of Pomoravije who had been suing each other for 30 years over insults began when one "gave a dirty look" to the other's pet dog.

> Last year the second district court in Belgrade was presented with 9000 suits over alleged slanders and insults. . . . Often the cases involve tenants crowded in apartment buildings. In one building in the Street of the October Revolution tenants began 53 suits against each other. Other causes of "spite" suits . . . included "a bent fence, a nasty look." Business enterprises are not immune and one court is handling a complaint of the Zastava Company of Knic over a debt of 10 dinars (less than 1 cent).

> In the countryside spite also appears in such petty forms as a brother who sued his sister because she gathered fruit fallen from a tree he regarded as his own. . . .
> Dr. Mirko Barjakterevic, professor of ethnology at Belgrade University . . . remarked that few languages had as many expressions for and about spite as Serbian and that at every turn one hears phrases like, "I'm going to teach him a lesson," and "I don't want to be made a fool of."

Consider, too, Frake's ("Litigation in Lipay: A Study in Subanum Law" quoted in Nader [1965:21]) account of the prominence of litigation among the Lipay of the Philippines:

> A large share, if not the majority, of legal cases deal with offenses so minor that only the fertile imagination of a Subanum legal authority can magnify them into a serious threat to some person or to society in general. . . . A festivity without litigation is almost as unthinkable as one without drink. If no subject for prosecution immediately presents itself, sooner or later, as the brew relaxes the tongues and actions, someone will make a slip.

> In some respects a Lipay trial is more comparable to an American poker game than to our legal proceedings. It is a contest of skill, in this case of verbal skill, accompanied by social merry-making, in which the loser pays a forfeit. He pays for much the same reason we pay a poker debt: so he can play the game again. Even if he does not

attitudes may affect the strategic situation of the parties. For example, the greater the distaste for litigation in a population, the greater the barriers to OSs pressing or defending claims, and the greater the RP advantages, assuming that such sentiments would affect OSs, who are likely to be individuals, more than RPs, who are likely to be organizations.[23]

It cannot be assumed that the observed variations in readiness to resort to official tribunals is directly reflective of a "rights consciousness" or appetite for vindication in terms of authoritative norms.[24] Consider the assertion that the low rate of litigation in Japan flows from an undeveloped "sense of justiciable rights" with the implication that the higher rate in the United States flows from such rights-consciousness.[25] But the high rate of settlements and the low rate of appeals in

> have the legal authority's ability to deal a verbalized "hand," he can participate as a defendant, plaintiff, kibitzer, singer, and drinker. No one is left out of the range of activities associated with litigation.

> Litigation nevertheless has far greater significance in Lipay than this poker-game analogy implies. For it is more than recreation. Litigation, together with the rights and duties it generates, so pervades Lipay life that one could not consistently refuse to pay fines and remain a functioning member of society. Along with drinking, feasting, and ceremonializing, litigation provides patterned means of interaction linking the independent nuclear families of Lipay into a social unit, even though there are no formal group ties of comparable extent. The importance of litigation as a social activity makes understandable its prevalence among the peaceful and, by our standards, "law-abiding" residents of Lipay.

[23] Generally, sentiments against litigation are less likely to affect organizations precisely because the division of labor within organizations means that litigation will be handled impersonally by specialists who do not have to conduct other relations with the opposing party (as customers, etc.). See Jacob (1969:78 ff.) on the separation of collection from merchandizing tasks as one of the determinants of creditor's readiness to avail of litigation remedies. And cf. the suggestion (note 16 above) that in complex organizations resort to litigation may be a way to externalize decisions that no one within the organization wants to assume responsibility for.

[24] Cf. Zeisel, Kalven & Buchholz (1959: Chap. 20). On the possibility of explaining differences in patterns of litigation by structural rather than cultural factors, see Kidder's (1971: Chap. IX) comparison of Indian and American litigation.

[25] Henderson (1968:488) suggests that in Japan, unlike America,

> . . . popular sentiment for justiciable rights is still largely absent. And, if dispute settlement is the context from which much of the growth, social meaning and political usefulness of justiciable rights derive—and American experience suggests it is—then the traditional tendency of the Japanese to rely on sublegal conciliatory techniques becomes a key obstacle in the path toward the rule-of-law envisioned by the new constitution.

He notes that

> In both traditional and modern Japan, conciliation of one sort or another has been and still is effective in settling the vast majority of disputes arising in the gradually changing social context. (1968:449).

Finding that Californians resorted to litigation about 23 times as often as Japanese, he concludes (1968:453) that traditional conciliation is employed to settle most "disputes that would go to court in a country with a developed sense of justiciable right." Henderson (1968:454) seems to imply that "in modern society [people] must comport thereselves according to reasonable and enforceable principles rather than haggling, negotiating and

the United States suggest it should not be regarded as having a population with great interest in securing moral victories through official vindication.[26] Mayhew (1973:14, Table I) reports a survey in which a sample of Detroit area residents were asked how they had wanted to see their "most serious problem" settled. Only a tiny minority (0% of landlord-tenant problems; 2% of neighborhood problems; 4% of expensive purchase problems; 9% of public organization problems; 31% of discrimination problems) reported that they sought "justice" or vindication of their legal rights: "most answered that they sought resolution of their problems in some more or less expedient way."

Paradoxically, low valuation of rule-outcomes in particular cases may co-exist with high valuation of rules as symbolic objects. Edelman (1967: chap. 2) distinguishes between remote, diffuse, unorganized publics, for whom rules are a source of symbolic gratification and organized, attentive publics directly concerned with the tangible results of their application. Public appetite for symbolic gratification by the promulgation of rules does not imply a corresponding private appetite for official vindication in terms of rules in particular cases. Attentive RPs on the other hand may be more inclined to regard rules instrumentally as assets rather than as sources of symbolic gratification.

* * *

We may think of litigation as typically involving various combinations of OSs and RPs. We can then construct a matrix such as Figure 1 and fill in the boxes with some well-known if only approximate American examples. (We ignore for the moment that the terms OS and RP represent ends of a continuum, rather than a dichotomous pair.)

On the basis of our incomplete and unsystematic examples, let us conjecture a bit about the content of these boxes:

Box I: OS vs. OS

The most numerous occupants of this box are divorces and insanity hearings. Most (over 90 per cent of divorces, for example) are uncontested.[27] A large portion of these are really pseudo-litigation, that is, a settlement is worked out between the parties and ratified in the guise of adjudication. When we get real litigation in Box I, it is often between parties who have some intimate tie with one another, fighting over some unsharable good, often with overtones of "spite" and "irrationality."

---

jockeying about to adjust personal relationships to fit an ever-shifting power balance among individuals."

Cf. Rabinowitz (1968: Part III) for a "cultural" explanation for the relative unimportance of law in Japanese society. (Non-egodeveloped personality, non-rational approach to action, extreme specificity of norms with high degree of contextual differentiation.)

[26] For an instructive example of response to a claimant who wants vindication rather than a tidy settlement, see Katz (1969:1492):

When I reported my client's instructions not to negotiate settlement at the pretrial conference, the judge appointed an impartial psychiatrist to examine Mr. Lin.

[27] For descriptions of divorce litigation, see Virtue (1956); O'Gorman (1963); Marshall and May (1932).

FIGURE 1
A TAXONOMY OF LITIGATION BY STRATEGIC
CONFIGURATION OF PARTIES

Initiator, Claimant

	One-Shotter	Repeat Player
One-Shotter	Parent v. Parent (Custody) Spouse v. Spouse (Divorce) Family v. Family Member (Insanity Commitment) Family v. Family (Inheritance) Neighbor v. Neighbor Partner v. Partner OS vs OS I	Prosecutor v. Accused Finance Co. v. Debtor Landlord v. Tenant I.R.S. v. Taxpayer Condemnor v. Property Owner RP vs OS II
Repeat Player	Welfare Client v. Agency Auto Dealer v. Manufacturer Injury Victim v. Insurance Company Tenant v. Landlord Bankrupt Consumer v. Creditors Defamed v. Publisher OS vs RP III	Union v. Company Movie Distributor v. Censorship Board Developer v. Suburban Municipality Purchaser v. Supplier Regulatory Agency v. Firms of Regulated Industry RP vs RP IV

Defendant

Courts are resorted to where an ongoing relationship is ruptured; they have little to do with the routine patterning of activity. The law is invoked *ad hoc* and instrumentally by the parties. There may be a strong interest in vindication, but neither party is likely to have much interest in the long-term state of the law (of, for instance, custody or nuisance). There are few appeals, few test cases, little expenditure of resources on rule-development. Legal doctrine is likely to remain remote from everyday practice and from popular attitudes.[28]

Box II: RP vs. OS

The great bulk of litigation is found in this box—indeed every really numerous kind except personal injury cases, insanity hearings, and divorces. The law is used for routine processing of claims by parties for whom the making of such claims is a regular business activity.[29] Often the cases here take the form of stereotyped mass

---

[28] For an estimate of the discrepancy between the law and popular attitudes in a "Box I" area, see Cohen, Robson and Bates (1958).

[29] Available quantitative data on the configuration of parties to litigation will be explored in a sequel to this essay. For the moment let me just say that the speculations here fit handily

processing with little of the individuated attention of full-dress adjudication. Even greater numbers of cases are settled "informally" with settlement keyed to possible litigation outcome (discounted by risk, cost, delay).

The state of the law is of interest to the RP, though not to the OS defendants. Insofar as the law is favorable to the RP it is "followed" closely in practice[30] (subject to discount for RP's transaction costs).[31] Transactions are built to fit the rules by creditors, police, draft boards and other RPs.[32] Rules favoring OSs may be less readily applicable, since OSs do not ordinarily plan the underlying transaction, or less meticulously observed in practice, since OSs are unlikely to be as ready or able as RPs to invest in insuring their penetration to the field level.[33]

---

with the available findings. For example, Wanner (1974), analyzing a sample of 7900 civil cases in three cities, found that business and governmental units are plaintiffs in almost six out of ten cases; and that they win more, settle less and lose less than individual plaintiffs. Individuals, on the other hand, are defendants in two thirds of all cases and they win less and lose more than do government or business units. A similar preponderance of business and governmental plaintiffs and individual defendants is reported in virtually all of the many studies of small claims courts. E.g., Pagter et al. (1964) in their study of a metropolitan California small claims court find that individuals made up just over a third of the plaintiffs and over 85% of defendants. A later survey of four small-town California small claims courts (Moulton 1969:1660) found that only 16% of plaintiffs were individuals—but over 93% of defendants.

[30] The analysis here assumes that, when called upon, judges apply rules routinely and relentlessly to RPs and OSs alike. In the event, litigation often involves some admixture of individuation, kadi justice, fireside equities, sentimentality in favor of the "little guy." (For a comparison of two small claims courts in one of which the admixture is stronger, see Yngvesson (1965)). It also involves some offsetting impurities in favor of frequent users. See note 9 above and note 59 below.

[31] Cf. Friedman (1967:806) on the zone of "reciprocal immunities" between, for example, landlord and tenant, afforded by the cost of enforcing their rights. The foregoing suggests that these immunities may be reciprocal, but they are not necessarily symmetrical. That is, they may differ in magnitude according to the strategic position of the parties. Cf. Vaughan's (1968:210) description of the "differential dependence" between landlord and low-income tenant. He regards this as reflecting the greater immediacy and constancy of the tenant's need for housing, the landlord's "exercise of privilege in the most elemental routines of the relationship," greater knowledge, and the fact that the landlord, unlike the tenant, does not have all his eggs in one basket (i.e., he is, in our terms, an RP).

> Whereas each tenant is dependent upon one landlord, the landlord typically diffuses his dependency among many tenants. As a result, the owner can rather easily retain an independent position in each relationship.

A similar asymmetry typically attends relations between employer and employee, franchiser and franchisee, insurer and insured, etc.

[32] See note 74 below. Cf. Skolnick's (1966:212ff) description of police adjustment to the exclusionary rule.

[33] Similarly, even OSs who have procured favorable judgments may experience difficulty at the execution stage. Even where the stakes loom large for OSs, they may be too small to enlist unsubsidized professional help in implementation. A recent survey of consumers who "won" in New York City's Small Claims Court found that almost a third were unable to collect. Marshals either flatly refused to accept such judgments for collection or "conveyed an impression that, even if they did take a small claims case, they would regard it as an annoyance and would not put much work into it." *New York Times,* Sept. 19, 1971. A subsequent survey (Community Service Society 1974:16) of 195 successful individual plaintiffs in two

Box III: OS vs. RP

All of these are rather infrequent types except for personal injury cases which are distinctive in that free entry to the arena is provided by the contingent fee.[34] In auto injury claims, litigation is routinized and settlement is closely geared to possible litigation outcome. Outside the personal injury area, litigation in Box III is not routine. It usually represents the attempt of some OS to invoke outside help to create leverage on an organization with which he has been having dealings but is now at the point of divorce (for example, the discharged employee or the cancelled franchisee).[35] The OS claimant generally has little interest in the state of the law; the RP defendant, however, is greatly interested.

Box IV: RP vs. RP

Let us consider the general case first and then several special cases. We might expect that there would be little litigation in Box IV, because to the extent that two RPs play with each other repeatedly,[36] the expectation of continued mutually benefcial interaction would give rise to informal bilateral controls.[37] This seems borne out by studies of dealings among businessmen[38] and in labor relations. Of-

---

Manhattan Small Claims Courts revealed that "only 50% of persons who received *judgments* were able to collect these through their own efforts or through use of sheriffs and marshals." (Plaintiffs who received settlements were more successful, collecting in 82% of the cases.) Cf. the finding of Hollingsworth, *et al.* (1973: Table 16) that of winning small claims plaintiffs in Hamilton County only 31% of individuals and unrepresented proprietorships collected half or more of the judgment amount; the corresponding figure for corporations and represented proprietorships was 55%.

[34] Perhaps high volume litigation in Box III is particularly susceptible to transformation into relatively unproblematic administrative processing when RPs discover that it is to their advantage and can secure a shift with some gains (or at least no losses) to OSs. Cf. the shift from tort to workman's compensation in the industrial accident area (Friedman and Ladinsky [1967]) and the contemporary shift to no-fault plans in the automobile injury area.

[35] Summers (1960:252) reports that "more than 3/4 of the reported cases in which individuals have sought legal protection of their rights under a collective agreement have arisen out of disciplinary discharge."

The association of litigation with "divorce" is clear in Macaulay (1963, 1969) and other discussions of commercial dealings. (Bonn 1972b:573 ff.). Consumer bankruptcy, another of the more numerous species of litigation in Box III, might be thought of as representing the attempt of the OS to effectuate a "divorce."

[36] For example, Babcock (1969:53–54) observes that what gives the suburb its greatest leverage on any one issue is the builder's need to have repeated contact with the regulatory powers of the suburb on various issues.

[37] The anticipated beneficial relations need not be with the identical party but may be with other parties with whom that party is in communication. RPs are more likely to participate in a network of communication which cheaply and rapidly disseminates information about the behavior of others in regard to claims and to have an interest and capacity for acquiring and storing that information. In this way RPs can cheaply and effectively affect the business reputation of adversaries and thus their future relations with relevant others. Leff (1970a; 26 ff.); Macaulay (1963:64).

[38] . . . why is contract doctrine not central to business exchanges?

Briefly put, private, between-the-parties sanctions usually exist, work and do not involve the costs of using contract law either in litigation or as a ploy in negotiations.

ficial agencies are invoked by unions trying to get established and by management trying to prevent them from getting established, more rarely in dealings between bargaining partners.[39] Units with mutually beneficial relations do not adjust their differences in courts. Where they rely on third parties in dispute-resolution, it is likely to take a form (such as arbitration or a domestic tribunal) detached from official sanctions and applying domestic rather than official rules.

However, there are several special cases. First, there are those RPs who seek not furtherance of tangible interests, but vindication of fundamental cultural commitments. An example would be the organizations which sponsor much church-state litigation.[40] Where RPs are contending about value differences (who is right) rather than interest conflicts (who gets what) there is less tendency to settle and less basis for developing a private system of dispute settlement.[41]

Second, government is a special kind of RP. Informal controls depend upon the ultimate sanction of withdrawal and refusal to continue beneficial relations.[42] To the extent that withdrawal of future association is not possible in dealing with government, the scope of informal controls is correspondingly limited. The development of informal relations between regulatory agencies and regulated firms is well known. And the regulated may have sanctions other than withdrawal which they can apply; for instance, they may threaten political opposition. But the more inclusive the unit of government, the less effective the withdrawal sanction and the greater the likelihood that a party will attempt to invoke outside allies by litigation even while sustaining the ongoing relationship. This applies also to monopolies,

---

. . . [M]ost importantly, there are relatively few one-shot, but significant, deals. A businessman usually cares about his reputation. He wants to do business again with the man he is dealing with and with others. Friedman and Macaulay (1967:805).

[39] Aspin (1966:2) reports that 70 to 75% of all complaints to the NLRB about the unfair labor practices of companies are under the single section [8(a)(3)] which makes it an unfair labor practice for employers to interfere with union organizing. These make up about half of *all* complaints of unfair labor practices.

[40] In his description of the organizational participants in church-state litigation, Morgan (1968:chap. 2) points out the difference in approach between value-committed "separationist purists" and their interest-committed "public schoolmen" allies. The latter tend to visualize the game as non-zero-sum and can conceive of advantages in alliances with their parochial-school adversaries. (1968:58n).

[41] Cf. Aubert's (1963:27 ff.) distinction between conflict careers based upon conflicts of interest and those arising from conflicts of value.

[42] This analysis is illuminated by Hirschman's distinction between two modes of remedial action by customers or members disappointed with the performance of organizations: (1) exit (that is, withdrawal of custom or membership); and (2) voice ("attempts at changing the practices and policies and outputs of the firm from which one buys or the organizations to which one belongs") [1970:30]. Hirschman attempts to discern the conditions under which each will be employed and will be effective in restoring performance. He suggests that the role of voice increases as the opportunities for exit decline, but that the possibility of exit increases the effectiveness of the voice mechanism. (1970:34, 83). Our analysis suggests that it is useful to distinguish those instances of voice which are "internal," that is, confined to expression to the other party, and those which are external, that is, seek the intervention of third parties. This corresponds roughly to the distinction between two-party and three-party dispute settlement. We might then restate the assertion to suggest that internal voice is effective where there is a plausible threat of sanction (including exit and external voice).

units which share the government's relative immunity to withdrawal sanctions.[43] RPs in monopolistic relationships will occasionally invoke formal controls to show prowess, to give credibility to threats, and to provide satisfactions for other audiences. Thus we would expect litigation by and against government to be more frequent than in other RP vs. RP situations. There is a second reason for expecting more litigation when government is a party. That is, that the notion of "gain" (policy as well as monetary) is often more contingent and problematic for governmental units than for other parties, such as businesses or organized interest groups. In some cases courts may, by proffering authoritative interpretations of public policy, redefine an agency's notion of gain. Hence government parties may be more willing to externalize decisions to the courts. And opponents may have more incentive to litigate against government in the hope of securing a shift in its goals.

A somewhat different kind of special case is present where plaintiff and defendant are both RPs but do not deal with each other repeatedly (two insurance companies, for example.) In the government/monopoly case, the parties were so inextricably bound together that the force of informal controls was limited; here they are not sufficiently bound to each other to give informal controls their bite; there is nothing to withdraw from! The large one-time deal that falls through, the marginal enterprise—these are staple sources of litigation.

Where there is litigation in the RP vs. RP situation, we might expect that there would be heavy expenditure on rule-development, many appeals, and rapid and elaborate development of the doctrinal law. Since the parties can invest to secure implementation of favorable rules, we would expect practice to be closely articulated to the resulting rules.

On the basis of these preliminary guesses, we can sketch a general profile of litigation and the factors associated with it. The great bulk of litigation is found in Box II; much less in Box III. Most of the litigation in these Boxes is mass routine processing of disputes between parties who are strangers (not in mutually beneficial continuing relations) or divorced[44]—and between whom there is a disparity in size.

[43] The potency of the monopolistic character of ties in promoting resort to third parties is suggested by the estimate that in the Soviet Union approximately one million contract disputes were arbitrated annually in the early 1960's. (Loeber, 1965:128, 133). Cf. Scott's (1965:63–64) suggestion that restricted mobility (defined in terms of job change) is associated with the presence of formal appeal systems in business organizations.

[44] That is, the relationship may never have existed, it may have "failed" in that it is no longer mutually beneficial, or the parties may be "divorced." On the incompatibility of litigation with ongoing relations between parties, consider the case of the lawyer employed by a brokerage house who brought suit against his employer in order to challenge New York State's law requiring fingerprinting of employees in the securities industry.

> They told me, "Don, you've done a serious thing: you've sued your employer." And then they handed me [severance pay] checks. They knew I had to sue them. Without making employer a defendant, it's absolutely impossible to get a determination in court. It was not a matter of my suing them for being bad guys or anything like that and they knew it. . . . [T]he biggest stumbling block is that I'm virtually blacklisted on Wall Street. . . .

His application for unemployment compensation was rejected on the ground that he had quit his employment without good cause, having provoked his dismissal by refusing to be fingerprinted. *New York Times*, March 2, 1970. It appears that, in the American setting at

One party is a bureaucratically organized "professional" (in the sense of doing it for a living) who enjoys strategic advantages. Informal controls between the parties are tenuous or ineffective; their relationship is likely to be established and defined by official rules; in litigation, these rules are discounted by transaction costs and manipulated selectively to the advantage of the parties. On the other hand, in Boxes I and IV, we have more infrequent but more individualized litigation between parties of the same general magnitude, among whom there are or were continuing multi-stranded relationships with attendant informal controls. Litigation appears when the relationship loses its future value; when its "monopolistic" character deprives informal controls of sufficient leverage and the parties invoke outside allies to modify it; and when the parties seek to vindicate conflicting values.

II. LAWYERS

What happens when we introduce lawyers? Parties who have lawyers do better.[45] Lawyers are themselves RPs. Does their presence equalize the parties, dispelling the advantage of the RP client? Or does the existence of lawyers amplify the advantage of the RP client? We might assume that RPs (tending to be larger units) who can buy legal services more steadily, in larger quantities, in bulk (by retainer) and at higher rates, would get services of better quality. They would have better information (especially where restrictions on information about legal services are present).[46] Not only would the RP get more talent to begin with, but he would on

---

any rate, litigation is not only incompatible with the maintenance of continuing relationships, but with their subsequent restoration. On the rarity of successful reinstatement of employees ordered reinstated by the NLRB, see Aspin (1966). Bonn (1972: 262) finds this pattern even among users of arbitration, which is supposedly less lethal to continuing relations than litigation. He found that in 78 cases of arbitration in textiles, "business relations were resumed in only fourteen." Cf. Golding's (1969:90) observation that jural forms of dispute-settlement are most appropriate where parties are not involved in a continuing relationship. But the association of litigation with strangers is not invariate. See the Yugoslav and Lipay examples in note 22 above. Cf. the Indian pattern described by Kidder (1971) and by Morrison (1975:39) who recounts that his North Indian villagers "commented scornfully that GR [a chronic litigant] would even take a complete stranger to law—proof that his energies were misdirected."

[45] For example, Ross (1970:193) finds that automobile injury claimants represented by attorneys recover more frequently than unrepresented claimants; that among those who recover, represented claimants recover significantly more than do unrepresented claimants with comparable cases. Claimants represented by firms recovered considerably more than claimants represented by solo practitioners; those represented by negligence specialists recovered more than those represented by firm attorneys. Similarly, Mosier and Soble (1973:35ff) find that represented tenants fare better in eviction cases than do unrepresented ones. The advantages of having a lawyer in criminal cases are well-known. See, for instance, Nagel (1973).

[46] As it happens, the information barriers vary in their restrictiveness. The American Bar Association's Code of Professional Responsibility permits advertising directed at corporations, banks, insurance companies, and those who work in the upper echelons of such institutions . . . [while proscribing] most forms of dissemination of information which would reach people of "moderate means" and apprise them of their legal rights and how they can find competent and affordable legal assistance to vindicate those rights. (Burnley 1973:77). On the disparate effect of these restrictions, cf. note 51.

the whole get greater continuity, better record-keeping, more anticipatory or pre-ventive work, more experience and specialized skill in pertinent areas, and more control over counsel.

One might expect that just how much the legal services factor would accen-tuate the RP advantage would be related to the way in which the profession was organized. The more members of the profession were identified with their clients (i.e., the less they were held aloof from clients by their loyalty to courts or an au-tonomous guild) the more the imbalance would be accentuated.[47] The more close and enduring the lawyer-client relationship, the more the primary loyalty of law-yers is to clients rather than to courts or guild, the more telling the advantages of accumulated expertise and guidance in overall strategy.[48]

What about the specialization of the bar? Might we not expect the existence of specialization to offset RP advantages by providing OS with a specialist who in pursuit of his own career goals would be interested in outcomes that would be advantageous to a whole class of OSs? Does the specialist become the functional equivalent of the RP? We may divide specialists into (1) those specialized by field

---

[47] The tension between the lawyer's loyalties to the legal system and to his client has been celebrated by Parsons (1954:381 ff.) and Horsky (1952: chap. 3). But note how this same deflection of loyalty from the client is deplored by Blumberg (1967) and others. The differ-ence in evaluation seems to depend on whether the opposing pull is to the autonomous legal tradition, as Parsons (1954) and Horsky (1972) have it, or to the maintanance of mutually beneficial interaction with a particular local institution whose workings embody some ad-mixture of the "higher law" (see note 82 below) with parochial understandings, institutional maintenance needs, etc.

[48] Although this is not the place to elaborate it, let me sketch the model that underlies this assertion. (For a somewhat fuller account, see International Legal Center, 1973:4ff.). Let us visualize a series of scales along which legal professions might be ranged:

		A		B
1.	Basis of Recruitment	Restricted	_____	Wide
2.	Barriers to Entry	High	_____	Low
3.	Division of Labor			
	a. Coordination	Low	_____	High
	b. Specialization	Low	_____	High
4.	Range of Services and Functions	Narrow	_____	Wide
5.	Enduring Relationships to Client	Low	_____	High
6.	Range of Institutional Settings	Narrow	_____	Wide
7.	Identification with Clients	Low	_____	High
8.	Identification with Authorities	High	_____	Low
9.	Guild Control	Tight	_____	Loose
10.	Ideology	Legalistic	_____	Problem-solving

It is suggested that the characteristics at the A and B ends of the scale tend to go together, so that we can think of the A and B clusters as means of describing types of bodies of legal professionals, for example, the American legal profession (Hurst 1950; Horsky 1952: Pt. V.; Carlin 1962, 1966; Handler 1967; Smigel 1969) would be a B type, compared to British bar-risters (Abel-Smith and Stevens 1967) and French *avocats* (LePaulle 1950); Indian lawyers (Galanter 1968–69), an intermediate case. It is suggested that some characteristics of Type B professions tend to accentuate or amplify the strategic advantages of RP parties. Consider-ation of, for instance, the British bar, should warn us against concluding that Type B profes-sions are necessarily more conservative in function than Type A. See text, at footnote 145.

of law (patent, divorce, etc.), (2) those specialized by the kind of party represented (for example, house counsel), and (3) those specialized by both field of law and "side" or party (personal injury plaintiff, criminal defense, labor). Divorce lawyers do not specialize in husbands or wives,[49] nor real-estate lawyers in buyers or sellers. But labor lawyers and tax lawyers and stockholders-derivative-suit lawyers do specialize not only in the field of law but in representing one side. Such specialists may represent RPs or OSs. Figure 2 provides some well-known examples of different kinds of specialists:

FIGURE 2
A TYPOLOGY OF LEGAL SPECIALISTS

Lawyer

	Specialized by Party	Specialized by Field and Party	Specialized by Field
RP Client	"House Counsel" or General Counsel for Bank, Insurance Co. etc. Corporation Counsel for Government Unit	Prosecutor Personal Injury Defendant Staff Counsel for NAACP Tax Labor/Management Collections	Patent
OS	"Poverty Lawyers" Legal Aid	Criminal Defense Personal Injury Plaintiff	Bankruptcy Divorce

Most specializations cater to the needs of particular kinds of RPs. Those specialists who service OSs have some distinctive features:

First, they tend to make up the "lower echelons" of the legal profession. Compared to the lawyers who provide services to RPs, lawyers in these specialties tend to be drawn from lower socio-economic origins, to have attended local, proprietary or part-time law schools, to practice alone rather than in large firms, and to possess low prestige within the profession.[50] (Of course the correlation is far from perfect; some lawyers who represent OSs do not have these characteristics and some representing RPs do. However, on the whole the difference in professional standing is massive).

Second, specialists who service OSs tend to have problems of mobilizing a clientele (because of the low state of information among OSs) and encounter "ethi-

---

[49] Which is not to deny the possibility that such "side" specialization might emerge. One can imagine "women's liberation" divorce lawyers—and anti-alimony ones—devoted to rule-development that would favor one set of OSs.

[50] On stratification within the American legal profession see Ladinsky (1963); Lortie (1959); Carlin (1966). But cf. Handler (1967).

cal" barriers imposed by the profession which forbids solicitation, advertising, referral fees, advances to clients, and so forth.[51]

Third, the episodic and isolated nature of the relationship with particular OS clients tends to elicit a stereotyped and uncreative brand of legal services. Carlin and Howard (1965:385) observe that:

> The quality of service rendered poorer clients is . . . affected by the non-repeating character of the matters they typically bring to lawyers (such as divorce, criminal, personal injury): this combined with the small fees encourages a mass processing of cases. As a result, only a limited amount of time and interest is usually expended on any one case—there is little or no incentive to treat it except as an isolated piece of legal business. Moreover, there is ordinarily no desire to go much beyond the case as the client presents it, and such cases are only accepted when there is a clear-cut cause of action; i.e., when they fit into convenient legal categories and promise a fairly certain return.

Fourth, while they are themselves RPs, these specialists have problems in developing optimizing strategies. What might be good strategy for an insurance company lawyer or prosecutor—trading off some cases for gains on others—is branded as unethical when done by a criminal defense or personal injury plaintiff lawyer.[52] It is not permissible for him to play his series of OSs as if they constituted a single RP.[53]

Conversely, the demands of routine and orderly handling of a whole series of OSs may constrain the lawyer from maximizing advantage for any individual OS. Rosenthal (1970:172) shows that "for all but the largest [personal injury] claims an attorney loses money by thoroughly preparing a case and not settling it early."

For the lawyer who services OSs, with his transient clientele, his permanent "client" is the forum, the opposite party, or the intermediary who supplies clients. Consider, for example, the dependence of the criminal defense lawyer on maintaining cooperative relations with the various members of the "criminal court community."[54] Similarly, Carlin notes that among metropolitan individual prac-

---

[51] See Reichstein (1965); Northwestern University Law Review (1953). On the differential impact of the "Canons of Ethics" on large law firms and those lawyers who represent OSs, see Carlin (1966); Shuchman (1968); Christianson (1970:136).

[52] ". . . the canons of ethics would prevent an attorney for a [oneshotter] . . . from trying to influence his client to drop a case that would create a bad precedent for other clients with similar cases. On the other hand, the canons of ethics do not prevent an attorney from advising a corporation that some of its cases should not be pursued to prevent setting a bad precedent for its other cases." (Rothstein 1974:502).

[53] Ross (1970:82) observes the possibility of conflict between client and

> the negligence specialist, who negotiates on a repeated basis with the same insurance companies. [H]is goal of maximizing the return from any given case may conflict with the goal of maximizing returns from the total series of cases he represents.

For a catalog of other potential conflicts in the relationship between specialists and OS clients, see O'Connell (1971:46–47).

[54] Blumberg (1967:47) observes

> [defense] counsel, whether privately retained or of the legal aid variety, have close and continuing relations with the prosecuting office and the court itself. Indeed, lines

titioners whose clientele consists of OSs, there is a deformation of loyalty toward the intermediary.

> In the case of those lawyers specializing in personal injury, local tax, collections, criminal, and to some extent divorce work, the relationship with the client ... is generally mediated by a broker or business supplier who may be either another lawyer or a layman. In these fields of practice the lawyer is principally concerned with pleasing the broker or winning his approval, more so than he is with satisfying the individual client. The source of business generally counts for more than the client, especially where the client is unlikely to return or to send in other clients. The client is then expendable: he can be exploited to the full. Under these conditions, when a lawyer receives a client ... he has not so much gained a client as a piece of business, and his attitude is often that of handling a particular piece of merchandise or of developing a volume of a certain kind of merchandise.[55]

The existence of a specialized bar on the OS side should overcome the gap in expertise, allow some economies of scale, provide for bargaining commitment and personal familiarity. But this is short of overcoming the fundamental strategic advantages of RPs—their capacity to structure the transaction, play the odds, and influence rule-development and enforcement policy.

Specialized lawyers may, by virtue of their identification with parties, become lobbyists, moral entrepreneurs, proponents of reforms on the parties' behalf. But lawyers have a cross-cutting interest in preserving complexity and mystique so that client contact with this area of law is rendered problematic.[56] Lawyers should not be expected to be proponents of reforms which are optimum from the point of view of the clients taken alone. Rather, we would expect them to seek to opti-

---

> of communication, influence and contact with those offices, as well as with the other subsidiary divisions of the office of the clerk and the probation division and with the press are essential to the practice of criminal law. Accused persons come and go in the court system, but the structure and its personnel remain to carry on their respective careers, occupational, and organizational enterprises. . . . [T]he accused's lawyer has far greater professional, economic, intellectual, and other ties to the various elements of the court system than to his own client.

Cf. Skolnick (1967); Battle (1971). On the interdependence of prosecutor and public defender, see Sudnow (1965:265, 273).

[55] Carlin (1962:161–62). On the "stranger" relationship between accident victim client and lawyer, see Hunting and Neuwirth (1962:109).

[56] Cf. Consumer Council (1970:19). In connection with the lawyer's attachment to (or at least appreciation of) the problematic character of the law, consider the following legend, carried at the end of a public service column presented by the Illinois State Bar Association and run in a neighborhood newspaper:

> No person should ever apply or interpret any law without consulting his attorney. Even a slight difference in the facts may change the result under the law. (*Woodlawn Booster*, July 31, 1963).

Where claims become insufficiently problematic they may drop out of the legal sphere entirely (such as social security). In high-volume and repetitive tasks which admit of economies of scale and can be rendered relatively unproblematic, lawyers may be replaced by entrepreneurs—title companies, bank trust departments—serving OSs on a mass basis (or even serving RPs, as do collection agencies). Cf. Johnstone and Hopson (1967:158ff).

mize the clients' position without diminishing that of lawyers. Therefore, specialized lawyers have an interest in a framework which keeps recovery (or whatever) problematic at the same time that they favor changes which improve their clients' position within this framework. (Consider the lobbying efforts of personal injury plaintiffs and defense lawyers.) Considerations of interest are likely to be fused with ideological commitments: the lawyers' preference for complex and finely-tuned bodies of rules, for adversary proceedings, for individualized case-by-case decision-making.[57] Just as the culture of the client population affects strategic position, so does the professional culture of the lawyers.

III. INSTITUTIONAL FACILITIES

We see then that the strategic advantages of the RP may be augmented by advantages in the distribution of legal services. Both are related to the advantages conferred by the basic features of the institutional facilities for the handling of claims: passivity and overload.

These institutions are passive, first, in the sense that Black refers to as "reactive"—they must be mobilized by the claimant—giving advantage to the claimant with information, ability to surmount cost barriers, and skill to navigate restrictive procedural requirements.[58] They are passive in a further sense that once in the door the burden is on each party to proceed with his case.[59] The presiding official acts as

---

[57] Stumpf, *et al.* (1971:60) suggest that professional responses to OEO legal services programs require explanation on ideological ("the highly individualized, case-by-case approach . . . as a prime article of faith") as well as pecuniary grounds. On the components of legalism as an ideology, see Shklar (1964:1–19). Of course this professional culture is not uniform but contains various subcultures. Brill's (1973) observations of OEO poverty lawyers suggest that crucial aspects of professional ideology (e.g., the emphasis on courts, rules and adjudication) are equally pronounced among lawyers who seek far-reaching change through the law.

[58] Black (1973:141) observes the departures from the passive or "reactive" stance of legal institutions tend to be skewed along class lines:

> . . . governments disproportionately adopt proactive systems of legal mobilization when a social control problem primarily involves the bottom of the social-class system. . . . The common forms of legal misconduct in which upper status citizens indulge, such as breach of contract and warranty, civil negligence, and various forms of trust violation and corruption, are usually left to the gentler hand of a reactive mobilization process.

[59] The passivity of courts may be uneven. Cf. Mosier and Soble's (1973:63) description of Detroit landlord-tenant court:

> If a tenant was unrepresented, the judge ordinarily did not question the landlord regarding his claims, nor did the judge explain defenses to the tenant. The most common explanation given a tenant was that the law permitted him only ten days to move and thus the judge's hands were tied. In addition, judges often asked tenants for receipts for rent paid and corroboration of landlord-breach claims. In contrast, the court supplied complaint and notice forms to the landlords and clerks at the court helped them to fill out the forms if necessary. In addition, the in-court observers noticed during the beginning of the study that the court would not dismiss a nonappearing landlord's case until completion of the docket call, which took approximately forty-five minutes (while the tenant sat and waited), but extended no similar courtesy to

umpire, while the development of the case, collection of evidence and presentation of proof are left to the initiative and resources of the parties.[60] Parties are treated as if they were equally endowed with economic resources, investigative opportunities and legal skills (Cf. Homberger [1971:641]). Where, as is usually the case, they are not, the broader the delegation to the parties, the greater the advantage conferred on the wealthier,[61] more experienced and better organized party.[62]

The advantages conferred by institutional passivity are accentuated by the chronic overload which typically characterizes these institutions.[63] Typically there are far more claims than there are institutional resources for full dress adjudication of each. In several ways overload creates pressures on claimants to settle rather than to adjudicate:

(a) by causing delay (thereby discounting the value of recovery);

(b) by raising costs (of keeping the case alive);

---

tardy tenants. However, once the surprised observers questioned the court personnel about the practice, it was changed; thereafter, tenants had thirty minutes after the call within which to appear.

The disparities in help given to landlords and tenants and the treatment of late land-lords and tenants are an indication of the perhaps inevitable bias of the court toward the landlord. Most of the judges and court personnel have a middle-class background and they have become familiar with many landlords and attorneys appearing regularly in the court. The court had years of experience as a vehicle for rent collection and eviction where no defenses could be raised. The judges and clerks repeatedly hear about tenants who fail to pay rent or did damage to the premises, while they probably never have the opportunity to observe the actual condition of the housing that the landlords are renting.

[60] Homberger (1970:31–31). For a description of more "active" courts see Kaplan, *et al.* (1958:1221 ff); Homberger (1970). Our description is of courts of the relatively passive variety typical of "common law" systems, but should not be taken as implying that "civil law" systems are ordinarily or typically different in practice. Cf. Merryman (1969:124). The far end of a scale of institutional "activism" might be represented by institutions like the Soviet Procuracy (Berman 1963:238ff). And, of course, even among common law courts passivity is relative and variable. Courts vary in the extent to which they exercise initiative for the purpose of developing a branch of the law (the "Lord Mansfield Syndrome"—see Lowry 1973) or actively protecting some class of vulnerable parties.

[61] As Rothstein (1974:506) sums it up, counsel fees and

[c]ourt costs, witness fees (especially for experts), investigation costs, court reporters fees, discovery costs, transcript costs, and the cost of any bond needed to secure opponents' damages, all make litigation an expensive task, thereby giving the advantage to those with large financial resources.

[62] A further set of institutional limitations should be mentioned here: limitations on the scope of matters that courts hear; the kind of relief that they can give; and on their capacity for systematic enforcement are discussed below (pp. 51 ff).

[63] On the limited supply of institutional facilities, consider Saari's (1967) estimate that in the early 1960's total governmental expenditures for civil and criminal justice in the United States ran about four to five billion dollars annually. (Of this, about 60% went for police and prosecution, about 20% for corrections, and 20% for courts.) This amounted to about 2.5% of direct expenditures of American governments. In 1965–66 expenditures for the judiciary represented 1/17 of 1% of the total federal budget; 6/10 of 1% of state budgets; something less than 6% of county and 3% of city budgets.

(c) by inducing institutional incumbents to place a high value on clearing dockets, discouraging full-dress adjudication in favor of bargaining, stereotyping and routine processing;[64]

(d) by inducing the forum to adopt restrictive rules to discourage litigation.[65]

Thus, overload increases the cost and risk of adjudicating and shields existing rules from challenge, diminishing opportunities for rule-change.[66] This tends to favor the beneficiaries of existing rules.

Second, by increasing the difficulty of challenging going practice, overload also benefits those who reap advantage from the neglect (or systematic violation) of rules which favor their adversaries.

Third, overload tends to protect the possessor—the party who has the money or goods—against the claimant.[67] For the most part, this amounts to favoring RPs over OSs, since RPs typically can structure transactions to put themselves in the possessor position.[68]

Finally, the overload situation means that there are more commitments in the

---

[64] The substitution of bargaining for adjudication need not be regarded as reflecting institutional deficiency. Even in criminal cases it may seem providential:

> It is elementary, historically and statistically, that systems of courts—the number of judges, prosecutors and courtrooms—have been based on the premise that approximately 90 percent of all [criminal] defendants will plead guilty, leaving only 10 percent, more or less, to be tried. . . . The consequences of what might seem on its face a small percentage change in the rate of guilty pleas can be tremendous. . . . [I]n Washington, D.C. . . . the guilty plea rate dropped to 65 percent. . . . [T]welve judges out of fifteen in active service were assigned to the criminal calendar and could barely keep up. . . . [T]o have this occur in the National Capital, which ought to be a model for the nation and show place for the world, was little short of disaster (Burger, 1970:931).

[65] On institutional coping with overload, see Friedman (1967:798ff).

[66] Cf. Foote (1956:645) on the rarity of appeal in vagrancy cases. Powell and Rohan (1968:177–78) observe that the ordinary week-to-week or month-to-month rental agreement

> is tremendously important sociologically in that occupancy thereunder conditions the home life of a very substantial fraction of the population. On the other hand, the financial smallness of the involved rights results in a great dearth of reported decisions from the courts concerning them. Their legal consequences are chiefly fixed in the 'over the counter' mass handling of "landlord and tenant" cases of the local courts. So this type of estate, judged sociologically is of great importance, but judged on the basis of its jurisprudential content is almost negligible.

[67] In the criminal process, too, the "possessor" (i.e., of defendant's mobility) enjoys great advantages. On the higher likelihood of conviction and of severe sentencing of those detained before trial, see Rankin (1964) and Wald (1964). Engle (1971) finds that among those convicted pre-trial status explains more of the variation in sentencing severity than any of 23 other factors tested.

[68] See Leff (1970a:22) on the tendency of RP creditors to put themselves in the possessor position, shifting the costs of "due process" to the OS debtor. There are, however, instances where OSs may use overload to advantage; for instance, the accused out on bail may benefit from delay. Cf. Engle's (1971) observation of the "weakening effect of time on the prosecutor's position." Rioters or rent-strikers may threaten to demand jury trials, but the effectiveness of this tactic depends on a degree of coordination that effectuates a change of scale.

formal system than there are resources to honor them—more rights and rules "on the books" than can be vindicated or enforced. There are, then, questions of priorities in the allocation of resources. We would expect judges, police, administrators and other managers of limited institutional facilities to be responsive to the more organized, attentive and influential of their constituents.[69] Again, these tend to be RPs.

Thus, overloaded and passive institutional facilities provide the setting in which the RP advantages in strategic position and legal services can have full play.[70]

IV. RULES[71]

We assume here that rules tend to favor older, culturally dominant interests.[72] This is not meant to imply that the rules are explicitly designed to favor these interests,[73] but rather that those groups which have become dominant have suc-

---

[69] For example, the court studied by Zeisel, *et al.* (1959:7) "had chosen to concentrate all of its delay in the personal injury jury calendar and to keep its other law calendars up to date, granting blanket preferment to all commercial cases . . . and to all non-jury personal injury cases." (Recovery in the latter was about 20% lower than jury awards in comparable cases [1959:119]).

[70] This analysis has not made separate mention of corruption, that is, the sale by incumbents of system outcomes divergent from those prescribed by authoritative norms. Insofar as such activities are analytically distinguishable from favorable priorities and "benign neglect" it should be noted that, since such enterprise on any considerable scale is confined to the organized, professional and wealthy, this provides yet another layer of advantage to some classes of "haves."

[71] I would like to emphasize that the term "rules" is used here as shorthand for all the authoritative normative learning. It is unnecessary for the purpose at hand to take a position on the question of whether all of that learning consists of rules or whether principles, policies, values, and standards are best understood as fundamentally different. It is enough for our purposes to note that this learning is sufficiently complex that the result in many cases is problematic and unknowable in advance.

[72] Even assuming that every instance of formulating rules represented a "fair" compromise among "have" and "have-not" interests, we should expect the stock of rules existing at any given time to be skewed toward those which favor "haves." The argument (cf. Kennedy 1973:384–5) goes like this: At the time of its formulation, each rule represents a current consensus about a just outcome as among competing interests. Over time the consensus changes, so that many rules are out of line with current understandings of fairness. Rule-makers (legislative, administrative and judicial) can attend to only some of all the possible readjustments. Which ones they will attend to depends in large measure on the initiative of those affected in raising the issue and mobilizing support to obtain a declaration of the more favorable current consensus. "Haves" (wealthy, professional, repeat players) enjoy a superior ability to elicit such declarations (cf. p. 100 ff.); they are thus likely to enjoy the timely benefits of shifts of social consensus in their favor. OSs, on the other hand, will often find it difficult to secure timely changes in the rules to conform to a new consensus more favorable to them. Thus RPs will be the beneficiaries of the timelag between crystallized rules and current consensus. Thus, even with the most favorable assumptions about rule-making itself, the mere fact that rules accrue through time, and that it requires expenditure of resources to overcome the lag of rules behind current consensus, provides RPs with a relatively more favorable set of rules than the current consensus would provide.

[73] This is sometimes the case; consider, for instance, the rules of landlord-tenant. Ohlhausen (1936) suggests that rules as to the availability of provisional remedies display a pronounced suc-

cessfully articulated their operations to pre-existing rules.[74] To the extent that rules are evenhanded or favor the "have-nots," the limited resources for their implementation will be allocated, I have argued, so as to give greater effect to those rules which protect and promote the tangible interests of organized and influential groups. Furthermore, the requirements of due process, with their barriers or protections against precipitate action, naturally tend to protect the possessor or holder against the claimant.[75] Finally, the rules are sufficiently complex[76] and problematic (or capable of being problematic if sufficient resources are expended to make them so) that differences in the quantity and quality of legal services will affect capacity to derive advantages from the rules.[77]

Thus, we arrive at Figure 3 which summarizes why the "haves" tend to come out ahead. It points to layers of advantages enjoyed by different (but largely overlapping) classes of "haves"—advantages which interlock, reinforcing and shielding one another.

---

pattern of favoring claims of types likely to be brought by the "well to do" over claims of types brought by the impecunious.

[74] Thus the modern credit seller-lender team have built their operation upon the destruction of the purchaser's defenses by the holder in due course doctrine originally developed for the entirely different purpose of insuring the circulation of commercial paper. See Rosenthal (1971:377 ff.). Shuchman (1971:761–62) points out how in consumer bankruptcies:

> Consumer creditors have adjusted their practices so that sufficient proof will be conveniently available for most consumer loans to be excepted from discharge under section 17a (2). They have made wide use of renewals, resetting, and new loans to pay off old loans, with the result that the consumers' entire debt will often be nondischargeable. Section 17a (2) constitutes, in effect, an enabling act—a skeletal outline that the consumer creditor can fill in to create nondischargeable debts—that operated to defeat the consumer's right to the benefits of a discharge in bankruptcy.

Similarly, Shuchman (1969) shows how RP auto dealers and financial institutions have developed patterns for resale of repossessed automobiles that meet statutory resale requirements but which permit subsequent profitable second sale and in addition produce substantial deficiency claims. More generally, recall the often-noted adaptive powers of regulated industry which manage, in Hamilton's (1957: chap. 2) terms, to convert "regulations into liberties" and "controls into sanctions."

[75] For some examples of possessor-defendants exploiting the full panoply of procedural devices to raise the cost to claimants, see Schrag (1969); Macaulay (1966:98). Large (1972) shows how the doctrines of standing, jurisdiction and other procedural hurdles, effectively obstruct application of favorable substantive law in environmental litigation. Facing these rules in serial array, the environmentalists win many skirmishes but few battles.

[76] Cf. the observation of Tullock (1971:48–49) that complexity and detail—the "maze" quality of legal rules—in itself confers advantages on "people of above average intelligence, with literary and scholarly interests"—and by extension on those who can develop expertise or employ professional assistance.

[77] For an example of the potency of a combination of complexity and expertise in frustrating recovery, see Laufer (1970). Of course, the advantage may derive not from the outcome, but from the complexity, expense and uncertainty of the litigation process itself. Borkin (1950) shows how, in a setting of economic competition among units of disparate size and resources, patent litigation may be used as a tactic of economic struggle. Cf. Hamilton (1957:75–76).

FIGURE 3
WHY THE "HAVES" TEND TO COME OUT AHEAD

Element	Advantages	Enjoyed by
PARTIES	– ability to structure transaction – specialized expertise, economies of scale – long-term strategy – ability to play for rules – bargaining credibility – ability to invest in penetration	– repeat players large, professional*
LEGAL SERVICES	– skill, specialization, continuity	– organized professional* wealthy
INSTITUTIONAL FACILITIES	– passivity – cost and delay barriers – favorable priorities	– wealthy, experienced, organized – holders, possessors – beneficiaries of existing rules – organized, attentive
RULES	– favorable rules – due process barriers	– older, culturally dominant – holders, possessors

* in the simple sense of "doing it for a living"

V. ALTERNATIVES TO THE OFFICIAL SYSTEM

We have been discussing resort to the official system to put forward (or defend against) claims. Actually, resort to this system by claimants (or initiators) is one of several alternatives. Our analysis should consider the relationship of the characteristics of the total official litigation system to its use *vis-à-vis* the alternatives. These include at least the following:

(1) Inaction—"lumping it," not making a claim or complaint. This is done all the time by "claimants" who lack information or access[78] or who knowingly decide gain is too low, cost too high (including psychic cost of litigating where such activity is repugnant). Costs are raised by lack of information or skill, and also include

---

[78] On the contours of "inaction," see Levine and Preston (1970); Mayhew and Riess (1969); Ennis (1967); Republic Research, Inc. (1970); Hallauer (1972).

risk. Inaction is also familiar on the part of official complainers (police, agencies, prosecutors) who have incomplete information about violations, limited resources, policies about *de minimus*, schedules of priorities, and so forth.[79]

(2) "Exit"—withdrawal from a situation or relationship by moving, resigning, severing relations, finding new partners, etc. This is of course a very common expedient in many kinds of trouble. Like "lumping it," it is an alternative to invocation of any kind of remedy system—although its presence as a sanction may be important to the working of other remedies.[80] The use of "exit" options depends on the availability of alternative opportunities or partners (and information about them), the costs of withdrawal, transfer, relocation, development of new relationships, the pull of loyalty to previous arrangements—and on the availability and cost of other remedies.[81]

(3) Resort to some unofficial control system—we are familiar with many instances in which disputes are handled outside the official litigation system. Here we should distinguish (a) those dispute-settlement systems which are normatively and institutionally appended to the official system (such as settlement of auto-injuries, handling of bad checks) from (b) those settlement systems which are relatively independent in norms and sanctions (such as businessmen settling disputes *inter se*, religious groups, gangs).

What we might call the "appended" settlement systems merge imperceptibly into the official litigation system. We might sort them out by the extent to which the official intervention approaches the adjudicatory mode. We find a continuum from situations where parties settle among themselves with an eye to the official rules and sanctions, through situations where official intervention is invoked, to those in which settlement is supervised and/or imposed by officials, to full-dress adjudication. All along this line the sanction is supplied by the official system (though not always in the manner prescribed in the "higher law")[82] and the norms or rules applied are a version of the official rules, although discounted for transaction costs and distorted by their selective use for the purposes of the parties.

---

[79] See Rabin (1972) and Miller (1969) (prosecutors); LaFave (1965) and Black (1971) (police); and generally, Davis (1969). Courts are not the only institutions in the legal system which are chronically overloaded. Typically, agencies with enforcement responsibilities have many more authoritative commitments than resources to carry them out. Thus "selective enforcement" is typical and pervasive; the policies that underlie the selection lie, for the most part, beyond the "higher law." On the interaction between enforcement and rule-development, see Gifford (1971).

[80] On exit or withdrawal as a sanction, see note 42 and text there. For an attempt to explore propensities to choose among resignation, exit, and voice in response to neighborhood problems, see Orbell and Uno (1972). "Exit" would seem to include much of what goes under the rubric of "self-help." Other common forms of self-help, such as taking possession of property, usually represent a salvage operation in the wake of exit by the other party. Yet other forms, such as force, are probably closer to the private dispute settlement systems discussed below.

[81] There are, of course, some cases (such as divorce or bankruptcy) in which exit can be accomplished only by securing official certification or permission; that is, it is necessary to resort to an official remedy system in order to effectuate exit.

[82] This term is used to refer to the law as a body of authoritative learning (rules, doctrines, principles) as opposed to the parochial embodiments of this higher law, as admixed with local understandings, priorities, and the like.

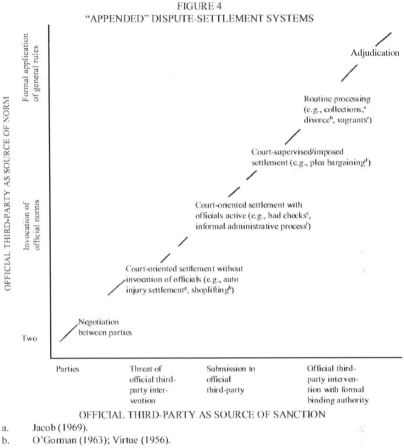

FIGURE 4
"APPENDED" DISPUTE-SETTLEMENT SYSTEMS

OFFICIAL THIRD-PARTY AS SOURCE OF SANCTION

a. Jacob (1969).
b. O'Gorman (1963); Virtue (1956).
c. Foote (1956); Spradley (1970).
d. Newman (1966: chap. 3); McIntyre and Lippman (1970).
e. Beutel (1957:287 ff.); cf. the operation of the Fraud and Complaint Department at McIntyre (1968:470-71).
f. Woll (1960); cf. the "formal informal settlement system" of the Motor Vehicles Bureau, described by Macaulay (1966:153 ff.).
g. Ross (1970).
h. Cameron (1964:32-36).

From these "appended" systems of discounted and privatized official justice, we should distinguish those informal systems of "private justice" which invoke other norms and other sanctions. Such systems of dispute-settlement are typical among people in continuing interaction such as an organized group, a trade, or a university.[83] In sorting out the various types according to the extent and the mode

---

[83] "Private" dispute settlement may entail mainly bargaining or negotiation between the parties (dyadic) or may involve the invocation of some third party in the decision-making position. It is hypothesized that parties whose roles in a transaction or relationship are complementary (husband-wife, purchaser-supplier, landlord-tenant) will tend to rely on dyadic processes in which group norms enter without specialized apparatus for announcing or enforcing norms. Precisely because of the mutual dependence of the parties, a capacity to

of intervention of third parties, we can distinguish two dimensions: the first is the degree to which the applicable norms are formally articulated, elaborated, and exposited, that is the increasingly organized character of the norms. The second represents the degree to which initiative and binding authority are accorded to the third party, that is, the increasingly organized character of the sanctions. Some conjectures about the character of some of the common types of private systems are presented in Figure 5.

Our distinction between "appended" and "private" remedy systems should not be taken as a sharp dichotomy but as pointing to a continuum along which we might range the various remedy systems.[84] There is a clear distinction between appended systems like automobile injury or bad check settlements and private systems like the internal regulation of the mafia (Cressey, 1969: Chaps. VIII, IX; Ianni, 1972), or the Chinese community.[85] The internal regulatory aspects of universities, churches and groups of businessmen lie somewhere in between.[86] It is as if we could visualize a scale stretching from the official remedy system through ones oriented to it through relatively independent systems based on similar values to independent systems based on disparate values.[87]

---

sanction is built into the relationship. On the other hand, parties who stand in a parallel position in a set of transactions, such as airlines or stockbrokers *inter se*, tend to develop remedy systems with norm exposition and sanction application by third parties. Again, this is because the parties have little capacity to sanction the deviant directly. This hypothesis may be regarded as a reformulation of Schwartz' (1954) proposition that formal controls appear where informal controls are ineffective and explains his finding of resort to formal controls on an Israeli moshav (cooperative settlement) but not in a kibbutz (collective settlement). In this instance, the interdependence of the kibbutzniks made informal controls effective, while the "independent" moshav members needed formal controls. This echos Durkheim's (1964) notion of different legal controls corresponding to conditions of organic and mechanical solidarity. A corollary to this is suggested by re-analysis of Mentschikoff's (1961) survey of trade association proclivity to engage in arbitration. Her data indicate that the likelihood of arbitration is strongly associated with the fungibility of goods (her categories are raw, soft and hard goods). Presumably dealings in more unique hard goods entail enduring purchaser-supplier relations which equip the parties with sanctions for dyadic dispute-settlement, sanctions which are absent among dealers in fungible goods. Among the latter, sanctions take the form of exclusion from the circle of traders, and it is an organized third party (the trade association) that can best provide this kind of sanction.

[84] The distinction is not intended to ignore the overlap and linkage that may exist between "appended" and "private" systems. See, for example, Macaulay's (1966:151 ff.) description of the intricate interweaving of official, appended and private systems in the regulation of manufacturer-dealer relations; Randall's (1968: chap. 8) account of the relation between official and industry censorship; Akers' (1968:470) observation of the interpenetration of professional associations and state regulatory boards.

[85] On internal regulation in Chinese communities in the United States, see Doo (1973); Light (1972, chap. 5, especially 89-94); Grace (1970).

[86] Cf. Mentschikoff's (1961) discussion of various species of commercial arbitration. She distinguishes casual arbitrations conducted by the American Arbitration Association which emphasize general legal norms and standards and where the "ultimate sanction . . . is the rendering of judgment on the award by a court. . . ." (1961:858) from arbitration within self-contained trade groups [where] the norms and standards of the group itself are being brought to bear by the arbitrators (1961:857) and the ultimate sanction is an intra-group disciplinary proceeding.

[87] The dotted extension of the scale in Figure 6 is meant to indicate the possibility of pri-

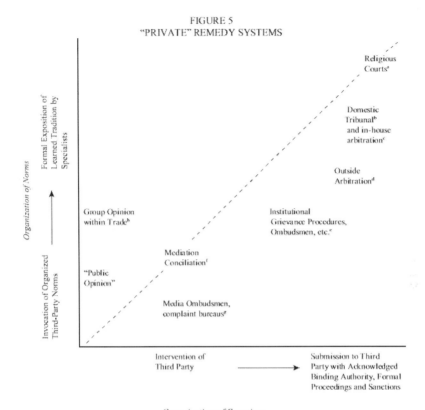

FIGURE 5
"PRIVATE" REMEDY SYSTEMS

Organization of Sanctions

a. Columbia J. of Law and Social Problems (1970, 1971); Shriver (1966); Ford (1970:457-79).
b. E.g., The International Air Transport Association (Gollan 1970); professional sports leagues and associations (Goldpaper 1971).
c. Mentschikoff (1961:859).
d. Bonn (1972); Mentschikoff (1961:856-57).
e. Gellhorn, 1966; Anderson (1969: chaps IV, V).
f. E.g., labor-management (Simkin [1971: chap. 3]); MacCallum (1967).
g. E.g., newspaper "action-line" columns, Better Business Bureaus.
h. Macaulay (1963:63-64); Leif (1970a:29 ff).

Presumably it is not accidental that some human encounters are regulated frequently and influentially by the official and its appended systems while others seem to generate controls that make resort to the official and its appended systems rare. Which human encounters are we likely to find regulated at the "official" end of our scale and which at the "private" end? It is submitted that location on our

vate systems which are not only structurally independent of the official system but in which the shared values comprise an oppositional culture. Presumably this would fit, for example, internal dispute settlement among organized and committed criminals or revolutionaries. Closer to the official might be the sub-cultures of delinquent gangs. Although they have been characterized as deviant sub-cultures, Matza (1964: chap. 2, esp. 59 ff.) argues that in fact the norms of these groups are but variant readings of the official legal culture. Such variant readings may be present elsewhere on the scale; for instance, businessmen may not recognize any divergence of their notion of obligatory business conduct from the law of contract.

scale varies with factors that we might sum up by calling them the "density" of the relationship. That is, the more inclusive in life-space and temporal span a relationship between parties,[88] the less likely it is that those parties will resort to the official system[89] and more likely that the relationship will be regulated by some independent "private" system.[90] This seems plausible because we would expect inclusive and enduring relationships to create the possibility of effective sanctions;[91] and we would expect participants in such relationships to share a value consensus[92] which provided standards for conduct and legitimized such sanctions in case of deviance.

---

[88] Since dealings between settlement specialists such as personal injury and defense lawyers may be more recurrent and inclusive than the dealings between parties themselves, one might expect that wherever specialist intermediaries are used, the remedy-system would tend to shift toward the private end of our spectrum. Cf. Skolnick (1967:69) on the "regression to cooperation" in the "criminal court community."

[89] Not only is the transient and simplex relationship more likely to be subjected to official regulation, it is apparently more amenable to formal legal control. See, for example, the greater success of antidiscrimination statutes in public accommodation than in housing and in housing than in employment (success here defined merely as a satisfactory outcome for the particular complainant). See Lockard (1968:91,122,138). Mayhew (1968:245 ff.; 278 ff.) provides an interesting demonstration of the greater impact of official norms in housing than in employment transactions in spite of the greater evaluative resistance to desegregation in the latter.

[90] The capacity of continuing or "on-going" relationships to generate effective informal control has been often noted (Macaulay 1963:63–64; Yngvesson 1976). It is not temporal duration *per se* that provides the possibility of control, but the serial or incremental character of the relationship, which provides multiple choice points at which parties can seek and induce adjustment of the relationship. The mortgagor-mortgagee relationship is an enduring one, but one in which there is heavy reliance on official regulation, precisely because the frame is fixed and the parties cannot withdraw or modify it. Contrast landlord-tenant, husband-wife or purchaser-supplier, in which recurrent inputs of cooperative activity are required, the withholding of which gives the parties leverage to secure adjustment. Schelling (1963:41) suggests a basis for this in game theory: threats intended to deter a given act can be delivered with more credibility if they are capable of being decomposed into a number of consecutive smaller threats.

[91] Conversely, the official system will tend to be used where such sanctions are unavailable, that is, where the claimee has no hope of any stream of benefits from future relations with the claimant (or those whose future relation with claimee will be influenced by his response to the claim). Hence the association of litigation with the aftermath of "divorce" (marital, commercial or organizational) or the absence of any "marriage" to begin with (e.g., auto injury, criminal). That is, government is the remedy agent of last resort and will be used in situations where one party has a loss and the other party has no expectation of any future benefit from the relationship.

[92] This does not imply that the values of the participants are completely independent of and distinct from the officially authoritative ones. More common are what we have referred to (note 87 above) as "variant readings" in which elements of authoritative tradition are re-ordered in the light of parochial understandings and priorities. For example, the understanding of criminal procedure by the police (Skolnick [1966:219 ff.]) or of air pollution laws by health departments (Goldstein and Ford [1971:20 ff.]). Thus the variant legal cultures of various legal communities at the field or operating level can exist with little awareness of principled divergence from the higher law.

FIGURE 6
A SCALE OF REMEDY SYSTEMS FROM OFFICIAL TO PRIVATE

REMEDY SYSTEMS

OFFICIAL		APPENDED			PRIVATE		
Adjudication	Routine Processing	Structurally Interstitial (Officials Participating)	Oriented to Official	Articulated to Official	Independent		Oppositional
	Collections Divorce	Plea bargaining, bad check recovery	Auto injury settlement	Businessmen	Churches, Chinese community	Gangs	Mafia, Revolutionaries

EXAMPLES

The prevalence of private systems does not necessarily imply that they embody values or norms which are competing or opposed to those of the official system. Our analysis does not impute the plurality of remedy systems to cultural differences as such. It implies that the official system is utilized when there is a disparity between social structure and cultural norm. It is used, that is, where interaction and vulnerability create encounters and relationships which do not generate shared norms (they may be insufficiently shared or insufficiently specific) and/or do not give rise to group structures which permit sanctioning these norms.[93]

Figure 7 sketches out such relationships of varying density and suggests the location of various official and private remedy systems.

---

[93] This comports with Bohannan's (1965:34 ff.) notion that law comprises a secondary level of social control in which norms are re-institutionalized in specialized legal institutions. But where Bohannan implies a constant relationship between the primary institutionalization of norms and their reinstitutionalization in specialized legal institutions, the emphasis here is on the difference in the extent to which relational settings can generate self-corrective remedy systems. Thus it suggests that the legal level is brought into play where the original institutionalization of norms is incomplete, either in the norms or the institutionalization.

Bohannan elaborates his analysis by suggesting (1965:37 ff.) that the legal realm can be visualized as comprising various regions of which the "Municipal systems of the sort studied by most jurists deal with a single legal culture within a unicentric power system." (In such a system, differences between institutional practice and legal prescription are matters of phase or lag.) Divergences from unity (cultural, political, or both) define other regions of the legal realm: respectively, colonial law, law in stateless societies and international law.

The analysis here suggests that "municipal systems" themselves may be patchworks in which normative consensus and effective unity of power converge only imperfectly. Thus we might expect a single legal system to include phenomena corresponding to other regions of his schema of the legal realm. The divergence of the "law on the books" and the "law in action" would not then be ascribable solely to lag or "phase" (1965:37) but rather would give expression to the discontinuity between culture and social structure.

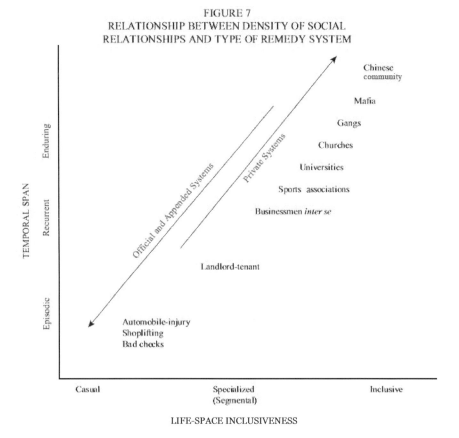

FIGURE 7
RELATIONSHIP BETWEEN DENSITY OF SOCIAL
RELATIONSHIPS AND TYPE OF REMEDY SYSTEM

It restates our surmise of a close association between the density of relationships and remoteness from the official system.[94] We may surmise further that on
the whole the official and appended systems flourish in connection with the disputes between parties of disparate size which give rise to the litigation in Boxes II

---

[94] The association postulated here seems to have support in connection with a number of
distinct aspects of legal process:

Presence of legal controls: Schwartz (1954) may be read as asserting that relational density (and the consequent effectiveness of informal controls) is inversely related to the presence of legal controls (defined in terms of the presence of sanction specialists).

Invocation (mobilization) of official controls: Black (1971:1097) finds that readiness to
invoke police and insistence of complainants on arrest is associated with "relational dis-
tance" between the parties. Cf. Kawashima's (1962:45) observation that in Japan, where
litigation was rare between parties to an enduring relationship regulated by shared ideals of
harmony, resort to officials was common where such ties were absent, as in cases of inter-
village and usurer-debtor disputes.

Elaboration of authoritative doctrine: Derrett (1959:54) suggests that the degree of elaboration of authoritative learned doctrine in classical Hindu law is related to the likelihood
that the forums applying such doctrine would be invoked, which is in turn dependent on the
absence of domestic controls.

and III of Figure I. Private remedy systems, on the other hand, are more likely to handle disputes between parties of comparable size.[95] The litigation in Boxes I and IV of Figure 1, then, seems to represent in large measure the breakdown (or inhibited development) of private remedy systems. Indeed, the distribution of litigation generally forms a mirror image of the presence of private remedy systems. But the mirror is, for the various reasons discussed here, a distorting one.

From the vantage point of the "higher law" what we have called the official system may be visualized as the "upper" layers of a massive "legal"[96] iceberg, something like this:

> Adjudication
> Litigation
> Appended Settlement Systems
> Private Settlement Systems
> Exit Remedies/Self Help
> Inaction ("lumping it")

The uneven and irregular layers are distinct although they merge imperceptibly into one another.[97] As we proceed to discuss possible reforms of the official system, we will want to consider the kind of impact they will have on the whole iceberg.

We will look at some of the connections and flows between layers mainly from the point of view of the construction of the iceberg itself, but aware that flows and connections are also influenced by atmospheric (cultural) factors such as appetite for vindication, psychic cost of litigation, lawyers' culture and the like.

VI. STRATEGIES FOR REFORM

Our categorization of four layers of advantage (Figure 3) suggests a typology of strategies for "reform" (taken here to mean equalization—conferring relative advantage on those who did not enjoy it before). We then come to four types of equalizing reform:

> (1) rule-change
> (2) improvement in institutional facilities
> (3) improvement of legal services in quantity and quality
> (4) improvement of strategic position of have-not parties

---

[95] There are, of course, exceptions, such as the automobile manufacturers' administration of warranty claims described by Whitford (1968) or those same manufacturers' internal dealer relations tribunals described by Macaulay (1966).

[96] The iceberg is not properly a legal one, hence the quotation marks. That is, I do not mean to impute any characteristics that might define the "legal" (officials, coercive sanctions, specialists, general rules) to all the instances in the iceberg. It is an iceberg of potential claims or disputes and the extent to which any sector of it is legalized is problematic. Cf. Abel (1974).

[97] Contrast the more symmetrical "great pyramid of legal order" envisioned by Hart and Sacks (1958:312). Where the Hart and Sacks pyramid portrays private and official decision-making as successive moments of an integrated normative and institutional order, the present "iceberg" model suggests that the existence of disparate systems of settling disputes is a reflection of cultural and structural discontinuities.

I shall attempt to sketch some of the possible ramifications of change on each of these levels for other parts of the litigation system and then discuss the relationship between changes in the litigation system and the rest of our legal iceberg. Of course such reforms need not be enacted singly, but may occur in various combinations. However, for our purposes we shall only discuss, first, each type taken in isolation and then, all taken together.

A. Rule-change

Obtaining favorable rule changes is an expensive process. The various kinds of "have-nots" (Figure 3) have fewer resources to accomplish changes through legislation or administrative policy-making. The advantages of the organized, professional, wealthy and attentive in these forums are well-known. Litigation, on the other hand, has a flavor of equality. The parties are "equal before the law" and the rules of the game do not permit them to deploy all of their resources in the conflict, but require that they proceed within the limiting forms of the trial. Thus, litigation is a particularly tempting arena to "have-nots," including those seeking rule change.[98] Those who seek change through the courts tend to represent relatively isolated interests, unable to carry the day in more political forums.[99]

Litigation may not, however, be a ready source of rule-change for "have-nots." Complexity, the need for high inputs of legal services and cost barriers (heightened by overloaded institutional facilities) make challenge of rules expensive. OS claimants, with high stakes in the tangible outcome, are unlikely to try to obtain rule changes. By definition, a test case—litigation deliberately designed to procure rule-change—is an unthinkable undertaking for an OS. There are some departures from our ideal type: OSs who place a high value on vindication by official rules or whose peculiar strategic situation makes it in their interest to pursue rule victories.[100] But

---

[98] Hazard (1970:246–47) suggests that the attractions of the courts include that they are open as of right, receptive to arguments based on principle and offer the advocate a forum in which he bears no responsibility for the consequences of having his arguments prevail.

[99] Dolbeare (1967:63). Owen (1971:68, 142) reports the parallel finding that in two Georgia counties "opinion leaders and influentials seldom use the court, except for economic retrieval." Cf. Howard's (1969:346) observation that ". . . adjudication is preeminently a method for individuals, small groups and minorities who lack access to or sufficient strength within the political arena to mobilize a favorable change in legislative coalitions."

[100] There are situations in which no settlement is acceptable to the OS. The most common case, perhaps, is that of the prisoner seeking post-conviction remedies. He has "infinite" costless time and nothing further to lose. Other situations may be imagined in which an OS stands only to gain by a test case and has the resources to expend on it. Consider, for example, the physician charged with ten counts of illegal abortion. Pleading guilty to one count if the state dropped the others and agreeing to a suspended sentence would still entail the loss of his license. Every year of delay is worth money, win or lose: the benefits of delay are greater than the costs of continued litigation.
When the price of alternatives becomes unacceptably high, we may find OSs swimming upstream against a clear rule and strategic disadvantage. (Cf. the explosion of selective service cases in the 1960's.) Such a process may be facilitated by, for example, the free entry afforded by the contingent fee. See Friedman and Ladinsky's (1967) description of the erosion of the fellow servant rule under the steady pounding of litigation by injured workman with no place else to turn and free entry.

generally the test case involves some organization which approximates an RP.[101]

The architecture of courts severely limits the scale and scope of changes they can introduce in the rules. Tradition and ideology limit the kinds of matters that come before them; not patterns of practice but individual instances, not "problems" but cases framed by the parties and strained through requirements of standing, case or controversy, jurisdiction, and so forth. Tradition and ideology also limit the kind of decision they can give. Thus, common law courts for example, give an all-or-none,[102] once-and-for-all[103] decision which must be justified in terms of a limited (though flexible) corpus of rules and techniques.[104] By tradition, courts cannot address problems by devising new regulatory or administrative machinery (and have no taxing and spending powers to support it); courts are limited to solutions compatible with the existing institutional framework.[105] Thus, even the most

---

[101] See Vose (1967) on the test-case strategy of the NAACP in the restrictive covenant area. By selecting clients to forward an interest (rather than serving the clients) the NAACP made itself an RP with corresponding strategic advantages over the opposite parties (neighborhood associations). The degree of such organizational support of litigation is a matter of some dispute. Participation by organized interest groups in litigation affecting municipal powers is described in Vose (1966); but Dolbeare (1967:40), in his study of litigation over public policy issues in a suburban county, found a total absence of interest-group sponsorship and participation in cases at the trial court level. Vose (1972:332) concludes a historical review by observing that:

> Most constitutional cases before the Supreme Court . . . are sponsored or supported by an identifiable voluntary association. . . . [This] has been markedly true for decades.

But Hakman (1966, 1969) found management of Supreme Court litigation by organized groups pursuing coherent long-range strategies to be relatively rare. But see Casper (1970) who contends that civil liberties and civil rights litigation in the Supreme Court is increasingly conducted by lawyers who are "group advocates" (that is, have a long-term commitment to a group with whose aims they identify) or "civil libertarians" (that is, have an impersonal commitment to the vindication of broad principles) rather than advocates. He suggests that the former types of representation lead to the posing of broader issues for decision.

[102] Although judicial decisions do often embody or ratify compromises agreed upon by the parties, it is precisely at the level of rule promulgation that such splitting the difference is seen as illegitimate. On the ideological pressures limiting the role of compromise in judicial decision see Coons (1964).

[103] Cf. Kalven (1958:165). There are, of course, exceptions, such as alimony, to this "once and for all" feature.

[104] Hazard (1970:248–50) points out that courts are not well-equipped to address problems by devising systematic legal generalizations. They are confined to the facts and theories presented by the parties in specific cases; after deciding the case before them, they lose their power to act; they have little opportunity to elicit commentary until after the event; and generally they can extend but not initiate legal principles. They have limited and rapidly diminishing legitimacy as devisers of new policy. Nor can courts do very much to stimulate and maintain political support for new rules.

[105] See generally Friedman (1967: esp. 821); Hazard (1970:248–50). The limits of judicial competence are by no means insurmountable. Courts do administer bankrupt railroads, recalcitrant school districts, offending election boards. But clearly the amount of such affirmative administrative re-ordering that courts can undertake is limited by physical resources as well as by limitations on legitimacy.

favorably inclined court may not be able to make those rule-changes most useful to a class of "have-nots."

Rule-change may make use of the courts more attractive to "have-nots." Apart from increasing the possibility of favorable outcomes, it may stimulate organization, rally and encourage litigants. It may directly redistribute symbolic rewards to "have-nots" (or their champions). But tangible rewards do not always follow symbolic ones. Indeed, provision of symbolic rewards to "have-nots" (or crucial groups of their supporters) may decrease capacity and drive to secure redistribution of tangible benefits.[106]

Rule-changes secured from courts or other peak agencies do not penetrate automatically and costlessly to other levels of the system, as attested by the growing literature on impact.[107] This may be especially true of rule-change secured by adjudication, for several reasons:

(1) Courts are not equipped to assess systematically the impact or penetration problem. Courts typically have no facilities for surveillance, monitoring, or securing systematic enforcement of their decrees. The task of monitoring is left to the parties.[108]

(2) The built-in limits on applicability due to the piecemeal character of adjudication. Thus a Mobilization for Youth lawyer reflects:

> ... What is the ultimate value of winning a test case? In many ways a result cannot be clearcut ... if the present welfare-residency laws are invalidated, it is quite possible that some other kind of welfare-residency law will spring up in their place. It is not very difficult to come up with a policy that is a little different, stated in different words, but which seeks to achieve the same basic objective. The results of test cases are not generally self-executing. . . . It is not enough to have a law invalidated or a policy declared void if the agency in question can come up with some variant of that policy, not very different in substance but sufficiently different to remove it from the effects of the court order.[109]

---

[106] See Lipsky (1970:176 ff.) for an example of the way in which provision of symbolic rewards to more influential reference publics effectively substituted for the tangible reforms demanded by rent-strikers. More generally, Edelman (1967:chap. 2) argues that it is precisely unorganized and diffuse publics that tend to receive symbolic rewards, while organized professional ones reap tangible rewards.

[107] For a useful summary of this literature, see Wasby (1970). Some broad generalizations about the conditions conducive to penetration may be found in Grossman (1970:545 ff.); Levine (1970:599 ff.).

[108] Cf. Howard's (1969:365 ff.) discussion of the relative ineffectualness of adjudication in voter registration and school integration (as opposed to subsequent legislative/administrative action) as flowing from judicial reliance on party initiative.

[109] Rothwax (1969:143). An analogous conclusion in the consumer protection field is reached by Leff (1970b:356). ("One cannot think of a more expensive and frustrating course than to seek to regulate goods or 'contract' quality through repeated law-suits against inventive 'wrongdoers.'") Leff's critique of Murray's (1969) faith in good rules to secure change in the consumer marketplace parallels Handler's (1966) critique of Reich's (1964a, 1964b) prescription of judicial review to secure change in welfare administration. Cf. Black's (1973:137) observation that institutions which are primarily reactive, requiring mobilization by citizens, tend to deal with specific instances rather than general patterns and, as a consequence,

(3) The artificial equalizing of parties in adjudication by insulation from the full play of political pressures—the "equality" of the parties, the exclusion of "irrelevant" material, the "independence" of judges—means that judicial outcomes are more likely to be at variance with the existing constellation of political forces than decisions arrived at in forums lacking such insulation. But resources that cannot be employed in the judicial process can reassert themselves at the implementation stage, especially where institutional overload requires another round of decision making (what resources will be deployed to implement which rules) and/or private expenditures to secure implementation. Even where "have-nots" secure favorable changes at the rule level, they may not have the resources to secure the penetration of these rules.[110] The impotence of rule-change, whatever its source, is particularly pronounced when there is reliance on unsophisticated OSs to utilize favorable new rules.[111]

Where rule-change promulgated at the peak of the system does have an impact on other levels, we should not assume any isomorphism. The effect on institutional facilities and the strategic position of the parties may be far different than we would predict from the rule change. Thus, Randall's study of movie censorship shows that liberalization of the rules did not make censorship boards more circumspect; instead, many closed down and the old game between censorship boards and distributors was replaced by a new and rougher game between exhibitors and local government-private group coalitions.[112]

B. Increase in Institutional Facilities

Imagine an increase in institutional facilities for processing claims such that there is timely full-dress adjudication of every claim put forward—no queue, no delay, no stereotyping. Decrease in delay would lower costs for claimants, taking away this advantage of possessor-defendants. Those relieved of the necessity of discounting recovery for delay would have more to spend on legal services. To the extent that settlement had been induced by delay (rather than insuring against the risk of unacceptable loss), claimants would be inclined to litigate more and settle less. More litigation without stereotyping would mean more contests, including more contesting of rules and more rule change. As discounts diminished, neither side could use settlement policy to prevent rule-loss. Such reforms would for the most part benefit OS claimants, but they would also improve the position of those

---

have little preventive capacity.

[110] Consider for example the relative absence of litigation about schoolroom religious practices clearly in violation of the Supreme Court's rules, as reported by Dolbeare and Hammond (1971). In this case RPs who were able to secure rule-victories were unable or unwilling to invest resources to secure the implementation of the new rules.

[111] See, for example, Mosier and Soble's (1973:61-64) study of the Detroit Landlord-Tenant Court, where even after the enactment of new tenant defenses (landlord breach, retaliation), landlords obtained all they sought in 97% of cases. The new defenses were raised in only 3% of all cases (13% of the 20% that were contested) although, the authors conclude, "many defendants doubtless had valid landlord breach defenses."

[112] Randall (1968:chap. 7). Cf. Macaulay's (1966:156) finding that the most important impact of the new rules was to provide leverage for the operation of informal and private procedures in which dealers enjoyed greater bargaining power in their negotiations with manufacturers.

RP claimants not already in the possessor position, such as the prosecutor where the accused is free on bail.

This assumes no change in the kind of institutional facilities. We have merely assumed a greater quantitative availability of courts of the relatively passive variety typical of (at least) "common law" systems in which the case is "tried by the parties before the court. . . ." (Homberger, 1970:31). One may imagine institutions with augmented authority to solicit and supervise litigation, conduct investigations, secure, assemble and present proof; which enjoyed greater flexibility in devising outcomes (such as compromise or mediation); and finally which had available staff for monitoring compliance with their decrees.[113] Greater institutional "activism" might be expected to reduce advantages of party expertise and of differences in the quality and quantity of legal services. Enhanced capacity for securing compliance might be expected to reduce advantages flowing from differences in ability to invest in enforcement. It is hardly necessary to point out that such reforms could be expected to encounter not only resistance from the beneficiaries of the present passive institutional style, but also massive ideological opposition from legal professionals whose fundamental sense of legal propriety would be violated.[114]

C. Increase in Legal Services

The reform envisaged here is an increase in quantity and quality of legal services to "have-nots" (including greater availability of information about these services).[115] Presumably this would lower costs, remove the expertise advantage, produce more litigation with more favorable outcomes for "have-nots," perhaps with more appeals and more rule challenges, more new rules in their favor. (Public defender, legal aid, judicare, and pre-payment plans approximate this in various fashions.) To the extent that OSs would still have to discount for delay and risk, their gains would be limited (and increase in litigation might mean even more delay). Under certain conditions, increased legal services might use institutional overload as leverage on behalf of "have-nots." Our Mobilization for Youth attorney observes:

---

[113] Some administrative agencies approximate this kind of "activist" posture. Cf. Nonet's (1969:79) description of the California Industrial Accident Commission:

> When the IAC in its early days assumed the responsibility of notifying the injured worker of his rights, of filing his application for him, of guiding him in all procedural steps, when its medical bureau checked the accuracy of his medical record and its referees conducted his case at the hearing, the injured employee was able to obtain his benefits at almost no cost and with minimal demands on his intelligence and capacities.

In the American setting, at least, such institutional activism seems unstable; over time institutions tend to approximate the more passive court model. See Nonet (1969: chaps. 6–7) and generally Bernstein (1955: chap. 7) on the "judicialization" of administrative agencies.

[114] Perhaps the expansive political role of the judiciary and the law in American society is acceptable precisely because the former is so passive and the latter so malleable to private goals. Cf. Selznick's (1969:225 ff.) discussion of the "privatization" and "voluntarization" of legal regulation in the United States.

[115] This would, of course, require the relaxation of barriers on information flow now imposed under the rubric of "professional ethics." See notes 46 and 51 above.

... if the Welfare Department buys out an individual case, we are precluded from getting a principle of law changed, but if we give them one thousand cases to buy out, that law has been effectively changed whether or not the law as written is changed. The practice is changed; the administration is changed; the attitude to the client is changed. The value of a heavy case load is that it allows you to populate the legal process. It allows you to apply un-remitting pressure on the agency you are dealing with. It creates a force that has to be dealt with, that has to be considered in terms of the decisions that are going to be made prospectively. It means that you are not somebody who will be gone tomorrow, not an isolated case, but a force in the community that will remain once this particular case has been decided.

As a result . . . we have been able, for the first time to participate along with welfare recipients . . . in a rule-making process itself . . . (Rothwax, 1969:140-41).

The increase in quantity of legal services was accompanied here by increased co-ordination and organization on the "have-not" side, which brings us to our fourth level of reform.

D. Reorganization of Parties

The reform envisaged here is the organization of "have-not" parties (whose position approximates OS) into coherent groups that have the ability to act in a co-ordinated fashion, play long-run strategies, benefit from high-grade legal services, and so forth.

One can imagine various ways in which OSs might be aggregated into RPs. They include (1) the membership association bargaining agent (trade unions, ten-ant unions); (2) the assignee-manager of fragmentary rights (performing rights associations like ASCAP); (3) the interest group-sponsor (NAACP, ACLU, envi-ronmental action groups).[116] All of these forms involve upgrading capacities for managing claims by gathering and utilizing information, achieving continuity and persistence, employing expertise, exercising bargaining skill and so forth. These advantages are combined with enhancement of the OS party's strategic position either by aggregating claims that are too small relative to the cost of remedies (consumers, breathers of polluted air, owners of performing rights); or by reduc-ing claims to manageable size by collective action to dispel or share unacceptable risks (tenants, migrant workers).[117] A weaker form of organization would be (4)

---

[116] For some examples of OSs organizing and managing claims collectively see Davis and Schwartz (1967) and various pieces in Burghardt (1972) (tenant unions); McPherson (1972) (Contract Buyers League); Shover (1966) (Farmers Holiday Association—mortgagors); Fink-lestein (1954) (ASCAP—performing rights); Vose (1967) (NAACP); Macaulay (1966) (auto-mobile dealers).

[117] A similar enhancement of prowess in handling claims may sometimes be provided com-mercially, as by collection agencies. Nonet (1969:71) observes that insurance coverage may serve as a form of organization:

When the employer buys insurance [against workman's compensation claims], he not only secures financial coverage for his losses, but he also purchases a claims ad-justment service and the legal defense he may need. Only the largest employers can adequately develop such services on their own. . . . Others find in their carrier a spe-cialized claims administration they would otherwise be unable to avail themselves

a clearing-house which established a communication network among OSs. This would lower the costs of information and give RPs a stake in the effect OSs could have on their reputation. A minimal instance of this is represented by the "media ombudsman"—the "action line" type of newspaper column. Finally, there is governmentalization—utilizing the criminal law or the administrative process to make it the responsibility of a public officer to press claims that would be unmanageable in the hands of private grievants.[118]

An organized group is not only better able to secure favorable rule changes, in courts and elsewhere, but is better able to see that good rules are implemented.[119] It can expend resources on surveillance, monitoring, threats, or litigation that would be uneconomic for an OS. Such new units would in effect be RPs.[120] Their encounters with opposing RPs would move into Box IV of Figure 1. Neither would enjoy the strategic advantages of RPs over OSs. One possible result, as we

---

of. . . . [T]o the employer, insurance constitutes much more than a way of spreading individual risks over a large group. One of its major functions is to pool the resources of possibly weak and isolated employers so as to provide them with effective means of self-help and legal defense.

[118] On criminalization as a mode of aggregating claims, see Friedman (1973:258). This is typically a weak form of organization, for several reasons. First, there is so much law that officials typically have far more to do than they have resources to do it with, so they tend to wait for complaints and to treat them as individual grievances. For example, the Fraud and Complaint Bureau described by McIntyre (1968) or the anti-discrimination commission described by Mayhew (1968). Cf. Selznick's (1969:225) observations on a general "tendency to turn enforcement agencies into passive recipients of privately initiated complaints. . . . The focus is more on settling disputes than on affirmative action aimed at realizing public goals." Second, enforcers have a pronounced tendency not to employ litigation against established and respectable institutions. Consider, for instance, the patterns of air pollution enforcement described by Goldstein and Ford (1971) or the Department of Justice position that the penal provisions of the Refuse Act should be brought to bear only on infrequent or accidental polluters, while chronic ones should be handled by more conciliatory and protracted administrative procedures. (1 Env't Rep Cur Dev No. 12 at 288 [1970]). Compare the reaction of Arizona's Attorney General to the litigation initiated by the overzealous chief of his Consumer Protection Division, who had recently started an investigation of hospital pricing policies.

I found out much to my shock and chagrin that anybody who is anybody serves on a hospital board of directors and their reaction to our hospital inquiry was one of defense and protection.

My policy concerning lawsuits . . . is that we don't sue anybody except in the kind of emergency situation that would involve [a business] leaving town or sequestering money or records. . . . I can't conceive any reason why hospitals in this state are going to make me sue them.

(*New York Times*, April 22, 1973).

[119] On the greater strategic thrust of group-sponsored complaints in the area of discrimination, see Mayhew (1968:168–73).

[120] Paradoxically, perhaps, the organization of OSs into a unit which can function as an RP entails the possibility of internal disputes with distinctions between OSs and RPs reappearing. On the reemergence of these disparities in strategic position within, for example, unions, see Atleson (1967:485 ff.) (finding it doubtful that Title I of the LMRDA affords significant protection to "single individuals"). Cf. Summers (1960); Atleson (1971) on the poor position of individual workers *vis-à-vis* unions in arbitration proceedings.

have noted in our discussion of the RP v. RP situation, is delegalization, that is, a movement away from the official system to a private system of dispute-settlement; another would be more intense use of the official system.

Many aspects of "public interest law" can be seen as approximations of this reform. (1) The class action is a device to raise the stakes for an RP, reducing his strategic position to that of an OS by making the stakes more than he can afford to play the odds on,[121] while moving the claimants into a position in which they enjoy the RP advantages without having to undergo the outlay for organizing. (2) Similarly, the "community organizing" aspect of public interest law can be seen as an effort to create a unit (tenants, consumers) which can play the RP game. (3) Such a change in strategic position creates the possibility of a test-case strategy for getting rule-change.[122] Thus "public interest law" can be thought of as a combination of community organizing, class action and test-case strategies, along with increase in legal services.[123]

VII. REFORM AND THE REST OF THE ICEBERG

The reforms of the official litigation system that we have imagined would, taken together, provide rules more favorable to the "have nots." Redress according to the official rules, undiscounted by delay, strategic disability, disparities of legal services and so forth could be obtained whenever either party found it to his advantage. How might we expect such a utopian upgrading of the official machinery to affect the rest of our legal iceberg?

---

[121] As an outspoken opponent of class actions puts it:

> When a firm with assets of, say, a billion dollars is sued in a class action with a class of several million and a potential liability of, say, $2 billion, it faces the possibility of destruction. . . . The potential exposure in broad class actions frequently exceeds the net worth of the defendants, and corporate management naturally tends to seek insurance against whatever slight chance of success plaintiffs may have (Simon, 1972:289–90).

He then cites "eminent plaintiffs' counsel" to the effect that:

> I have seen nothing so conducive to settlement of complex litigation as the establishment by the court of a class . . . whereas, if there were no class, it would not be disposed of by settlement.

[122] The array of devices for securing judicial determination of broad patterns of behavior also includes the "public interest action" in which a plaintiff is permitted to vindicate rights vested in the general public (typically by challenging exercises of government power). (Homberger, 1974). Unlike the class action, plaintiff does not purport to represent a class of particular individuals (with all the procedural difficulties of that posture) and unlike the classic test case he is not confined to his own grievance, but is regarded as qualified by virtue of his own injury to represent the interests of the general public.

[123] However, there may be tensions among these commitments. Wexler (1970), arguing for the primacy of "organizing" (including training in lay advocacy) in legal practice which aims to help the poor, points to the seductive pull of professional notions of the proper roles and concerns of the lawyer. Cf. Brill's (1973) portrayal of lawyers' professional and personal commitment to "class action" cases (in which the author apparently includes all "test cases") as undercutting their avowed commitment to facilitate community organization. On the inherent limits of "organizing" strategies, see note 127.

We would expect more use of the official system. Those who opted for inaction because of information or cost barriers and those who "settled" at discount rates in one of the "appended" systems would in many instances find it to their advantage to use the official system. The appended systems, insofar as they are built on the costs of resort to the official system, would either be abandoned or the outcomes produced would move to approximate closely those produced by adjudication.[124]

On the other hand, our reforms would, by organizing OSs, create many situations in which *both* parties were organized to pursue their long-run interest in the litigation arena. In effect, many of the situations which occupied Boxes II and III of Figure 1 (RP v. OS, OS v. RP)—the great staple sources of litigation—would now be moved to Box IV (RP v. RP). We observed earlier that RPs who anticipate continued dealings with one another tend to rely on informal bilateral controls. We might expect then that the official system would be abandoned in favor of private systems of dispute-settlement.[125]

Thus we would expect our reforms to produce a dual movement: the official and its appended systems would be "legalized"[126] while the proliferation of private systems would "delegalize" many relationships. Which relationships would we expect to move which way? As a first approximation, we might expect that the less "inclusive" relationships currently handled by litigation or in the appended systems would undergo legalization, while relationships at the more inclusive end of the scale (Figure 7) would be privatized. Relationships among strangers (casual, episodic, non-recurrent) would be legalized; more dense (recurrent, inclusive) relationships between parties would be candidates for the development of private systems.

Our earlier analysis suggests that the pattern might be more complex. First, for various reasons a class of OSs may be relatively incapable of being organized. Its size, relative to the size and distribution of potential benefits, may require disproportionately large inputs of coordination and organization.[127] Its shared inter-

---

[124] That is, the "reciprocal immunities" (Friedman 1967:806) built on transaction costs of remedies would be narrowed and would be of the same magnitude for each party.

[125] This is in Boxes II and III of Figure 1, where both parties are now RPs. But presumably in some of the litigation formerly in Box I, one side is capable of organization but the other is not, so new instances of strategic disparity might emerge. We would expect these to remain in the official system.

[126] That is, in which the field level application of the official rules has moved closer to the authoritative "higher law" (see note 82).

[127] Olson (1965) argues that capacity for coordinated action to further common interests decreases with the size of the group: ". . . relatively small groups will frequently be able voluntarily to organize and act in support of their common interests, and some large groups normally will not be able to do so." (1965:127). Where smaller groups can act in their common interest, larger ones are likely to be capable of so acting only when they can obtain some coercive power over members or are supplied with some additional selective incentives to induce the contribution of the needed inputs of organizational activity. (On the reliance of organizations on these selective incentives, see Salisbury [1969] and Clark and Wilson [1961].) Such selective incentives may be present in the form of services provided by a group already organized for some other purpose. Thus many interests may gain the benefits of organization only to the extent that those sharing them overlap with those with a more organizable interest (consider, for instance, the prominence of labor unions as lobbyists for consumer interests).

est may be insufficiently respectable to be publicly acknowledged (for instance, shoplifters, homosexuals until very recently). Or recurrent OS roles may be staffed by a shifting population for whom the sides of the transaction are interchangeable.[128] (For instance, home buyers and sellers, negligent motorists and accident victims.)[129] Even where OSs are organizable, we recall that not all RP v. RP encounters lead to the development of private remedy systems. There are RPs engaged in value conflict; there are those relationships with a governmental or other monopoly aspect in which informal controls may falter; and finally there are those RPs whose encounters with one another are non-recurring. In all of these we might expect legalization rather than privatization.

Whichever way the movement in any given instance, our reforms would entail changes in the distribution of power. RPs would no longer be able to wield their strategic advantages to invoke selectively the enforcement of favorable rules while securing large discounts (or complete shielding by cost and overload) where the rules favored their OS opponents.

Delegalization (by the proliferation of private remedy and bargaining systems) would permit many relationships to be regulated by norms and understandings that departed from the official rules. Such parochial remedy systems would be insulated from the impingement of the official rules by the commitment of the parties to their continuing relationship. Thus, delegalization would entail a kind of pluralism and decentralization. On the other hand, the "legalization" of the official and appended systems would amount to the collapse of species of pluralism and decentralization that are endemic in the kind of (unreformed) legal system we have postulated. The current prevalence of appended and private remedy systems reflects the inefficiency, cumbersomeness and costliness of using the official system. This inefficient, cumbersome and costly character is a source and shield of a kind of decentralization and pluralism. It permits a selective application of the "higher law" in a way that gives effect at the operative level to parochial norms and concerns which are not fully recognized in the "higher law" (such as the right to ex-

---

[128] Cf. Fuller's (1969:23) observation that the notion of duty is most understandable and acceptable in a society in which relationships are sufficiently fluid and symmetrical so that duties "must in theory and practice be reversible."

[129] Curiously these relationships have the character which Rawls (1958:98) postulates as a condition under which parties will agree to be bound by "just" rules; that is, no one knows in advance the position he will occupy in the proposed "practice." The analysis here assumes that while high turnover and unpredictable interchange of roles may approximate this condition in some cases, one of the pervasive and important characteristics of much human arranging is that the participants have a pretty good idea of which role in the arrangement they will play. Rawls (1971:136–141) suggests that one consequence of this "veil of ignorance" (". . . no one knows his place in society, his class position or social status; nor does he know his fortune in the distribution of natural assets and abilities, his intelligence and strength and the like") is that "the parties have no basis for bargaining in the usual sense" and concludes that without such restriction "we would not be able to work out any definite theory of justice at all. . . . . If knowledge of particulars is allowed, then the outcome is biased by arbitrary contingencies." If we posit knowledge of particulars as endemic, we may surmise that a "definite theory of justice" will play at most a minor role in explaining the legal process.

clude low status neighbors,[130] or police dominance in encounters with citizens[131]). If the insulation afforded by the costs of getting the "higher law" to prevail were eroded, many relationships would suddenly be exposed to the "higher law" rather than its parochial counterparts. We might expect this to generate new pressures for explicit recognition of these "subterranean" values or for explicit decentralization.

These conjectures about the shape that a "reformed" legal system might take suggest that we take another look at our unreformed system, with its pervasive disparity between authoritative norms and everyday operations. A modern legal system of the type we postulated is characterized structurally by institutional unity and culturally by normative universalism. The power to make, apply and change law is reserved to organs of the public, arranged in unified hierarchic relations, committed to uniform application of universalistic norms.

There is, for example, in American law (that is, in the higher reaches of the system where the learned tradition is propounded) an unrelenting stress on the virtues of uniformity and universality and a pervasive distaste for particularism, compromise and discretion.[132] Yet the cultural attachment to universalism is wedded to and perhaps even intensifies diversity and particularism at the operative level.[133]

The unreformed features of the legal system then appear as a device for maintaining the partial dissociation of everyday practice from these authoritative institutional and normative commitments. Structurally (by cost and institutional overload) and culturally (by ambiguity and normative overload) the unreformed system effects a massive covert delegation from the most authoritative rule-makers to field level officials (and their constituencies) responsive to other norms and priorities than are contained in the "higher law."[134] By their selective application of rules in a context of parochial understandings and priorities, these field level

---

[130] On exclusion of undesirable neighbors, see Babcock (1969); of undesirable sojourners, see the banishment policy described in Foote (1956).

[131] See the anguished discovery (Seymour 1971:9) of this by a former United States Attorney in his encounter with local justice:

> When the police officer had finished his testimony and left the stand, I moved to dismiss the case as a matter of law, pointing out that the facts were exactly the same as in the case cited in the annotation to the statute. I asked the judge to please look at the statute and read the case under it. Instead he looked me straight in the eye and announced, "Motion denied."

[132] It seems hardly necessary to adduce examples of this pervasive distaste of particularism. But consider Justice Frankfurter's admonition that "We must not sit like a kadi under a tree dispensing justice according to conditions of individual expediency." *Terminiello v. Chicago,* 337 U.S. 1, 11 (1948). Or Wechsler's (1959) castigation of the Supreme Court for departing from the most fastidiously neutral principles.

[133] As Thurman Arnold observed, our law "compels the necessary compromises to be carred on *sub rosa,* while the process is openly condemned. . . . Our process attempts to outlaw the 'unwritten law.'" (1962:162). On the co-existence of stress on uniformity and rulefulness with discretion and irregularity, see Davis (1969).

[134] Cf. Black's (1973:142–43) observations on "reactive" mobilization systems as a form of delegation which perpetuates diverse moral subcultures as well as reinforces systems of social stratification (141).

legal communities produce regulatory outcomes which could not be predicted by examination of the authoritative "higher law."[135]

Thus its unreformed character articulates the legal system to the discontinuities of culture and social structure: it provides a way of accommodating cultural heterogeneity and social diversity while propounding universalism and unity; of accommodating vast concentrations of private power while upholding the supremacy of public authority; of accommodating inequality in fact while establishing equality at law; of facilitating action by great collective combines while celebrating individualism. Thus "unreform"—that is, ambiguity and overload of rules, overloaded and inefficient institutional facilities, disparities in the supply of legal services, and disparities in the strategic position of parties—is the foundation of the "dualism"[136] of the legal system. It permits unification and universalism at the symbolic level and diversity and particularism at the operating level.[137]

VIII. IMPLICATIONS FOR REFORM: THE ROLE OF LAWYERS

We have discussed the way in which the architecture of the legal system tends to confer interlocking advantages on overlapping groups whom we have called the "haves." To what extent might reforms of the legal system dispel these advantages? Reforms will always be less total than the utopian ones envisioned above. Reformers will have limited resources to deploy and they will always be faced with the necessity of choosing which uses of those resources are most productive of equalizing change. What does our analysis suggest about strategies and priorities?

Our analysis suggests that change at the level of substantive rules is not likely in itself to be determinative of redistributive outcomes. Rule change is in itself

---

[135] Some attempts at delineating and comparing such "local legal cultures'" are found in Jacob (1969); Wilson (1968); Goldstein and Ford (1971). It should be emphasized that such variation is not primarily a function of differences at the level of rules. All of these studies show considerable variation among localities and agencies governed by the same body of rules.

[136] I employ this term to refer to one distinctive style of accommodating social diversity and normative pluralism by combining universalistic law with variable application, local initiative and tolerated evasion. (Cf. the kindred usage of this term by Rheinstein [1972: chaps. 4, 10] to describe the divorce regime of contemporary western nations characterized by a gap between "the law of the books and the law in action;" and by tenBroek [1964a, 1965] to describe the unacknowledged co-existence of diverse class-specific bodies of law.) This dualistic style might be contrasted to, among others, (a) a "millet" system in which various groups are explicitly delegated broad power to regulate their own internal dealings through their own agencies (cf. Reppetto, 1970); (b) official administration of disparate bodies of "special law" generated by various groups (for example, the application of their respective "personal laws'" to adherents of various religions in South Asian countries. See Galanter [1968]). Although a legal system of the kind we have postulated is closest to dualism, it is not a pure case, but combines all three. For some observations on changes in the relation of government law to other legal orderings, see Weber (1954: 16–20, 140–49).

[137] The durability of "dualism" as an adaptation is reinforced by the fact that it is "functional" not only for the larger society, but that each of its "moieties" gives support to the other: the "higher law" masks and legitimates the "operating level"; the accommodation of particularistic interests there shields the "higher law" from demands and pressures which it could not accommodate without sacrificing its universalism and semblance of autonomy. I do not suggest that this explains why some societies generate these "dual" structures.

likely to have little effect because the system is so constructed that changes in the rules can be filtered out unless accompanied by changes at other levels. In a setting of overloaded institutional facilities, inadequate costly legal services, and unorganized parties, beneficiaries may lack the resources to secure implementation; or an RP may restructure the transaction to escape the thrust of the new rule. (Leff, 1970b; Rothwax, 1969:143; Cf. Grossman, 1970). Favorable rules are not necessarily (and possibly not typically) in short supply to "have-nots"; certainly less so than any of the other resources needed to play the litigation game.[138] Programs of equalizing reform which focus on rule-change can be readily absorbed without any change in power relations. The system has the capacity to change a great deal at the level of rules without corresponding changes in everyday patterns of practice[139] or distribution of tangible advantages. (See, for example, Lipsky, 1970: chap. 4, 5.) Indeed rule-change may becom a symbolic substitute for redistribution of advantages. (See Edelman, 1967:40.)

The low potency of substantive rule-change is especially the case with rule-changes procured from courts. That courts can sometimes be induced to propound rule-changes that legislatures would not make points to the limitations as well as the possibilities of court-produced change. With their relative insulation from retaliation by antagonistic interests, courts may more easily propound new rules which depart from prevailing power relations. But such rules require even greater inputs of other resources to secure effective implementation. And courts have less capacity than other rule-makers to create institutional facilities and re-allocate resources to secure implementation of new rules. Litigation then is unlikely to shape decisively the distribution of power in society. It may serve to secure or solidify symbolic commitments. It is vital tactically in securing temporary advantage or protection, providing leverage for organization and articulation of interests and conferring (or withholding) the mantle of legitimacy.[140] The more divided the other holders of power, the greater the redistributive potential of this symbolic/tactical role. (Dahl, 1958:294).

Our analysis suggests that breaking the interlocked advantages of the "haves" requires attention not only to the level of rules, but also to institutional facilities, legal services and organization of parties. It suggests that litigating and lobbying have to be complemented by interest organizing, provisions of services and invention of new forms of institutional facilities.[141]

---

[138] Indeed the response that reforms must wait upon rule-change is one of the standard ploys of targets of reform demands. See, for example, Lipsky's (1970: 94-96) housing officials' claim that implementation of rent-strikers' demands required new legislation, when they already had the needed power.

[139] Compare Dolbeare and Hammond's (1971:151) observation, based on their research into implementation of the school prayer decisions, that "images of change abound while the status quo, in terms of the reality of people's lives, endures."

[140] On litigation as an organizational tool, see the examples given by Gary Bellow in *Yale Law Journal* (1970:1087–88).

[141] Cf. Cahn and Cahn's (1970:1016 ff.) delineation of the "four principal areas where the investment of . . . resources would yield critically needed changes: the creation (and legitimation) of new justice-dispensing institutions, the expansion of the legal manpower supply . . . the development of a new body of procedural and substantive rights, and the

The thrust of our analysis is that changes at the level of parties are most likely to generate changes at other levels. If rules are the most abundant resource for reformers, parties capable of pursuing long-range strategies are the rarest. The presence of such parties can generate effective demand for high grade legal services—continuous, expert, and oriented to the long run—and pressure for institutional reforms and favorable rules. This suggests that we can roughly surmise the relative strategic priority of various rule-changes. Rule changes which relate directly to the strategic position of the parties by facilitating organization, increasing the supply of legal services (where these in turn provide a focus for articulating and organizing common interests) and increasing the costs of opponents—for instance authorization of class action suits, award of attorneys' fees and costs, award of provisional remedies—these are the most powerful fulcrum for change.[142] The intensity of the opposition to class action legislation and autonomous reform-oriented legal services[143] such as California Rural Legal Assistance indicates the "haves" own estimation of the relative strategic impact of the several levels.[144]

The contribution of the lawyer to redistributive social change, then, depends upon the organization and culture of the legal profession. We have surmised that court-produced substantive rule-change is unlikely in itself to be a determinative element in producing tangible redistribution of benefits. The leverage provided by litigation depends on its strategic combination with inputs at other levels. The question then is whether the organization of the profession permits lawyers to develop and employ skills at these other levels. The more that lawyers view themselves exclusively as courtroom advocates, the less their willingness to undertake new tasks and form enduring alliances with clients and operate in forums other than courts, the less likely they are to serve as agents of redistributive change. Paradoxically, those legal professions most open to accentuating the advantages of the "haves" (by allowing themselves to be "captured" by recurrent clients) may be most able to become (or have room for, more likely) agents of change, precisely because they provide more license for identification with

development of forms of group representation as a means of enfranchisement," and the rich catalog of examples under each heading.

[142] The reformer who anticipates "legalization" (see text at note 126 above) looks to organization as a fulcrum for expanding legal services, improving institutional facilities and eliciting favorable rules. On the other hand, the reformer who anticipates "de-legalization" and the development of advantageous bargaining relationships/private remedy systems may be indifferent or opposed to reforms of the official remedy system that would make it more likely that the official system would impinge on the RP v. RP relationship.

[143] It is clear, e.g. that what Agnew (1972:930) finds objectionable is the redistributive thrust of the legal services program:

. . . the legal services program has gone way beyond the idea of a governmentally funded program to make legal remedies available to the indigent. . . . We are dealing, in large part, with a systematic effort to redistribute societal advantages and disadvantages, penalties and rewards, rights and resources.

[144] Summed up neatly by the head of OEO programs in California, who, defending Governor Reagan's veto of the California Rural Legal Assistance program, said:

What we've created in CRLA is an economic leverage equal to that of a large corporation. Clearly that should not be.

Quoted at Stumpf, *et al.* (1971:65).

clients and their "causes" and have a less strict definition of what are properly professional activities.[145]

REFERENCES

ABEL, Richard L. (1974) "A Comparative Theory of Dispute Institutions in Society," 8 *Law & Society Review* 217.

ABEL-SMITH, Brian and Robert STEVENS (1967) *Lawyers and the Courts: A Sociological Study of the English Legal System, 1750–1965.* Cambridge: Harvard University Press.

AGNEW, Spiro (1972) "What's Wrong with the Legal Services Program," 58 *A.B.A. Journal* 930.

AKERS, Ronald L. (1968) "The Professional Association and the Legal Regulation of Practice," 2 *Law & Society Review* 463.

ANDERSON, Stanley (1969) *Ombudsman Papers: American Experience and Proposals, With a Comparative Analysis of Ombudsmen Offices by Kent M. Weeks.* Berkeley: Univ. of Cal. Inst. of Govt. Studies.

ARNOLD, Thurman (1962) *The Symbols of Government.* New York: Harcourt Brace and World (First publication, 1935).

ASPIN, Leslie (1966) *A Study of Reinstatement Under the National Labor Relations Act.* Unpublished dissertation, Mass. Inst. of Tech., Dept. of Economics.

ATLESON, James B. (1971) "Disciplinary Discharges, Arbitration and NLRB Deference," 20 *Buffalo Law Review* 355.

———. (1967) "A Union Member's Right of Free Speech and Assembly: Institutional Interests and Individual Rights," 51 *Minnesota Law Review* 403.

AUBERT, Vilhelm (1967) "Courts and Conflict Resolution," 11 *Journal of Conflict Resolution* 40.

———. (1963) "Competition and Dissensus: Two Types of Conflict Resolution," 7 *Journal of Conflict Resolution* 26.

BABCOCK, Richard S. (1969) *The Zoning Game: Municipal Practices and Policies.* Madison: University of Wisconsin Press.

BATTLE, Jackson B. (1971) "In Search of the Adversary System—The Cooperative Practices of Private Criminal Defense Attorneys," 50 *Texas Law Review* 60.

BERMAN, Harold J. (1963) *Justice in the U.S.S.R.: An Interpretation of Soviet Law.* Revised Ed., Enlarged. New York: Vintage Books.

BERNSTEIN, Marver H. (1955) *Regulating Business by Independent Commission.* Princeton: Princeton University Press.

---

[145] Cf. note 48 above. It is submitted that legal professions that approximate "Type B" will not only accentuate the "have" advantages, but will also be most capable of producing redistributive change.

BEUTEL, Frederick K. (1957) *Some Potentialities of Experimental Jurisprudence as a New Branch of Social Science*. Lincoln: University of Nebraska Press.

BLACK, Donald J. (1973) "The Mobilization of Law," 2 *Journal of Legal Studies* 125.

— — —. (1971) "The Social Organization of Arrest," 23 *Stanford Law Review* 1087.

— — —. (1970) "Production of Crime Rates," 35 *American Sociological Review* 733.

BLANKENBURG, Erhard, Viola BLANKENBURG and Hellmut MORASON (1972) "Der lange Weg in die Berufung," in Rolf BENDER (ed.) *Tatsachen Forschung in der Justiz*. Tubingen: C.B. Mohr, 1972.

BLUMBERG, Abraham S. (1967a) *Criminal Justice*. Chicago: Quadrangle Books.

— — —. (1967b) "The Practice of Law as a Confidence Game," 1 *Law & Society Review* 15.

BOHANNAN, Paul J. (1965) "The Differing Realms of the Law," in Laura NADER (ed.) *The Ethnography of Law* (Special Publication of *American Anthropologist*, Vol. 67, No. 6, Part 2): 33-42.

BONN, Robert L. (1972a) "Arbitration: An Alternative System for Handling Contract Related Disputes," 17 *Administrative Sciences Quarterly* 254.

— — —. (1972b) "The Predictability of Nonlegalistic Adjudication," 6 *Law & Society Review* 563.

BORKIN, Joseph (1950) "The Patent Infringement Suit—Ordeal by Trial," 17 *University of Chicago Law Review* 634.

BRILL, Harry (1973) "The Uses and Abuses of Legal Assistance," No. 31 (Spring) *The Public Interest* 38.

BRUFF, Harold H. (1973) "Arizona's Inferior Courts," 1973 *Law and the Social Order* 1.

BURGER, Warren (1970) "The State of the Judiciary—1970," 56 *A.B.A. Journal* 929.

BURGHARDT, Stephen (ed.) (1972) Tenants and the Urban Housing Crisis. Dexter, Mich.: The New Press.

BURNLEY, James H. IV (1973) "Comment, Solicitation by the Second Oldest Profession: Attorneys and Advertising," 8 *Harvard Civil Rights-Civil Liberties Law Review* 77.

CAHN, Edgar S. and Jean Camper CAHN (1970) "Power to the People or the Profession?—The Public Interest in Public Interest Law," 79 *Yale Law Journal* 1005.

CAMERON, Mary Owen (1964) *The Booster and the Snitch: Department Store Shoplifting*. New York: Free Press of Glencoe.

CARLIN, Jerome E. (1966) *Lawyers' Ethics: A Survey of the New York City Bar*. New York: Russell Sage Foundation.

— — —. (1962) *Lawyers on Their Own: A Study of Individual Practitioners in Chicago*. New Brunswick: Rutgers University Press.

CARLIN, Jerome E. and Jan HOWARD (1965) "Legal Representation and Class Justice," 12 *U.C.L.A. Law Review* 381.

CASPER, Jonathan D. (1970) "Lawyers Before the Supreme Court: Civil Liberties and Civil Rights, 1957–66," 22 *Stanford Law Review* 487.

CHRISTIANSON, Barlow F. (1970) *Lawyers for People of Moderate Means: Some Problems of Availability of Legal Services.* Chicago: American Bar Foundation.

CLARK, Peter B. and James Q. WILSON (1961) "Incentive Systems: A Theory of Organizations," 6 *Administrative Sciences Quarterly* 129.

COHEN, Julius, Reginald A.H. ROBSON and Alan BATES (1958) *Parental Authority: The Community and the Law.* New Brunswick: Rutgers University Press.

COHN, Bernard S. (1959) "Some Notes on Law and Change in North India," 8 *Economic Development and Cultural Change* 79.

COLUMBIA JOURNAL OF LAW AND SOCIAL PROBLEMS (1971) "Roman Catholic Ecclesiastical Courts and the Law of Marriage," 7 *Columbia Journal of Law and Social Problems* 204.

———. (1970) "Rabbinical Courts: Modern Day Solomons," 6 *Columbia Journal of Law and Social Problems* 49.

COMMUNITY SERVICE SOCIETY, Department of Public Affairs, Special Committee On Consumer Protection (1974) *Large Grievances About Small Causes: New York City's Small Claims Court—Proposals for Improving the Collection of Judgments.* New York: New York City Community Service Society.

CONARD, Alfred F., James N. MORGAN, Robert W. PRATT, JR., Charles F. VOLTZ and Robert L. BOMBAUGH (1964) *Automobile Accident Costs and Payments: Studies in the Economics of Injury Reparation.* Ann Arbor: University of Michigan Press.

CONSUMER COUNCIL (1970) *Justice Out of Reach: A Case for Small Claims Courts.* London: Her Majesty's Stationery Office.

COONS, John E. (1964) "Approaches to Court-Imposed Compromise—The Uses of Doubt and Reason," 58 *Northwestern University Law Review* 750.

CRESSEY, Donald R. (1969) *Theft of the Nation: The Structure and Operations of Organized Crime in America.* New York: Harper and Row.

DAHL, Robert A. (1958) "Decision-making in a Democracy: The Supreme Court as a National Policy-maker," 6 *Journal of Public Law* 279.

DAVIS, Gordon J. and Michael W. SCHWARTZ (1967) "Tenant Unions: An Experiment in Private Law Making," 2 *Harvard Civil Rights-Civil Liberties Law Review* 237.

DAVIS, Kenneth Culp (1969) *Discretionary Justice: A Preliminary Inquiry.* Baton Rouge: Louisiana State University Press.

DERRETT, J. Duncan M. (1959) "Sir Henry Maine and Law in India," 1959 (Part I) *Juridical Review* 40.

DIBBLE, Vernon K. (1973) "What Is, and What Ought to Be: A Comparison of Certain Formal Characteristics of the Ideological and Legal Styles of Thought," 79 *American Journal of Sociology* 511.

DOLBEARE, Kenneth M. (1969) "The Federal District Courts and Urban Public Policy: An Exploratory Study (1960–1967)," in J. GROSSMAN and J. TANENHAUS (eds.) *Frontiers of Judicial Research.* New York: John Wiley.

———. (1967) *Trial Courts in Urban Politics: State Court Policy Impact and Function in a Local Political*

System. New York: John Wiley.

DOLBEARE, Kenneth M. and Phillip E. HAMMOND (1971) *The School Prayer Decisions: From Court Policy to Local Practice.* Chicago: University of Chicago Press.

DOO, Leigh-Wei (1973) "Dispute Settlement in Chinese-American Communities," 21 *American Journal of Comparative Law* 627.

DURKHEIM, Émile (1964) *The Division of Labor in Society.* New York: Free Press.

EDELMAN, Murray (1967) *The Symbolic Uses of Politics.* Urbana: University of Illinois Press.

EHRLICH, Eugen (1936) *Fundamental Principles of the Sociology of Law.* New York: Russell and Russell Publishers.

ENGLE, C. Donald (1971) *Criminal Justice in the City.* Unpublished dissertation, Department of Political Science, Temple University.

ENNIS, Phillip H. (1967) *Criminal Victimization in the United States: A Report of a National Survey.* (President's Commission on Law Enforcement and Administration of Justice, Field Survey II). Washington: Government Printing Office.

FELSTINER, William L.F. (1974) "Influences of Social Organization on Dispute Processing," 9 *Law & Society Review* 63.

FINKLESTEIN, Herman (1954) "The Composer and the Public Interest—Regulation of Performing Rights Societies," 19 *Law and Contemporary Problems* 275.

FOOTE, Caleb (1956) "Vagrancy-type Law and Its Administration," 104 *University of Pennsylvania Law Review* 603.

FORD, Stephen D. (1970) *The American Legal System.* Minneapolis: West Publishing Company.

FRANK, Jerome (1930) *Law and the Modern Mind.* New York: Coward-McCann.

FRANKLIN, Marc, Robert H. CHANIN and Irving MARK (1961) "Accidents, Money and the Law. A Study of the Economics of Personal Injury Litigation," 61 *Columbia Law Review* 1.

FRIEDMAN, Lawrence M. (1973) *A History of American Law.* New York: Simon and Shuster.

———. (1969) "Legal Culture and Social Development," 4 *Law & Society Review* 29.

———. (1967) "Legal Rules and the Process of Social Change," 19 *Stanford Law Review* 786.

FRIEDMAN, Lawrence M. and Jack LADINSKY (1967) "Social Change and the Law of Industrial Accidents," 67 *Columbia Law Review* 50.

FRIEDMAN, Lawrence M. and Stewart MACAULAY (1967) "Contract Law and Contract Teaching: Past, Present, and Future," 1967 *Wisconsin Law Review* 805.

FULLER, Lon L. (1969) *The Morality of Law.* Revised ed., New Haven: Yale University Press.

GALANTER, Marc (1968–69) "Introduction: The Study of the Indian Legal Profession," 3 *Law & Society Review* 201.

———. (1968) "The Displacement of Traditional Law in Modern India," 24 *Journal of Social Issues* 65.

GELLHORN, Walter (1966) *When Americans Complain: Governmental Grievance Procedures.* Cambridge: Harvard University Press.

GIFFORD, Daniel J. (1971) "Communication of Legal Standards, Policy Development and Effective Conduct Regulation," 56 *Cornell Law Review* 409.

GOLDING, Martin P. (1969) "Preliminaries to the Study of Procedural Justice," in G. HUGHES (ed.) *Law, Reason and Justice.* New York: New York University Press.

GOLDSTEIN, Paul and Robert FORD (1971) "The Management of Air Quality: Legal Structures and Official Behavior," 21 *Buffalo Law Review* 1.

GRACE, Roger (1970) "Justice, Chinese Style," 75 *Case and Comment* 50.

GROSSMAN, Joel (1970) "The Supreme Court and Social Change: A Preliminary Inquiry," 13 *American Behavioral Scientist* 535.

HAHM, Pyong-Choon (1969) "The Decision Process in Korea," in G. SCHUBERT and D. DANELSKI (eds.) *Comparative Judicial Behavior: Cross-Cultural Studies of Political Decision-Making in the East and West.* New York: Oxford University Press.

HALLAUER, Robert Paul (1972) "Low Income Laborers as Legal Clients: Use Patterns and Attitudes Toward Lawyers," 49 *Denver Law Journal* 169.

HAKMAN, Nathan (1969) "The Supreme Court's Political Environment: The Processing of Noncommercial Litigation," in J. GROSSMAN and J. TANENHAUS (eds.) *Frontiers of Judicial Research.* New York: John Wiley and Sons.

———. (1966) "Lobbying the Supreme Court—An Appraisal of Political Science Folklore," 35 *Fordham Law Review* 15.

HANDLER, Joel (1967) *The Lawyer and his Community: The Practicing Bar in a Middle-sized City.* Madison: University of Wisconsin Press.

———. (1966) "Controlling Official Behavior in Welfare Administration," in Jacobus TEN-BROEK, *et al.* (eds.) *The Law of the Poor.* San Francisco: Chandler Publishing Co.

HANDLER, Milton (1971a) "The Shift from Substantive to Procedural Innovations in Antitrust Suits," 26 *Record of N.Y.C. Bar Association* 124.

———. (1971b) "Twenty-Fourth Annual Antitrust Review," 26 *Record of N.Y.C. Bar Association* 753.

HART, Henry M., JR. and Albert M. SACKS (1958) *The Legal Process: Basic Problems in the Making and Application of Law.* Cambridge, Mass.: Harvard Law School, Tentative Edition (Mimeographed).

HAZARD, Geoffrey C., JR. (1970) "Law Reforming in the Anti-Poverty Effort," 37 *University of Chicago Law Review* 242.

———. (1965) "After the Trial Court—the Realities of Appellate Review," in Harry JONES (ed.) *The Courts, the Public and the Law Explosion.* Englewood Cliffs: Prentice Hall.

HENDERSON, Dan Fenno (1968) "Law and Political Modernization in Japan," in Robert E. WARD (ed.) *Political Development in Modern Japan.* Princeton: Princeton University Press.

HIRSCHMAN, Albert O. (1970) *Exit, Voice, and Loyalty: Responses to Decline in Firms, Organizations and States.* Cambridge: Harvard University Press.

HOLLINGSWORTH, Robert J., William B. FELDMAN and David C. CLARK (1974) "The Ohio Small Claims Court: An Empirical Study," 42 *University of Cincinnati Law Review* 469.

HOMBERGER, Adolf (1974) "Private Suits in the Public Interest in the United States of America,"

23 *Buffalo Law Review* 343.

———. (1971) "State Class Actions and the Federal Rule," 71 *Columbia Law Review* 609.

———. (1970) "Functions of Orality in Austrian and American Civil Procedure," 20 *Buffalo Law Review* 9.

HORSKY, Charles (1952) *The Washington Lawyer*. Boston: Little, Brown and Co.

HOWARD, J. Woodford, JR. (1969) "Adjudication Considered as a Process of Conflict Resolution: A Variation on Separation of Powers," 18 *Journal of Public Law* 339.

HUNTING, Roger Bryand and Gloria S. NEUWIRTH (1962) *Who Sues in New York City? A Study of Automobile Accident Claims*. New York: Columbia University Press.

HURST, James Willard (1950) *The Growth of American Law: The Law Makers*. Boston: Little, Brown and Co.

IANNI, Francis A.J. (1972) *A Family Business: Kinship and Control in Organized Crime*. New York: Russell Sage Foundation and Basic Books.

INTERNATIONAL LEGAL CENTER (1973) *Newsletter No. 9*, July 1973. New York: International Legal Center.

JACOB, Herbert (1969) *Debtors in Court: The Consumption of Government Services*. Chicago: Rand McNally and Co.

JOHNSTONE, Quintin and Dan HOPSON, JR. (1967) *Lawyers and Their Work: An Analysis of the Legal Profession in the United States and England*. Indianapolis: Bobbs Merrill Co.

KALVEN, Harry, JR. (1958) "The Jury, the Law and the Personal Injury Damage Award," 19 *Ohio State Law Journal* 158.

KAPLAN, Benjamin, Arthur T. von MEHREN and Rudolf SCHAEFER (1958) "Phases of German Civil Procedure," 71 *Harvard Law Review* 1193-1268, 1443-72.

KATZ, Marvin (1969) "Mr. Lin's Accident Case: A Working Hypothesis on the Oriental Meaning of Face in International Relations and the Grand Scheme," 78 *Yale Law Journal* 1491.

KAWASHIMA, Takeyoshi (1963) "Dispute Resolution in Contemporary Japan," in A.T. von MEHREN (ed.) *Law in Japan: The Legal Order in a Changing Society*. Cambridge: Harvard University Press.

KENNEDY, Duncan (1973) "Legal Formality," 2 *Journal of Legal Studies* 351.

KIDDER, Robert L. (1974) "Formal Litigation and Professional Insecurity: Legal Entrepreneurship in South India," 9 *Law & Society Review* 11.

———. (1973) "Courts and Conflict in an Indian City: A Study in Legal Impact," 11 *Journal of Commonwealth Political Studies* 121.

———. (1971) *The Dynamics of Litigation: A Study of Civil Litigation in South Indian Courts*. Unpublished Dissertation, Northwestern University.

LADINSKY, Jack (1963) "Careers of Lawyers, Law Practice and Legal Institutions," 28 *American Sociological Review* 47.

LAFAVE, Wayne R. (1965) *Arrest: The Decision to Take a Suspect into Custody*. Boston: Little, Brown and Co.

LARGE, Donald W. (1972) "Is Anybody Listening? The Problem of Access in Environmental Litigation," 1972 *Wisconsin Law Review* 62.

LAUFER, Joseph (1970) "Embattled Victims of the Uninsured: In Court with New York's MVAIC, 1959–69," 19 *Buffalo Law Review* 471.

LE VAR, C. Jeddy (1973) "The Small Claims Court: A Case Study of Process, Politics, Outputs and Factors Associated with Businessmen Usage." Unpublished Paper.

LEFF, Arthur A. (1970a) "Injury, Ignorance, and Spite—The Dynamics of Coercive Collection," 80 *Yale Law Journal* 1.

———. (1970b) "Unconscionability and the Crowd-Consumers and the Common Law Tradition," 31 *University of Pittsburgh Law Review* 349.

LePAULLE, Pierre George (1950) "Law Practice in France," 50 *Columbia Law Review* 945.

LEVINE, Felice J. and Elizabeth PRESTON (1970) "Community Resource Orientation Among Low Income Groups," 1970 *Wisconsin Law Review* 80.

LEVINE, James P. (1970) "Methodological Concerns in Studying Supreme Court Efficacy," 4 *Law & Society Review* 583.

LIGHT, Ivan H. (1972) *Ethnic Enterprise in America: Business and Welfare Among Chinese, Japanese and Blacks.* Berkeley: University of California Press.

LIPSKY, Michael (1970) *Protest in City Politics: Rent Strikes, Housing, and the Power of the Poor.* Chicago: Rand McNally and Co.

LOBENTHAL, Joseph S., JR. (1970) *Power and Put-On: The Law in America.* New York: Outerbridge and Dienstfrey.

LOCKARD, Duane (1968) *Toward Equal Opportunity: A Study of State and Local Antidiscrimination Laws.* New York: Macmillan Co.

LOEBER, Dietrich A. (1965) "Plan and Contract Performance in Soviet Law," in W. LAFAVE (ed.) *Law in the Soviet Society.* Urbana: University of Illinois Press.

LORTIE, Dan C. (1959) "Laymen to Lawmen: Law School, Careers, and Professional Socialization," 29 *Harvard Educational Review* 352.

LOWRY, S. Todd (1973) "Lord Mansfield and the Law Merchant," 7 *Journal of Economic Issues* 605.

LOWY, Michael J. (n.d.) "A Good Name is Worth More than Money: Strategies of Court Use in Urban Ghana." Unpublished paper.

MACAULAY, Stewart (1966) *Law and the Balance of Power: The Automobile Manufacturers and Their Dealers.* New York: Russell Sage Foundation.

———. (1963) "Non-Contractual Relations in Business: A Preliminary Study," 28 *American Sociological Review* 55.

MacCALLUM, Spencer (1967) "Dispute Settlement in an American Supermarket," in Paul BOHANNAN (ed.) *Law and Warfare.* Garden City, N.Y.: Natural History Press for American Museum of Natural History.

MARSHALL, Leon C. and Geoffrey MAY (1932) *The Divorce Court: Volume One—Maryland.* Baltimore: The Johns Hopkins Press.

MATZA, David (1964) *Delinquency and Drift.* New York: John Wiley.

MAYHEW, Leon H. (1973) "Institutions of Representation." A paper prepared for delivery at the Conference on the Delivery and Distribution of Legal Services, State University of New York at Buffalo, October 12, 1973.

———. (1971) "Stability and Change in Legal Systems," in Alex INKELES and Bernard BARBER (eds.) *Stability and Social Change.* Boston: Little, Brown and Co.

———. (1968) *Law and Equal Opportunity: A Study of the Massachusetts Commission Against Discrimination.* Cambridge: Harvard University Press.

MAYHEW, Leon and Albert J. REISS, JR. (1969) "The Social Organization of Legal Contacts," 34 *American Sociological Review* 309.

McINTYRE, Donald M. (1968) "A Study of Judicial Dominance of the Charging Process," 59 *Journal of Criminal Law, Criminology and Police Science* 463.

McINTYRE, Donald M. and David LIPPMAN (1970) "Prosecutors and Early Disposition of Felony Cases," 56 *A.B.A. Journal* 1154.

McPHERSON, James Alan (1972) "In My Father's House There are Many Mansions, and I'm Going to Get Me Some of Them, Too! The Story of the Contract Buyers League," 229(4) *Atlantic Monthly* 51.

MENTSCHIKOFF, Soia (1961) "Commercial Arbitration," 61 *Columbia Law Review* 846.

MERRYMAN, John Henry (1969) *The Civil Law Tradition: An Introduction to the Legal Systems of Western Europe and Latin America.* Stanford, Cal.: Stanford University Press.

MILLER, Frank W. (1969) *Prosecution: the Decision to Charge a Suspect with a Crime.* Boston: Little, Brown and Co.

MORGAN, Richard S. (1968) *The Politics of Religious Conflict: Church and State in America.* New York: Pegasus.

MORRISON, Charles (1974) "Clerks and Clients: Paraprofessional Roles and Cultural Identities in Indian Litigation," 9 *Law & Society Review* 39.

MOSIER, Marilyn Miller and Richard A. SOBLE (1973) "Modern Legislation, Metropolitan Court, Miniscule Results: A Study of Detroit's Landlord-Tenant Court," 7 *University of Michigan Journal of Law Reform* 6.

MOULTON, Beatrice A. (1969) "The Persecution and Intimidation of the Low-Income Litigant as Performed by the Small Claims Court in California," 21 *Stanford Law Review* 1657.

MURPHY, Walter (1959) "Lower Court Checks on Supreme Court Power," 53 *American Political Science Review* 1017.

MURRAY, John E., Jr. (1969) "Unconscionability: Unconscionability." 31 *University of Pittsburgh Law Review* 1.

NADER, Laura (1965) "The Anthropological Study of Law," in Laura NADER (ed.) *The Ethnography of Law* (= Part 2 of *American Anthropologist*, Volume 67, No. 6).

NAGEL, Stuart S. (1973) "Effects of Alternative Types of Counsel on Criminal Procedure Treatment," 48 *Indiana Law Journal* 404.

NEWMAN, Donald J. (1966) *Conviction: The Determination of Guilt or Innocence Without Trial.* Boston: Little, Brown and Co.

NEW YORK TIMES (1973) "Arizona Losing Consumer Chief," April 22, 1973, p. 39.

NONET, Philippe (1969) *Administrative Justice: Advocacy and Change in a Government Agency.* New York: Russell Sage Foundation.

NORTHWESTERN UNIVERSITY LAW REVIEW (1953) "Settlement of Personal Injury Cases in the Chicago Area," 47 *Northwestern University Law Review* 895.

O'CONNELL, Jeffrey (1971) *The Injury Industry and the Remedy of No-Fault Insurance.* Chicago: Commerce Clearing House.

O'GORMAN, Hubert (1963) *Lawyers and Matrimonial Cases: A Study of Informal Pressures in Private Professional Practice.* New York: Free Press.

OHLHAUSEN, George C. (1936) "Rich and Poor in Civil Procedure," 11 *Science and Society* 275.

OLSON, Mancur, JR. (1965) *The Logic of Collective Action: Public Goods and the Theory of Groups.* Cambridge: Harvard University Press.

ORBELL, John M. and Toro UNO (1972) "A Theory of Neighborhood Problem Solving: Political Action *vs.* Residential Mobility," 66 *American Political Science Review* 471.

OWEN, Harold J., JR. (1971) *The Role of Trial Courts in the Local Political System: A Comparison of Two Georgia Counties.* Unpublished dissertation, Department of Political Science, University of Georgia.

PAGTER, C.R., R. McCLOSKEY and M. REINIS (1964) "The California Small Claims Court," 52 *California Law Review* 876.

PARSONS, Talcott (1954) "A Sociologist Looks at the Legal Profession," in *Essays in Sociological Theory.* New York: Free Press.

POWELL, Richard R. and Patrick J. ROHAN (1968) *Powell on Real Property.* One Volume Ed. New York: Mathew Bender.

RABIN, Robert L. (1972) "Agency Criminal Referrals in the Federal System: An empirical study of prosecutorial discretion," 24 *Stanford Law Review* 1036.

RABINOWITZ, Richard W. (1968) "Law and the Social Process in Japan," in *Transactions of the Asiatic Society of Japan,* Third Series, Volume X. Tokyo.

RANDALL, Richard S. (1968) *Censorship of the Movies: Social and Political Control of a Mass Medium.* Madison: University of Wisconsin Press.

RANKIN, Anne (1964) "The Effect of Pretrial Detention," 39 *N.Y.U. Law Review* 641.

RAWLS, John (1971) *A Theory of Justice.* Cambridge: Harvard University Press.

———. (1958) "Justice as Fairness," 68 *The Philosophical Review* 80.

REICH, Charles (1964a) "The New Property," 73 *Yale Law Journal* 733.

———. (1964b) "Individual Rights and Social Welfare: The Emerging Legal Issues," 74 *Yale Law Journal* 1245.

REICHSTEIN, Kenneth J. (1965) "Ambulance Chasing: A Case Study of Deviation Within the Legal Profession," 3 *Social Problems* 3.

REPPETTO, Thomas (1970) "The Millet System in the Ottoman and American Empires," 5 *Public Policy* 629.

REPUBLIC RESEARCH, INC. (1970) "Claims and Recovery for Product Injury Under the Common Law," in National Commission on Product Safety, Supplemental Studies, Vol. III: *Product Safety Law and Administration: Federal, State, Local and Common Law.* Washington: U.S. Government Printing Office, 237.

ROSENTHAL, Albert J. (1971) "Negotiability—Who Needs It?," 71 *Columbia Law Review* 375.

ROSENTHAL, Douglas E. (1970) *Client Participation in Professional Decision: the Lawyer-Client Relationship in Personal Injury Cases.* Unpublished dissertation, Yale University.

ROSS, H. Laurence (1970) *Settled Out of Court: The Social Process of Insurance Claims Adjustment.* Chicago: Aldine.

ROTHSTEIN, Lawrence E. (1974) "The Myth of Sisyphus: Legal Services Efforts on Behalf of the Poor," 7 *University of Michigan Journal of Law Reform* 493.

ROTHWAX, Harold J. (1969) "The Law as an Instrument of Social Change," in Harold H. WEISSMAN (ed.) *Justice and the Law in the Mobilization for Youth Experience.* New York: New York Association Press.

SAARI, David J. (1967) "Open Doors to Justice—An Overview of Financing Justice in America," 50 *Journal of the American Judicature Society* 296.

SALISBURY, Robert H. (1969) "An Exchange Theory of Interest Groups," 13 *Midwest Journal of Political Science* 1.

SCHELLING, Thomas C. (1963) *The Strategy of Conflict.* New York: Oxford University Press.

SCHRAG, Philip G. (1969) "Bleak House 1968: A Report on Consumer Test Litigation," 44 *N.Y.U. Law Review* 115.

SCHWARTZ, Richard D. (1954) "Social Factors in the Development of Legal Control: A Case Study of Two Israeli Settlements," 63 *Yale Law Journal* 471.

SCIGLIANO, Robert (1971) *The Supreme Court and the Presidency.* New York: Free Press.

SCOTT, William G. (1964) *The Management of Conflict: Appeal Systems in Organizations.* Homewood, Ill.: Irwin/Dorsey.

SELZNICK, Philip, with the collaboration of Philippe NONET and Howard M. VOLLMER (1969), *Law, Society and Industrial Justice.* Russell Sage Foundation.

SEYMOUR, Whitney North, JR. (1974) "Frontier Justice: A Run-In with the Law," *The New York Times,* July 21, 1974.

SHKLAR, Judith N. (1964) *Legalism.* Cambridge: Harvard University Press.

SHOVER, John L. (1966) *Cornbelt Rebellion: The Farmers' Holiday Association.* Urbana: University of Illinois Press.

SHRIVER, George H. (ed.) (1966) *America's Religious Heretics: Formal and Informal Trials in American Protestantism.* Nashville: Abingdon Press.

SHUCHMAN, Philip (1971) "The Fraud Exception in Consumer Bankruptcy," 23 *Stanford Law Review* 735.

———. (1969) "Profit on Default: An Archival Study of Automobile Repossession and Resale," 22 *Stanford Law Review* 20.

———. (1968) "Ethics and Legal Ethics: The Propriety of the Canons as a Group Moral Code," 37 *George Washington Law Review* 244.

SIMKIN, William E. (1971) *Mediation and the Dynamics of Collective Bargaining.* Washington: Bureau of National Affairs.

SIMON, William (1972) "Class Actions—Useful Tool or Engine of Destruction," 55 *Federal Rules Decisions* 375.

SKOLNICK, Jerome (1967) "Social Control in the Adversary Process," 11 *Journal of Conflict Resolution* 52.

———. (1966) *Justice Without Trial: Law Enforcement in a Democratic Society.* New York: John Wiley.

SMALL CLAIMS STUDY GROUP (1972) "Little Injustices: Small Claims Courts and the American Consumer." A preliminary report to The Center for Auto Safety, Cambridge, Mass.

SMIGEL, Erwin O. (1969) *The Wall Street Lawyer: Professional Organization Man?* Bloomington: Indiana University Press.

SMITH, Regan G. (1970) *The Small Claims Court: A Sociological Interpretation.* Unpublished dissertation, Department of Sociology, University of Illinois.

SPRADLEY, James P. (1970) *You Owe Yourself a Drunk: An Ethnography of Urban Nomads.* Boston: Little, Brown and Co.

STUMPF, Harry P., Henry P. SCHROERLUKE and Forrest D. DILL (1971) "The Legal Profession and Legal Services: Explorations in Local Bar Politics," 6 *Law & Society Review* 47.

SUDNOW, David (1965) "Normal Crimes: Sociological Features of the Penal Code in a Public Defender Office," 12 *Social Problems* 255.

SUMMERS, Clyde (1960) "Individual Rights in Collective Agreements: A Preliminary Analysis," 9 *Buffalo Law Review* 239.

TANNER, Nancy (1970) "Disputing and the Genesis of Legal Principles: Examples from Minangkabau," 26 *Southwestern Journal of Anthropology* 375.

tenBROEK, Jacobus (1964–65) "California's Dual System of Family Law: Its Origin, Development and Present Status," 16 *Stanford Law Review* 257-317, 900-81; 17 *Stanford Law Review* 614-82.

TRUBEK, David M. (1972) "Toward a Social Theory of Law: An Essay on the Study of Law and Development," 82 *Yale Law Journal* 1.

TULLOCK, Gordon (1971) *Logic of the Law.* New York: Basic Books, Inc.

VAUGHAN, Ted R. (1968) "The Landlord-Tenant Relationship in a Low-Income Area," 16 *Social Problems* 208.

VIRTUE, Maxine Boord (1956) *Family Cases in Court: A Group of Four Court Studies Dealing with Judicial Administration.* Durham: Duke University Press.

VOSE, Clement E. (1972) *Constitutional Change: Amendment Politics and Supreme Court Litigation Since 1900.* Lexington, Mass.: D.C. Heath.

— — —. (1967) *Caucasians Only: The Supreme Court, the NAACP, and the Restrictive Covenant Cases.* Berkeley: University of California Press.

— — —. (1966) "Interest Groups, Judicial Review, and Local Government," 19 *Western Political Quarterly* 85.

WALD, Patricia (1964) "Foreword: Pretrial Detention and Ultimate Freedom," 39 *N.Y.U. Law Review* 631.

WANNER, Craig (1974a) "The Public Ordering of Private Relations: Part I: Initiating Civil Cases in Urban Trial Courts," 8 *Law & Society Review* 421.

— — —. (1974b) "The Public Ordering of Private Relations: Part II: Winning Civil Cases in Urban Trial Courts," 9 *Law & Society Review* 293.

— — —. (1973) "A Harvest of Profits: Exploring the Symbiotic Relationship between Urban Civil Trial Courts and the Business Community," Paper prepared for delivery at the 1973 Annual Meeting of the American Political Science Association.

WASBY, Stephen L. (1970) *The Impact of the United States Supreme Court: Some Perspectives.* Homewood, Ill.: The Dorsey Press.

WEBER, Max (1954), Max RHEINSTEIN (ed.) *Max Weber on Law in Economy and Society.* Cambridge: Harvard University Press.

WECHSLER, Herbert (1959) "Toward Neutral Principles of Constitutional Law," 73 *Harvard Law Review* 1.

WEXLER, Stephen (1973) "Practicing Law for Poor People," 79 *Yale Law Journal* 1049.

WHITFORD, William C. (1968) "Law and the Consumer Transaction: A Case Study of the Automobile Warranty," 1968 *Wisconsin Law Review* 1006.

WILSON, James Q. (1968) *Varieties of Police Behavior: The Management of Law and Order in Eight Communities.* Cambridge: Harvard University Press.

WOLL, Peter (1960) "Informal Administrative Adjudication: Summary of Findings," 7 *U.C.L.A. Law Review* 436.

YALE LAW JOURNAL (1970) "The New Public Interest Lawyers," 79 *Yale Law Journal* 1069.

YNGVESSON, Barbara (1976) "Responses to Grievance Behavior: Extended Cases in a Fishing Community," 3 *American Ethnologist* 353-373.

— — —. (1965) "The Berkeley-Albany and Oakland-Piedmont Small Claims Courts: A Comparison of Role of the Judge and Social Function of the Courts." Unpublished paper.

ZEISEL, Hans, Harry KALVEN, JR., and Bernard BUCHHOLZ (1959) *Delay in the Court.* Boston: Little, Brown and Co.

PLANET OF THE APs:
REFLECTIONS ON THE SCALE OF LAW AND ITS USERS

Marc Galanter

> [O]ne can no more predict the outcome of a case from the facts and the
> law than one can predict the outcome of a game of chess from the posi-
> tions of the pieces and the rules of the game. In either case, one needs
> to know who is playing.
>
> Lynn M. LoPucki & Walter O. Weyrauch[1]

I. THE ASCENT OF THE APs

Our human world is populated by several kinds of creatures: the most familiar are we natural, biological, individual humans. But the world also contains artificial "corporate" actors. Blackstone sums up the distinction neatly:

> Natural persons are such as the God of nature formed us: artificial are such as
> are created and devised by human laws for the purposes of society and govern-
> ment; which are called corporations or bodies politic.[2]

In the course of a typical day each of us consumes the products and employs the services of innumerable corporations, which supply us with foodstuffs, medications, television programs, and books as well as telephones, automobiles, insurance, banking services, and on and on. My normal progress through the day would be unsustainable without these creatures that routinely deliver unimaginable prodigies of organization and performance. These corporate creatures or artificial persons (APs) are one of humanity's great inventions. They have proved a tool for complex and coordinated action of a scale, consistency, and perseverance vastly beyond the range of biological individuals or informal groupings.

---

[1] *A Theory of Legal Strategy*, 49 DUKE L.J. 1405, 1472 (2000).

[2] WILLIAM BLACKSTONE, 1 COMMENTARIES *119.

The James McCormick Mitchell Lecture, University at Buffalo Law School, April 18, 2005. The themes of this lecture have been percolating with me intermittently for a number of years. I am indebted to the Mitchell Lecture committee for providing an opportunity to bring it to long-postponed fruition and to Jim Wooten for his bountiful assistance in the run-up to the lecture. I am grateful to the participants in several workshops and seminars at various institutions. I would like to mention particularly the helpfulness of Stephen M. Bainbridge and the excellent research assistance of William B. Turner. Cited as 53 BUFF. L. REV. 1369 (2006).

But these creatures are more than passive instruments serving our needs and desires. Their presence changes our world and it changes us. Like Dr. Frankenstein's creation, they both reflect and escape from the purposes of their creators. I propose to examine the way that the growing presence of APs affects the character of our legal world, especially its institutions of civil justice.

Before moving to these questions it may be helpful to address in a preliminary way the question of the "reality" of APs. In what sense are APs entities that can act and can pursue interests or goals? A great deal of energy has been expended in theorizing about the nature of the corporation: The terminology differs, but the basic controversy is over whether a corporation is (1) a merely nominal entity; (2) a group or partnership of natural persons (NPs); (3) a natural entity or "person" in its own right. Over time the third has come to predominate in official and popular usage.[3]

The personhood of the corporation is denied by a theory popular among academics which regards the corporation as a nexus or web of explicit and implicit contracts.[4] "The description of the corporation as a nexus of contracts not only de-personalizes the corporation, it denies that there is any body there at all. . . . [I]t denies that there is anything distinctive out there to regulate. All there are are natural people engaged in their own individualized wealth-maximizing activities."[5] In the nexus view, reference to corporations as actors is a fiction or reification.[6] But the equal and opposite sin to reification is reductionism. Applying the same analysis, is not a contract merely a nexus of expectations, which in turn are nexuses of perceptions, and so forth? Why are contracts more fundamental building blocks of the "real" than corporations? Or than the law of California, for that matter, which is after all just a nexus of expectations about what courts and other officials will do? Are corporations to be singled out for deconstructive treatment that could be applied equally to all institutions? To show that something is made up of constituent elements is not much of a trick. The question is not, it seems to me, what corporations "really" are, but whether it makes sense to address entities at this level for the purposes of assigning entitlements and fashioning controls.

Like the common law tradition, ordinary English speech concurs in attributing a distinct moral status to corporations: analysis of linguistic usage shows that "extension of human properties to corporate bodies is woven into the very fabric of language."[7] While the use of physiological references in connection with institutions is taken as metaphoric or metonymic, "cognitive verbs and many activity

---

[3] *See* Morton J. Horwitz, *Santa Clara Revisited: The Development of Corporate Theory*, 88 W. Va. L. Rev. 173 (1985); Carl J. Mayer, *Personalizing the Impersonal: Corporations and the Bill of Rights*, 41 Hastings L.J. 577 (1990); Sanford A. Schane, *The Corporation is a Person: The Language of a Legal Fiction*, 61 Tul. L. Rev. 563 (1987).

[4] *See* Henry N. Butler, *The Contractual Theory of the Corporation*, 11 Geo. Mason L. Rev. 99, 99–100 (1989); Frank H. Easterbrook & Daniel Fischel, *The Corporate Contract*, 89 Colum. L. Rev. 1416, 1426 (1989).

[5] David Millon, *Personifying the Corporate Body*, 2 Graven Images 116, 123 (1995).

[6] For a richer view of corporations as political entities with law-making and law-applying capacities, see Dalia Tsuk, *From Pluralism to Individualism: Berle and Means and 20th-Century American Legal Thought*, 30 Law & Soc. Inquiry 179 (2005).

[7] Schane, *supra* note 3, at 594–95.

words, when used with institutional nouns, have precisely the same meanings that they have with person nouns."[8]

> [N]ouns such as "corporation" occupy their own special class. Institutional nouns have unique properties. First, although physiological verbs, in their literal senses, are inappropriate with them, cognitive verbs reign supreme. So far as language is concerned, institutions do not have bodies—they indeed are incorporeal and intangible—but they certainly do have minds. They think and they feel and they say. Next, there are many activity verbs that are compatible with, and literally applicable to, institutional nouns, so that, linguistically, the institutions are viewed as competent to perform the designated acts. To be sure, language does not regard institutions as fully human, but it does impute important human characteristics to them—mentalities and the ability to pursue social activities. As a consequence, language treats the ensuing thoughts and actions as belonging to the institutions themselves—and not to the hidden members. This perspective from language turns out to be most congenial to the personal [i.e., entity] theory of corporate personality.[9]

That corporations are regarded as actors in their own right does not imply that moral standing equivalent to that of natural persons need be attributed to them. Nor are they necessarily regarded as the bearers of equal legal rights and responsibilities. For example, researchers describe jurors holding corporations to higher standards of responsibility in keeping with their greater perceived capacity to foresee and prevent harm.[10]

In other ways, too, APs may be more complete or competent persons. To a far greater extent than natural persons, APs may be capable of acting in the purposeful, rational, calculating fashion that the legal system prefers to ascribe to actors.[11] James Coleman describes APs as less susceptible to the lapses of willpower that are endemic to the activities of natural persons.[12] Chris Guthrie suggests that institutional litigants, "repeat players with active caseloads who are likely to view litigation primarily as a financial matter," are less likely than NPs to be emotionally disabled by "regret aversion" in pursuing litigation.[13] But APs suffer their own distinctive infirmities (what sociologists might label "goal displacement" and economists might view as "agency problems") that impede the optimal pursuit of their corporate interests or goals. These include the concealment or distortion of

---

[8] *Id.* at 606.

[9] *Id.* at 607.

[10] *See* VALERIE P. HANS, BUSINESS ON TRIAL: THE CIVIL JURY AND CORPORATE RESPONSIBILITY (2000); Robert J. MacCoun, *Differential Treatment of Corporate Defendants by Juries: An Examination of the "Deep-Pockets" Hypothesis*, 30 LAW & SOC'Y REV. 121 (1996).

[11] *See* Hans Geser, *Organisationen als soziale Akteure* [Organizations as Social Actors], 19 ZEITSCHRIFT FÜR SOZIOLOGIE 401 (1990) (F.R.G.), available at http://socio.ch/arbeit/t_hgeser5.htm.

[12] JAMES S. COLEMAN, FOUNDATIONS OF SOCIAL THEORY 548 (1990) (defining willpower as "the power to prevent short-term interests from overwhelming long-term interests"). He observes that the power asymmetry in interactions between NPs and APs is due in part to the fact that "one actor is a corporate actor, constructed differently from natural persons. The consequence is that a corporate actor is in a unique position to exploit weakness of will in natural persons, even to exploit the potential for such weakness by encouraging impulsive action." *Id.* at 549.

[13] Chris Guthrie, *Better Settle Than Sorry: The Regret Aversion Theory of Litigation Behavior*, 1999 U. ILL. L. REV 43, 82 (1999).

information as it flows up the organizational hierarchy,[14] the perpetuation of un-realistic belief systems,[15] excessive optimism,[16] and a bias against relinquishing commitments, even in the face of contrary evidence[17]—traits that flourish in the small group setting of corporate decision-making.[18]

Of course, APs are staffed by NPs. APs have proven proficient in mobilizing the energies and engaging the loyalties of NPs, providing a sense of meaning and purpose, and even inspiring personal sacrifice. NPs often fuse their personal goals with those of APs, finding them vehicles for fulfillment of their central personal aspirations. Loyalty to APs may induce individuals to act contrary to the interests of NPs such as themselves—and sometimes indeed to their very selves.[19]

APs are not the only kinds of collectivities in which natural persons partici-pate. APs are outnumbered, even now, by much more widespread and pervasive "primordial" institutions—families, religious fellowships, networks of transac-tors, neighbors, and friends. Until very recently these "spontaneous," "communal" institutions were the predominant forms of social organization. Some APs were present—governmental bodies, religious institutions, and a scatter of incorpo-rated utilities, banks, and commercial enterprises—but most human activity was conducted through these informal groupings.[20] Over the course of the last century there has been a dramatic transformation in the organization of social life from primordial institutions to "purposively constructed" organizations with specific goals and formal structures.[21] The family-owned corner grocery has been replaced

---

[14] *See* Donald C. Langevoort, *Organized Illusions: A Behavioral Theory of Why Corporations Mislead Stock Market Investors (And Cause Other Social Harms)*, 146 U. PA. L. REV. 122 (1997).

[15] *Id.* at 133.

[16] *Id.* at 139-40.

[17] *Id.* at 142-43; *see also* John M. Darley, *How Organizations Socialize Individuals into Evildo-ing*, in CODES OF CONDUCT: BEHAVIORAL RESEARCH INTO BUSINESS ETHICS 13 (David M. Messick & Ann E. Terbrunsel eds., 1994).

[18] *See* John C. Coffee, Jr., *"No Soul to Damn: No Body to Kick": An Unscandalized Inquiry into the Problem of Corporate Punishment*, 79 MICH. L. REV. 386 (1981); Darley, *supra* note 17, at 13-43 (1996).

[19] For example, consider the story of Victor Crawford, a former Tobacco Institute lobbyist who died of lung cancer (after conversion to anti-tobacco activism). Jason Vest, *No More Smoke Screens: Cancer, Then Remorse, Strikes an Ex-Tobacco Lobbyist*, WASH. POST, Mar. 4, 1995, at C1. Or Frank Cornelius, an insurance lobbyist who led a successful effort to limit recoveries in Indiana before becoming the victim of catastrophic medical injuries. Andrew Blum, *Ex-Tort Re-former's Son Carries on the Fight*, NAT'L L.J., Apr. 17, 1995, at A10.

[20] On the regulatory aspects of these, in contemporary society, see Marc Galanter, *Justice in Many Rooms: Courts, Private Ordering and Indigenous Law*, 19 J. LEGAL PLURALISM 1 (1981); Stewart Macaulay, *Private Government*, in LAW AND THE SOCIAL SCIENCES 445 (Leon Lipson & Stanton Wheeler eds., 1986); Sally Falk Moore, *Law and Social Change: The Semi-Autonomous Social Field as an Appropriate Subject of Study*, 7 LAW & SOC'Y REV. 719 (1973).

[21] James S. Coleman, *The Rational Reconstruction of Society: 1992 Presidential Address*, AM. SOC. REV., Feb. 1993, at 1. I do not regard this as necessarily implying a loss of "community." Arthur Stinchcombe points out that rather than being mutually inimical, "the solidarity of com-munal groups is intimately dependent on their degree of formal organization." Arthur Stinch-combe, *Social Structure and Organizations*, in HANDBOOK OF ORGANIZATIONS (James E. March ed., 1965). Nor should the shift from enclosed self-contained inclusive communities to looser, overlapping, partial communities be deplored as a loss of human autonomy or amenity. *Cf.* SALLY ENGLE MERRY, GETTING JUSTICE OR GETTING EVEN: LEGAL CONSCIOUSNESS AMONG WORKING-CLASS AMERICANS 172-76 (1990).

by the supermarket, which is now being challenged by the national big-box re-
tailer; the neighborhood doctor has become part of a Health Maintenance Organization (HMO); local musicians have been overshadowed by the fare provided by
entertainment conglomerates. An increasing portion of our encounters, transactions, and relationships are with APs.[22]

The emergence of APs entails a change in our relationship to the law. If primordial or communal institutions are "socially constructed," artificial persons
such as corporations and governments are legally constructed. In addition to the
front line activity of, for example, manufacturing and selling widgets, the corporate actor contains devices for governing and modifying this activity. Like H.L.A.
Hart's legal systems, they contain a combination of primary rules and secondary
rules (rules about the making, changing, and application of rules).[23] They contain
rules about their internal operations and about relations with suppliers, customers, and employees. Not only are these corporate creatures themselves little legal
systems, but they enjoy an affinity with the big, public legal system. They resemble
that system in their reliance upon bureaucratic organization, written records, and
formal rules.

The increasing presence of APs in our world makes law more salient. Relations with APs are regulated more by law than are relationships among NPs and
primordial institutions, in which the admixture of "informal" norms and reciproci-
ties is higher. Where APs are involved, regulation is more formal and more likely
to rely upon, be modeled on, or invoke law. Where public law is not immediately
present, it is mirrored in great webs of rules (for example in the coverage provisions of HMOs) or *faux* law (for example in airlines' frequent-flier programs).

As more of our encounters and relationships are with APs, an increasing portion of our troubles and disputes are with APs, rather than with other NPs. Conflicts arising from such relationships increasingly come to the legal system and
are regulated by public law as well as by the law-like rules generated within APs.
(Regulated here doesn't mean "determined"; law can be present, needing to be
"taken into account," even where it is not "in charge.")

Thus an increasing portion of matters taken up by legal institutions are conflicts between individuals and organizations (i.e., between NPs and APs). Great
parts of the civil justice system are populated by claims of APs against NPs, mostly
routine matters of debt collection, foreclosure, replevin, and so forth.[24] And other

---

[22] The population of APs has been increasing more rapidly than the population of NPs. In 1950,
there were 629,314 active corporations in the United States; in 2001, there were 5,136,000. If
we eliminate the 2,986,000 S corporations, that leaves a total of some 2,150,000 active corporations—more than three times the total half a century earlier. Of these, some 26,000 had receipts
of more than $50 million in 2001. U.S. CENSUS BUREAU, STATISTICAL ABSTRACT OF THE UNITED
STATES tbls.725, 726 & 955 (2004-2005), http://www. census.gov/prod/www/statistical-ab-
stract-2001_2005.html. (The NP population of the United States grew by 86% during the second
half of the twentieth century.) A rough measure of the increasing prominence of APs in innovative
economic activity is provided by figures on patents for invention. In 1980, corporations were the
recipients of 46,000 (76%) of the 66,200 patents issued for inventions by the U.S. Patent Office.
In 2003, corporations received 148,000 (88%) of the 169,000 invention patents. In other words,
patents issued to individuals rose by more than one-third from 1980 to 2003, while patents issued
to corporations more than tripled. U.S. CENSUS BUREAU, *supra*, at tbl.744.

[23] H.L.A. HART, THE CONCEPT OF LAW (1961).

[24] PUBLIC CITIZEN, FREQUENT FLIERS: CORPORATE HYPOCRISY IN ACCESSING THE COURTS (2004)

sectors of the civil justice system are devoted mainly to individuals seeking to hold APs to account. A study of civil litigation in the state courts of general jurisdiction of the seventy-five most populous counties of the United States found that in 1992, APs were the plaintiffs in some 73% of contracts cases and only 6% of torts cases, while they defended 60% of contracts cases and more than half of torts cases.[25] In the federal courts, Gillian Hadfield estimates that in 1970 organizations were plaintiffs in some 43% of civil cases and defendants in some 67%. In that year 41% of cases involved individual plaintiffs suing organizational defendants. By 2000, organizational defendants had increased to 83% but organization plaintiffs had decreased to 30%, so that 60% of cases were now individual plaintiffs versus organizational defendants.[26] There is no comparable data for the state courts where the vast majority of cases are located, but we have some indication that the overall configuration of parties is similar. In 60% of civil jury trials in the seventy-five counties in 1992 individual plaintiffs were opposed to organizational defendants.[27]

II. A SWOLLEN HEMISPHERE

Over the past half-century there has been a dramatic change in scale in many aspects of the legal world: the amount and complexity of legal regulation; the frequency of litigation; the amount of authoritative legal material; the number, coordination, and productivity of lawyers; the number of legal actors and the resources that they devote to legal activity; the amount of information about law and the velocity with which it circulates.[28] A crude but useful summary measure of the scope of legal activity is provided by looking at spending on law. The receipts of what the Census Bureau calls the legal services industry (basically, lawyers in private practice) grew from about four-tenths (0.4%) of one percent of the Gross Domestic Product (GDP) in 1978 to about one and eight-tenths percent (1.8%) in 2003.[29] This understates total spending on legal services for it does not include in-

---

(cases of types typically filed by businesses against individuals greatly outnumber case types typically filed by individuals against businesses).

[25] CAROL J. DEFRANCES ET AL., U.S. DEP'T OF JUST., CIVIL JUSTICE SURVEY OF STATE COURTS, 1992: CONTRACT CASES IN LARGE COUNTIES tbl.4 (1996); STEVEN K. SMITH, ET AL., U.S. DEP'T OF JUST., CIVIL JUSTICE SURVEY OF STATE COURTS, 1992: TORT CASES IN LARGE COUNTIES tbl.6 (1995), available at http://www.ojp. usdoj.gov/bjs/pub/pdf/tcilc.pdf. In the tort cases, non-individuals (who I am for the moment equating with APs) were 49.7% of defendants, but we can safely assume that insurers were interested parties in a large portion of the other half of cases in which the nominal defendants were overwhelmingly individuals. *Id.* at tbl.6.

[26] Gillian Hadfield, *Exploring Economic and Democratic Theories of Civil Litigation: Differences between Individual and Organizational Litigants in the Disposition of Federal Civil Cases*, 57 STAN. L. REV. 1275, 1298, 1304 (2005).

[27] CAROL J. DEFRANCES ET AL., U.S. DEPT. OF JUSTICE, CIVIL JUSTICE SURVEY OF STATE COURTS, 1992: CIVIL JURY CASES AND VERDICTS IN LARGE COUNTIES 3 (1995). These magnitudes are confirmed by Gross and Syverud's study of trials-to-verdict in California in 1985-86 and 1990-91, where individuals made up about 94% of plaintiffs in both periods and only 30.6% (1985-86) and 32.6% (1990-91) of the defendants. Samuel R. Gross & Kent D. Syverud, *Don't Try: Civil Jury Verdicts in a System Geared to Settlement*, 44 UCLA L. REV. 1, 15, 18 (1996).

[28] *See* Marc Galanter, *Law Abounding: Legalisation Around the North Atlantic*, 55 MOD. L. REV. 1 (1992).

[29] See sources cited *infra* Figure 1.

house legal services consumed by businesses or governments. In-house corporate lawyers and government lawyers (including judges) make up about one-fifth of all practicing lawyers. If we assume that they are as productive as lawyers in private practice, we can estimate that the "legal services" portion of GDP is now about two and a quarter percent—a portion over four times as large as it was a quarter-century earlier.

Figure 1. Expenditures on Legal Services as Percent of Gross Domestic Product, 1978-2003

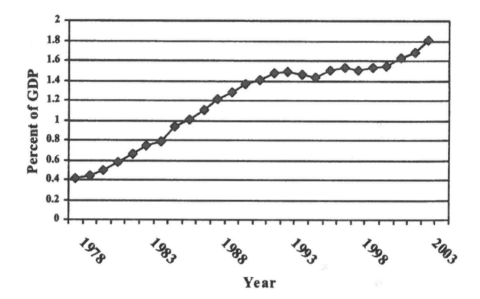

Sources: Legal Services data from U.S. Census Bureau, Current Business Reports: Service Annual Survey, 1983 to Present. The Census Bureau routinely revises published data in these reports from one year to the next. Where multiple figures were available, the most recent one was used. GDP data is in 2000 chained dollars, available from U.S. Department of Commerce, Bureau of Economic Analysis, http://www.bea.gov/bea/dn/homegdp.htm (last visited March 9, 2006).

Given the substantial growth of the underlying economy, this growth in share represents a very substantial increase in the absolute size of the legal services industry. In constant 2000 dollars, the gross receipts of the U.S. law firms increased 649% from $22.15 billion in 1967 to $166.1 billion in 2002. Legal services expenditures grew much more rapidly than the economy as a whole. Figure 2 displays the growth of law (measured by legal services receipts) relative to the whole economy. Using 1967 as our baseline (n=100), legal services receipts reached 749 in 2002, while the GDP reached 289.

Figure 2. Growth of Gross Domestic Product Compared with Receipts of Legal Services Industry, 1967-2002, Five Year Intervals

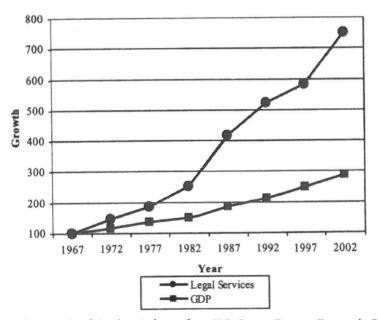

Sources: Legal Services Industry from U.S. Census Bureau, Economic Census: Professional, Scientific, and Technical Services, 1972 to 2002; GDP data is in 2002 chained dollars, available from http://www.bea.gov/bea/dn/home/gdp.home/htm (last visited March 9, 2006).

The provision of legal services to NPs and APs is performed by different lawyers, who are organized in different ways. Lawyers in the United States nominally form a single profession. But it is a profession that is intensely stratified. With due allowance for exceptions, the upper strata of the bar consist mostly of large firms whose members are recruited mainly from elite schools and who serve organizational clients; the lower strata practice as individuals or small firms, are drawn from less prestigious schools, and service individual clients. Law practice is a bifurcated structure, organized around different kinds of clients. Much of the variation within the profession, Heinz and Laumann conclude, is accounted for by

> one fundamental distinction—the distinction between lawyers who represent large organizations (corporations, labor unions, or government) and those who represent individuals. The two kinds of law practice are two hemispheres of the profession. Most lawyers reside exclusively in one hemisphere or the other and seldom, if ever, cross the equator.[30]

In the corporate hemisphere, a wider range of services is supplied over a longer duration; there is more specialization and coordination; research and investi-

---

[30] JOHN H. HEINZ & EDWARD O. LAUMANN, CHICAGO LAWYERS: THE SOCIAL STRUCTURE OF THE BAR 319 (1982).

gation are more elaborate; tactics can be more innovative and less routine, etc.[31]

During recent decades there has been a dramatic increase in the presence of lawyers. From 1960 to 2000 the number of lawyers in the United States more than tripled.[32] The law firms that service APs have multiplied, grown, and flourished while the sectors of the profession that serve individuals have been relatively stagnant in earnings and growth.[33] In 1960 the section of the profession consisting of large firms devoted to serving corporate clients consisted of just a few thousand lawyers but by 2000 over one hundred thousand lawyers worked in such firms.[34]

The increasing predominance of organizations as users of law is dramatically displayed by Heinz and Laumann's studies of the Chicago bar. They estimated that in 1975 more than half (53 percent) of the total effort of Chicago's bar was devoted to the corporate client sector, and a smaller but still substantial proportion (40 percent) was expended on the personal client sector."[35] When the researchers returned to the field twenty years later, they found that there were roughly twice as many lawyers working in Chicago. But in 1995, about 64% of the total effort of all Chicago lawyers was devoted to the corporate client sector and only 29% to the personal/small business sector.[36] Since the number of lawyers in Chicago had doubled, this meant that the total effort devoted to the personal sector had increased by 45%. But the corporate sector grew by 126%. To the extent that lawyers serving the corporate sector were able to combine more staff and support services with their effort, these figures understate the gap in services delivered.

Is this pattern peculiar to Chicago? Or to the largest metropolitan areas? The generality of both the contours of distribution and the patterns of change are suggested by census data. As the size of the legal services "pie" was increasing, businesses were buying a greater share of that pie. In 1967, individuals bought 55% of the product of the legal services industry and businesses bought 39%. In 2002, individual purchases had fallen to 41.4% and business purchases has risen to 47.4% of a much-enlarged total.[37] Table 1 summarizes these changes. Figures 2 and 3 depict the change in the portion of purchases of legal services by different categories of buyers.

---

[31] On the contrasting styles of ordinary lawyering and mega-lawyering, see Marc Galanter, *Mega-Law and Mega-Lawyering in the Contemporary United States*, in the SOCIOLOGY OF THE PROFESSIONS: LAWYERS, DOCTORS AND OTHERS 152 (Robert Dingwall & Philip Lewis eds., 1983 [rptd. 2014]).

[32] The lawyer population increased 235% from 285,933 in 1960 to 1,066,328 in 2000. There was one lawyer for every 627 people in 1960 and one for every 264 people in 2000. CLARA N. CARSON, THE LAWYER STATISTICAL REPORT: THE U.S. LEGAL PROFESSION IN 2000 1 (2004).

[33] *See* Richard H. Sander & E. Douglass Williams, *Why Are There So Many Lawyers? Perspectives on a Turbulent Market*, 14 LAW & SOC. INQUIRY 431 (1989).

[34] In 1957 there were just thirty-eight law firms in the United States with more than fifty lawyers. ERWIN O. SMIGEL, THE WALL STREET LAWYER: PROFESSIONAL ORGANIZATION MAN? 43 (1969). In 2000 over 122,000 lawyers (some 36% of firm lawyers and 18% of all lawyers in private practice) worked in the 737 firms with fifty-one or more lawyers. CARSON, *supra* note 32, at 9, 15.

[35] HEINZ & LAUMANN, *supra* note 30, at 42.

[36] John P. Heinz et al., *The Changing Character of Lawyers' Work: Chicago in 1975 and 1995*, 32 LAW & SOC'Y REV. 751, 765 tbl.3 (1998).

[37] From 1967 to 1992, with each subsequent five-year period, the business portion has increased and the share consumed by individuals declined. The apparent sharp reversal in 1997 (visible in Figure 3) is due to reporting error (as explained in the note to Figure 3, *infra*).

Table 1. Receipts of Legal Services Industry by Class of Client, 1967-2002 (Billions of Dollars)

	Total Suppliers	Total Receipts	Individuals	Business	Government	Other
1967						
2000 Dollars		$22.15	$12.20	$8.64	$1.31	*
Actual Dollars		$5.23	$2.88	$2.04	$0.31	*
% of Receipts		100%	55%	39%	6%	*
1972	77,282					
2000 Dollars		$32.47	$17.06	$13.73	$0.94	$0.74
Actual Dollars		$9.67	$5.08	$4.09	$0.28	$0.22
% of Receipts		100%	53%	42%	2.90%	2.30%
% Change from 1967		46.59%	39.85%	58.96%	-28.39%	
1977	94,882					
2000 Dollars		$41.03	$19.38	$18.23	$1.34	$0.98
Actual Dollars		$17.15	$8.10	$7.62	$0.56	$0.41
% of Receipts		100%	49%	46%	3.30%	2.50%
% Change from 1972		26.37%	13.61%	32.75%	42.51%	32.79%
1982	115,407					
2000 Dollars		$55.76	$24.81	$27.11	$1.79	$2.03
Actual Dollars		$34.32	$15.27	$16.69	$1.10	$1.25
% of Receipts		100%	45%	50%	3.30%	3.70%
% Change from 1977		35.88%	28.00%	48.72%	33.38%	107.01%
1987	138,222					
2000 Dollars		$92.42	$38.78	$47.07	$3.19	$3.39
Actual Dollars		$66.99	$28.11	$34.12	$2.31	$2.46
% of Receipts		100%	42%	51%	3.40%	3.70%
% Change from 1982		65.75%	56.32%	73.60%	78.33%	67.12%
1992	142,606					
2000 Dollars		$115.65	$46.70	$60.04	$4.46	$4.44
Actual Dollars		$99.14	$40.03	$51.47	$3.82	$3.81
% of Receipts		100%	40%	51%	3.80%	3.80%
% Change from 1987		25.14%	20.42%	27.56%	39.84%	30.97%
1997	165,757					
2000 Dollars		$129.00	$63.43	$54.47	$3.96	$1.73
Actual Dollars		$122.62	$60.29	$51.78	$3.76	$1.64
% of Receipts		100%	49.62%	42.20%	3.10%	1.30%
% Change from 1992		23.68%	50.61%	0.60%	-1.57%	-56.96%
2002	179,346					
2000 Dollars		$166.10	$68.73	$79.61	$6.28	$4.15
Actual Dollars		$171.83	$71.10	$82.36	$6.50	$4.29
% of Receipts		100.00%	41.40%	47.90%	3.80%	2.50%
% Change from 1997		40.13%	17.93%	59.06%	72.87%	161.59%

Sources: Legal Services Industry from U.S. Census Bureau, Economic Census: Professional, Scientific, and Technical Services, 1972 through 2002; Price de-

flator for 2000 dollar values from http://research.stlouisfed.org/fred2/data/
GDPDEF.txt (last visited March 9, 2006). For 1967 only total receipts overall are
available from the U.S. Census. Percentages for classes of clients are taken from
Richard H. Sander & E. Douglas Williams, *Why Are There So Many Lawyers?
Perspectives on a Turbulent Market*, 14 LAW & SOC. INQUIRY 431, 441 (1989).
In their analyses, government and other are combined categories, thus the 6%
figure includes both categories. Calculations of percentage change of these cat-
egories from 1967 to 1972 combines government and other.

Table 1 indicates that individuals' expenditures on legal services (in constant
dollars) increased 463% from 1967 to 1992, while law firms' receipts from businesses increased by 821% during that period. Even this higher rate of growth understates the growth of business expenditures on legal services, for it includes only
outside lawyers and does not include in-house legal expenditures, which greatly
increased during this period.[38] Figures 3 and 4 display the relative growth in legal
services receipts from the various kinds of clients.

Figure 3. Receipts of Legal Service Industry by Client, 1967-2002

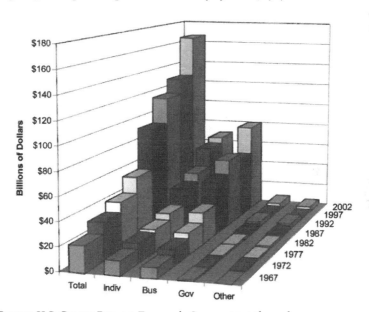

Source: U.S. Census Bureau, Economic Census, 1972 through 2002.

Note: The component figures for 1997 are plainly anomalous: the clear trend of
receipts from business growing faster than receipts from individuals over the
entire period suddenly reverses in 1997 and reverts in 2002. This is the result of
reporting error. According to Holly C. Higgins, Survey Statistician, U.S. Bureau
of the Census, a number of firms that year entered all of their receipts on the line,
"All other fees received," which appears on the form as a sub-category of Individuals. For the firms so reporting, receipts that came from Business, Government,
or Other sources were counted as receipts from Individuals, which explains why

---

[38] For exclusion of in-house legal services from Census of Service Industries, see the introduction
to the U.S. DEP'T OF COMMERCE, BUREAU OF THE CENSUS, 1982 CENSUS OF SERVICE INDUSTRIES,
iii-vi (1984).

the figure for Individuals grew much faster than the figure for Business in 1997. E-mail from Holly C. Higgins, Survey Statistician, U.S. Bureau of the Census, to William B. Turner (Aug. 11, 2005) (on file with author).

We may think that the presence of dedicated "public interest lawyers" or "cause lawyers" and the "pro bono" exertions of corporate firms help to offset this imbalance. Pro bono volunteers "do a tremendous service representing individual poor clients in routine matters and lending their institutional resources to support the reform agendas of public interest groups."[39] But pro bono work is ultimately constrained by the interests of the provider firms, who are vigorous advocates for corporate clients. Public interest law firms may be free of such constraint, but it should be noted that the public interest law format has been successfully borrowed by groups aligned with corporate parties, so that there now is at least as much "public interest" lawyering on behalf of corporations and their allies as there is on behalf of their antagonists.[40]

As law, driven by corporate expenditures, becomes more technical, complex, and expensive, individuals are just the wrong size to use legal services effectively.[41] It is a rare instance in which the kinds of options that are routine for large organizations are feasible and effective for individuals. "[T]he market for lawyers," Gillian Hadfield observes, "overwhelmingly allocates legal resources to clients with interests backed by corporate aggregations of wealth."[42] The aspects of the legal system most responsive to the needs and aspirations of individuals absorb less of its energy and attention as "the legal system prices itself out of the reach of all in-

[39] Scott L. Cummings, *The Politics of Pro Bono*, 52 UCLA L. REV. 1, 147 (2004). Estimating the scale of pro bono activity, Deborah Rhode concludes that "the best available research finds that American lawyers average less than half an hour of work per week and under half a dollar per day in support of pro bono legal services." Deborah L. Rhode, *Pro Bono in Principle and in Practice*, 26 HAMLINE J. PUB. L. & POL'Y 315, 328 (2005).

[40] BRIAN Z. TAMANAHA, LAW AS A MEANS TO AN END: THREAT TO THE RULE OF LAW, ch. 8 (2006).

[41] For example, the legal aid attorney who prevailed in the landmark unconscionability case of Williams v. Walker-Thomas Furniture Co., 350 F.2d 445 (D.C. Cir. 1965), reported that the case required 210 hours of legal work. Robert H. Skilton & Orrin L. Helstad, *Protection of the Installment Buyer of Goods under the Uniform Commercial Code*, 65 MICH. L. REV. 1465, 1480 n.38 (1967). At a modest (for the 1960s) hourly fee of $25, protection of Mrs. William's $1800 worth of purchases would have cost her $5250 in lawyers' fees alone. An even more daunting example is provided by the experience of A. Ernest Fitzgerald, the Air Force cost analyst who disclosed the multibillion dollar cost overrun in the C-5A transport. In the course of winning his six-year fight for reinstatement (with back pay) in his $31,000 per year job, he accumulated lawyers' fees of more than $400,000:

> [A] small army of Government lawyers was set to work against Mr. Fitzgerald—lawyers representing the Air Force, the Department of Defense, the Justice Department, the United States Attorney's Office and the Civil Service Commission.

> These lawyers delayed hearings, refusing to turn over documents, appealed every concession made, filed motions that required scores of time-consuming proceedings taking up time—and all the while Mr. Fitzgerald's attorneys were costing him $125 an hour.

Broad Effects Seen From Award of Legal Fees to Pentagon Aide, N.Y. TIMES, Jan. 2, 1976, at 8. A more recent example is provided by the inability of well-resourced individuals like the Clintons to finance their legal fees. *See* Stuart Taylor, *"Brother, Can You Spare Some Fees?"*, LEGAL TIMES, Mar. 18, 1996, at 23.

[42] Gillian Hadfield, *The Price of Law: How the Market for Lawyers Distorts the Justice System*, 98 MICH. L. REV. 953, 998 (2000).

dividuals except those with a claim on corporate wealth."[43] So the system is "heavily, and it seems increasingly, skewed towards managing the economy rather than safeguarding just relationships and democratic institutions."[44] As the courts focus more on economic issues, the message is that this is what adjudication should be about. Tort reform campaigns attack the propriety of "non-economic" damages with the implication that "noneconomic" items like pain, suffering, and disfigurement are unmeasurable, unsubstantial, and illusory.

III. THE WINNING WAYS OF APs

Not only do APs occupy more of the legal realm, they are more resourceful and more successful users of law than NPs. Unsurprisingly, in those arenas like lobbying[45] or administrative hearings[46] where actors can deploy the full range of their assets, recurrent organizational players fare better than individuals. Such advantages appear also in the judicial forum, in which parties are ostensibly on an equal footing. Some years ago, I attempted to identify some of the advantages enjoyed by recurrent (usually organizational) players ("repeat-players") over infrequent individual players ("one-shotters").[47] Briefly, my catalog included:

- ability to utilize advance intelligence, structure the next transaction, build a record and so forth.

- ability to develop expertise; ready access to specialists; economies of scale and low start-up costs for any case.

- opportunity to develop facilitative informal relations with institutional incumbents.

- ability to establish and maintain credibility as a combatant. With no bargaining reputation to maintain, the one-time litigant has greater difficulty in convincing establishing commitments to his bargaining positions.[48]

---

[43] *Id.*

[44] *Id.* at 1004.

[45] See Lester M. Salamon & John J. Siegfried, *Economic Power and Political Influence: The Impact of Industry Structure on Public Policy*, 71 AM. POL. SCI. REV. 1026 (1977).

[46] *See* Erasmus H. Kloman, *Public Participation in Technology Assessment*, 35 PUB. ADMIN. REV. 67 (1975).

[47] Marc Galanter, *Why the "Haves" Come Out Ahead: Speculations on the Limits of Legal Change*, 9 LAW & SOC'Y REV. 95, 97 (1974). A number of scholars have identified further advantages of the corporate player in the legal arena, including the ability to impede less formidable opponents from using the legal process by bringing "SLAPP suits" ("Strategic Litigation Against Public Participation"). *See, e.g.*, GEORGE W. PRING & PENELOPE CANAN, SLAPPs: GETTING SUED FOR SPEAKING OUT (1996); FIONA J. L. DONSON, LEGAL INTIMIDATION: A SLAPP IN THE FACE OF DEMOCRACY (2000). Alternatively, repeat-players (who are almost always APs) may raise the barrier to challenges by manipulating the conflict of interest rules to prevent opponents from obtaining high-quality specialized representation. SUSAN P. SHAPIRO, TANGLED LOYALTIES: CONFLICT OF INTEREST IN LEGAL PRACTICE 182-84 (2002). Again, sheer scale may enable an AP to play for rules simultaneously and strategically in a number of different subject areas, carrying favorable rules "established in one substantive law area . . . to others." Lea VanderVelde, *Wal-Mart as a Phenomenon in the Legal World: Matters of Scale, Scale Matters*, in WAL-MART WORLD (Stanley Braun ed., 2006).

[48] H. LAWRENCE ROSS, SETTLED OUT OF COURT: THE SOCIAL PROCESS OF INSURANCE CLAIMS AD-

- ability to play the odds. The larger the matter at issue looms for the one-shotter, the more likely he is to avoid risk (that is, minimize the probability of maximum loss). The greater size of these recurrent organizational litigants means that the stakes are both absolutely larger (and thus justify greater expenditures) and relatively smaller, so they can adopt strategies calculated to maximize gain over a long series of cases, even where this involves the risk of maximum loss in some cases. (This advantage is an application of a much more general capacity of corporate actors to utilize actuarial practices that "allow power to be exercised more effectively and at lower political cost.")[49]

- ability to play for rules as well as immediate gains. It is worthwhile for a recurrent litigant to expend resources in influencing the making of relevant rules by lobbying and so forth.[50] Recurrent litigants can also play for rules in litigation itself whereas a onetime litigant is unlikely to do so.

In the years since these speculations were first published, many researchers have attempted to test the presence and magnitude of such advantages.[51] In the current American setting, the well-resourced repeat-player (RP) is in almost all cases an organization, so that researchers have variously operationalized RPs as organizations, businesses, etc. A body of evidence has accumulated showing that organizations do better than individuals in almost every kind of litigation, at almost every stage, and as both plaintiffs and defendants.

JUSTMENT 156 (1970); THOMAS C. SHELLING, THE STRATEGY OF CONFLICT 22, 41 (1963).

[49] Jonathan Simon, *The Ideological Effects of Actuarial Practices*, 21 LAW & SOC'Y REV. 771 (1988).

[50] Lobbying may be subtle and may be directed to judges as well as legislators and administrators. On the organized provision of "educational" junkets for judges by corporate partisans, see DOUGLAS T. KENDALL & JASON C. RYLANDER, COMMUNITY RIGHTS COUNSEL, TAINTED JUSTICE: HOW PRIVATE JUDICIAL TRIPS UNDERMINE PUBLIC TRUST IN THE FEDERAL JUDICIARY (2004); ALLIANCE FOR JUSTICE, JUSTICE FOR SALE: SHORTCHANGING THE PUBLIC INTEREST FOR PRIVATE GAIN (1993). Gary Edmond and David Mercer describe the role of corporate-sponsored think-tanks and polemicists in promoting the convergence of judicial attitudes about expert evidence and civil liability with "legal weapons [that] were crafted and refined in corporate foundries." Gary Edmond & David Mercer, *Daubert and the Exclusionary Ethos: The Convergence of Corporate and Judicial Attitudes towards the Admissibility of Expert Evidence in Tort Litigation*, 26 LAW & POL'Y 231, 251 (2004). The latest variation of "lobbying" the judiciary is "seeding" the research of independent scholars in the hope of producing literature that would be useful ammunition for advocacy. Thus the Exxon Corporation promoted and supported extensive research on punitive damages by prominent scholars. See Alan Zarembo, *Funding Studies to Suit Need: In the 1990s, Exxon Began Paying for Research into Juries and the Damages they Award. The Findings Have Served the Firm Well in Court*, L.A. TIMES, Dec. 3, 2003, at A-1; see also William R. Freudenburg, *Seeding Science, Courting Conclusions: Reexamining the Intersection of Science, Corporate Cash, and the Law*, 20 SOC. F. 3 (2005). The findings of this research have been deployed in advocacy aimed at curtailing punitive damages, such as those facing the corporate sponsor in the Exxon Valdez oil spill case. See Brief of Certain Leading Business Corporations as Amici Curiae Supporting Petitioner, State Farm Mutual Automobile Insurance Company v. Curtis B. Campbell & Inez Preece Campbell, 537 U.S. 1042 (2002) (No. 01-1289).

[51] See, e.g., Symposium, *Do the "Haves" Still Come Out Ahead?*, 33 LAW & SOC'Y REV. 793 (1999); IN LITIGATION: DO THE "HAVES" STILL COME OUT AHEAD? (Herbert M. Kritzer & Susan S. Silbey eds., 2003). Research along these lines is surveyed in Brian J. Glenn, *The Varied and Abundant Progeny*, in IN LITIGATION, *supra*, at 371.

Two recent studies of federal court litigation suggest that organizational litigants win more frequently and lose less often than do individuals. Terence Dunworth and Joel Rogers compared the litigation of the largest corporations with that of all other parties in the federal courts for a twenty-year period. The largest corporations were more successful both as plaintiffs and as defendants: they won 79% of the federal cases in which they were plaintiffs, compared to 62% won by all other parties.[52] As defendants, the gap was even greater: the largest corporations won some 62% of the time while other parties won only 33% of their cases.[53]

In a comparison of performance confined to diversity cases, Dunworth and Rogers were able to separate business from non-business parties. As Table 2 shows, businesses outperformed non-business parties as both plaintiffs and defendants. The largest businesses actually won a smaller percentage of their plaintiff cases than did other businesses, but maintained their winning ways as defendants. Other businesses outperformed non-business parties by a wide margin as plaintiffs and a more modest one as defendants.

Table 2. Percentage of Cases Won by Various Kinds of Parties in Federal District Courts, 1971-1991

		As Plaintiffs	As Defendants
All Cases	Fortune 2000	79%	62%
	Other Parties	62%	33%
Diversity Cases	Fortune 2000	71%	61%
	Other Business Parties	80%	36%
	Non-Business Parties	64%	28%

Source: Dunworth and Rogers, *supra* note 52, at 557-558.

In another study of federal diversity cases, Theodore Eisenberg and Henry Farber eliminated personal injury cases (because corporations are so infrequently plaintiffs) and compared the performance of corporations and individuals as plaintiffs.[54] Again, corporations won some 83% and individuals some 60% of the cases in which they were plaintiffs. Eisenberg and Farber divide their cases according to the configuration of the parties and present the plaintiff-win rates for the various match-ups between individuals and organizations. These are shown in Table 3.

---

[52] Terence Dunworth & Joel Rogers, *Corporations in Court: Big Business Litigation in U.S. Federal Courts, 1971-1991*, 21 LAW & SOC. INQUIRY 497, 557 (1996).

[53] *Id.*

[54] Theodore Eisenberg & Henry S. Farber, *The Litigious Plaintiff Hypothesis: Case Selection and Resolution*, 28 RAND J. ECON. S92, S99 (1997).

Table 3. Plaintiff Win Rates by Configuration of Parties, Federal District Courts, Non-Personal Injury Diversity Cases, 1986-1994

Overall Plaintiff Win Rate (Win Rate at Trial) [Trial Rate]	Defendant		
	Individual	Corporation	TOTAL
Individual	72.4% (63.3.%) [3.61%]	50.1% (56.0%) [4.49%]	60.8% (58.6%) [4.12%]
Corporation	90.8% (66.2%) [2.52%]	74.8% (64.0%) [3.41%]	83.6% (64.8%) [3.04%]
TOTAL	83.4% (64.5%) [3.07%]	63.2% (59.3%) [3.95%]	73.7% (61.2%) [3.58%]

Source: Eisenberg & Farber, *supra*, note 54 at S103 tbl. 2.

We see that not only do corporate plaintiffs win more, they win even more frequently as both plaintiffs and defendants when opposing individuals than when opposing other corporations. They won 90% of the cases in which they sued individuals and lost only 50% of the cases in which individuals sued them. The differentials are less for that small subset (3.58%) of cases that went to trial. (Interestingly, the individual plaintiff vs. corporate defendant match-up was the only configuration in which plaintiffs won more frequently at trial than at the pre-trial stages.)

These patterns are not peculiar to federal district courts. Studying three urban trial courts, Craig Wanner found that business and government plaintiffs win more often and more quickly than do individual plaintiffs.[55] Not only are they more successful overall, which might be attributed to differences in the kinds of cases they bring, but they are more successful in almost every one of the heavily litigated categories of cases. Organizations did strikingly better not only as plaintiffs, but also as defendants.[56] This general pattern is confirmed by Harold Owen's study of two Georgia trial courts: individual plaintiffs win less often and individual defendants lose more often than their organizational counterparts.[57]

Corporations not only get better results, but they do so at lower cost—i.e., with pre-tax dollars. As Jeffrey Stempel observes,

[55] Craig Wanner, *The Public Ordering of Private Relations: Part II: Winning Civil Court Cases,* 9 Law & Soc'y Rev. 293, 305 tbl.9 (1975).

[56] *Id.* at 302 tbl.7.

[57] Harold J. Owen, Jr., The Role of Trial Courts in The Local Political System: A Comparison of Two Georgia Counties (1971) (unpublished Ph.D. dissertation, University of Georgia) (on file with author).

commercial litigants have a natural economic advantage in litigation with natural persons. The litigation expenditures (indeed, all dispute resolution expenditures) of the commercial litigant are almost certain to be successfully characterized as business expenses deductible in the year in which they are incurred. Thus, the money spent on litigation . . . effectively reduces the litigant company's taxes by as much as one-third. By contrast, an individual claiming tortious injury, breach of consumer contract, discrimination, or fraud is normally unable to have his or her disputing costs partially subsidized by the government.[58]

It is widely believed that juries are resolutely hostile to corporations. Actually juries find more frequently in favor of corporations, but where they do find corporations liable, they award higher damages than against other parties for comparable injuries.[59] Experimental studies suggest that this is not so much a "deep pocket" effect as an effect of jurors' estimation of corporations as being equipped with greater capacity to foresee and prevent harm.[60]

The advantages of organized and powerful players in the judicial arena are not peculiar to federal courts, or to trial courts, nor to the present era. Analyzing outcomes in state supreme courts over the period 1870-1970, Wheeler et al. found

that parties with greater resources—relatively speaking, the "haves"—generally fared better than those with fewer resources. In match-ups between stronger and weaker parties, the stronger consistently and on a variety of different measures won an advantage averaging 5 percent.[61]

They also concluded that

the more sharply party disparity can be delineated, the larger the net advantage of the stronger parties, and some of those advantages are really substantial. Thus the consistent advantage to the "haves" in our results probably *understates* their true advantage.[62]

In a study of the success of appellants before U.S. Courts of Appeals (4th, 7th, and 11th circuits in 1986), Donald Songer and Reginald Sheehan found that "[t]he success rates of appellants consistently increase with each incremental increase in their strength relative to the strength of the respondent."[63] They discovered that "the relative advantages of the 'haves' were generally found to be several times as great in the courts of appeals as they were in [Wheeler et al.'s] state supreme

[58] Jeffrey W. Stempel, *Contracting Access to the Courts: Myth of Reality? Boon or Bane?*, 40 ARIZ. L. REV. 965, 998 (1998).

[59] For example, "[b]usinesses were somewhat more successful with juries than were individuals, both as plaintiffs and defendants." AUDREY CHIN & MARK A. PETERSON, DEEP POCKETS,EMPTY POCKETS: WHO WINS IN COOK COUNTY JURY TRIALS? 25 (1985). But awards against corporate defendants were considerably higher than against individuals. *Id.* at 27.

[60] See Valerie P. Hans, *The Contested Role of the Civil Jury in Business Litigation*, 79 JUDICATURE 242 (1996); Robert J. MacCoun, *Differential Treatment of Corporate Defendants by Juries: An Examination of the "Deep Pockets" Hypothesis*, 30 LAW & SOC'Y REV. 121 (1996).

[61] Stanton Wheeler et al., *Do the "Haves" Come Out Ahead? Winning and Losing in State Supreme Courts, 1870-1970*, 21 LAW & SOC'Y REV. 403, 443 (1987).

[62] *Id.*

[63] Donald R. Songer & Reginald S. Sheehan, *Who Wins on Appeal? Upperdogs and Underdogs in the United States Courts of Appeals*, 36 AM. J. POL. SCI. 235, 246 (1992).

courts."[64]

Kevin Clermont and Theodore Eisenberg looked at the propensity of federal appellate courts in thirteen categories of non-personal injury diversity trials and found that plaintiffs and defendants fare very differently in the appeals process.[65] Where a plaintiff wins in the trial courts, defendant appellants secure reversals almost twice as frequently as do plaintiff appellants in cases where defendants win at trial (28.4% vs. 14.8%).[66] Corporate losers at the trial court level appeal more frequently than individual losers (28.5% vs. 20.2% as plaintiffs, 22.4% vs. 17.1% as defendants) and more of these appeals lead to reversals (21.5% for corporate plaintiffs vs. 12.5% for individual plaintiffs, 27.5% for corporate defendants vs. 24% for individual defendants).[67] Reversals of jury verdicts at the instance of defendants are almost twice as frequent as reversals at the instance of plaintiffs. Clermont and Eisenberg conclude that the most plausible explanation is appellate judges' mistaken attribution of pro-plaintiff bias on the part of juries.[68] We have seen that increasingly the plaintiffs in federal civil cases are NPs and the defendants are APs. So the "plaintiphobia" of the appellate courts, as Clermont and Eisenberg call it, becomes another layer of advantage for APs.

Do these disparities in success in the judicial forum necessarily reflect the differences in "party capability" or "the relational effects of asymmetric parties"?[69] The universe of disputes and litigation is frequently and usefully visualized as a pyramid made up of successive layers including perceived injuries, grievances, claims, disputes, filings, trials, and appeals.[70] There is attrition—often very pro-

---

[64] *Id.* at 255. Such consistent advantages for "haves" parties were not found in the U.S. Supreme Court when the effects of ideology were controlled. *See id.* at 235-58.

[65] Kevin M. Clermont & Theodore Eisenberg, *Plaintiphobia in the Appellate Courts: Civil Rights Really Do Differ from Negotiable Instruments*, 2002 U. ILL. L. REV. 947 (2002) (summarizing and analyzing results). See especially their earlier study, *Appeal from Jury or Judge Trial: Defendants' Advantage*, 3 AM. L. & ECON. REV. 125 (2001).

[66] *Id.* at 131 tbl.1.

[67] *Id.* at 138 nn.22-23.

[68] *Id.* at 138.

[69] Such effects are not confined to courts in the United States. Studies of the Supreme Court and the Provincial Courts of Appeal in Canada found clear confirmation of the party capability thesis. Peter McCormick, *Party Capability Theory and Appellate Success in the Supreme Court of Canada, 1949-1992*, 26 CAN. J. POL. SCI. 523 (1993); Peter McCormick, *Who Wins and Who Loses in the Provincial Courts of Appeal? A Statistical Analysis, 1920-1990*, CAN. J.L. & SOC'Y, Fall 1994, at 21. Outcomes in the English Court of Appeal reflect "the relational effects of asymmetric parties." Burton M. Atkins, *A Cross National Perspective on the Structuring of Trial Court Outputs: The Case of the English High Court*, in COMPARATIVE JUDICIAL SYSTEMS 143 (John R. Schmidhauser ed., 1987); *see also* Burton M. Atkins, *Party Capability Theory as an Explanation for Intervention Behavior in the English Court of Appeal*, 35 AM. J. POL. SCI. 881 (1991).

[70] A brief summation of the "pyramid" analysis may be found at Marc Galanter, *Reading the Landscape of Disputes: What We Know and Don't Know (and Think We Know) about Our Allegedly Contentious and Litigious Society*, 31 UCLA L. REV. 4, 12-32 (1983). *See also* Marc Galanter, *Adjudication, Litigation and Related Phenomena*, in LAW AND THE SOCIAL SCIENCES 151, 183-203 (Leon Lipson & Stanton Wheeler eds., 1986). *See generally* William L.F. Felstiner et al., *The Emergence and Transformation of Disputes: Naming, Blaming, Claiming...*, 15 LAW & SOC'Y REV. 631 (1980-81) (providing a conceptual framework for studying the emergence and transformation of disputes); Neil Vidmar, *Justice Motives and Other Psychological Factors in the Development and Resolution of Disputes*, in THE JUSTICE MOTIVE IN SOCIAL BEHAVIOR: ADAPTING TO TIMES OF SCARCITY AND CHANGE 395, 409-13 (Melvin J. Lerner & Sally C. Lerner eds., 1981).

nounced—as cases move up the pyramid; only a fraction of the possible cases run the whole course to trials and appeals. As matters proceed up the pyramid, there is selection.[71] The cases that survive to the next layer are not entirely representative of the cohort at a given level. For example, such survivors may involve larger injuries or involve parties that are more knowledgeable, more contentious, less risk-averse or better supplied with resources.

Some portion of the observed difference in gross rates of success is attributable to the make-up of the litigation portfolios of organizations and individuals. Organizations bring more cases of the kinds that are easiest to win (such as collections, foreclosures, etc.) and organizations bring not only different cases but "better" cases. As plaintiffs, they can avoid weak cases by forbearance to bring suit or by readily accepting a low settlement; as defendants, they can settle the more meritorious and attractive cases against them—perhaps before filing. So their portfolio tends to consist of cases in which the evidence is stronger and the claim more firmly located within accepted lines of recovery. Stronger evidence, more cut-and-dried claims, and unassailable defenses are the result of advance planning and good record-keeping, as well as of the intrinsic merit of the claim. A calculating settlement policy reflects their capacity as litigants as much as the virtues of their conduct in the underlying transaction. Their capacity is enhanced by lawyering that involves more preventive work, continuity of attention, specialized expertise, economies of scale, and shrewd investment in rule development in judicial, legislative, and administrative settings. This is not a new phenomenon. Describing federal diversity litigation in the late nineteenth century, Edward Purcell observes that

> [c]orporations had the time, resources, incentives and sophistication both to litigate selectively in order to maximize their chances of developing favorable common law rules and to lobby the legislatures persistently in an effort to have statutory law tailored most closely to their interests.[72]

Difference in the "merits" of cases, then, is in large measure not an alternative explanation of party success, but a specification of one of the ways in which party

---

The first major empirical application of this method was undertaken by Richard E. Miller & Austin Sarat, *Grievances, Claims and Disputes: Assessing the Adversary Culture*, 15 LAW & SOC'Y REV. 525 (1980-81) (reporting on a survey of households estimating the rates of grievances, claims, and disputes that could have been brought to a civil court of general jurisdiction). *See also* Herbert M. Kritzer, *Propensity to Sue in England and the United States of America: Blaming and Claiming in Tort Cases*, 18 J.L. & SOC'Y 400 (1991); Herbert M. Kritzer et al., *The Aftermath of Injury: Cultural Factors in Compensation Seeking in Canada and the United States*, 25 LAW & SOC'Y REV. 499, 501-02 (1991); Herbert M. Kritzer et al., *To Confront or Not to Confront: Measuring Claiming Rates in Discrimination Grievances*, 25 LAW & SOC'Y REV. 875, 879-82 (1991).

[71] *See, e.g.*, George L. Priest & Benjamin Klein, *The Selection of Disputes for Litigation*, 13 J. LEGAL STUD. 1 (1984); *see also* Donald Wittman, *Is the Selection of Cases for Trial Biased?*, 14 J. LEGAL STUD. 185 (1985) (proposing a model for the distribution of litigant estimates of outcomes that differs from Priest and Klein's model and leads to contrary conclusions about the litigation process); Samuel R. Gross & Kent D. Syverud, *Getting to No: A Study of Settlement Negotiations and the Selection of Cases for Trial*, 90 MICH. L. REV. 319 (1991) (explaining why a good part of the Priest and Klein framework is at odds with the data and presenting data on failed pretrial negotiations).

[72] EDWARD A. PURCELL, JR., LITIGATION AND INEQUALITY: FEDERAL DIVERSITY JURISDICTION IN INDUSTRIAL AMERICA, 1870-1958, at 29 (1992).

capability affects the profile of litigation.

Which is not to say that "merit" is illusory or that the courts are biased against individuals. Courts are like the referees in a basketball game between an NP team of six-foot tall players and an AP team of equally-talented seven-footers. The seven-foot AP team doesn't get its baskets dishonestly, and sometimes the six-footers win the game, but over the long haul the disparity in resources is reflected in the scores. In sports like basketball and football, we tolerate gross disparities of physical stature (relying on schedulers to preserve the element of genuine contest?), while in other sports, such as boxing, this is considered unfair and the contest is conducted in weight classes (or in gender divisions, as in golf, tennis, swimming, and track). Adjudication resembles professional team sports in this respect: no allowance is made for the difference in height or reach. In basketball and football, the game is dominated by ever-taller and ever-heavier players; fewer short and light players can compete. In baseball, the richest teams collect the best players and win more frequently.[73] Similarly, in the legal arena, organizational players are crowding out individual ones and they are more frequently successful.

When I say corporations and other APs are on the whole more capable players of the law game, I am not attributing to them a preternatural competence and freedom from error. Corporations blunder just as do individuals and the blundering reflects the structure of corporations: their problems of coordination, the necessity of acting through agents with their own limited perspectives and separate ambitions. But their performance suggests that on the whole the corporate entity's incremental increase in capability as a legal actor outweighs these distractions. In short, our institutions of legal remedy are not exempt from the working of the general phenomenon of cumulative advantage.[74]

Party capacity to litigate not only affects the outcome of individual cases, but

---

[73] "Of the 13 major league clubs with the highest payrolls during the 1998 season, only Baltimore finished below .500. Of the 17 others, only St. Louis and Toronto were above .500." Jeff Miller, *Too Many Franchises Asking: Why Bother?*, Wisc. St. J., Apr. 4, 1999, at 1D. From 1996 to 1999, teams in the fourth payroll quartile won a median of seventy-two games (in a 162 game season), a number which progressed steadily by quartiles to a median of 95 for teams in the first payroll quartile. Paul L. Caron & Rafael Gely, *What Law Schools Can Learn from Billy Beane and the Oakland Athletics*, 82 Tex. L. Rev. 1483, 1489 (2004) (reviewing Michael Lewis, Moneyball: The Art of Winning an Unfair Game (2003)).

[74] The cumulative advantage phenomenon has been observed in many settings. Merton and Zuckerman identified what they called the "Matthew effect": "[T]he process by which those who have been given some advantages come to be given still more." William J. Goode, The Celebration of Heroes: Prestige as a Social Control System 279 (1978). In the sociology of science, such cumulative advantage is understood to be present, but there is still uncertainty about the precise mechanism. *See* Paul D. Allison, J. Scott Long & Tad K. Krauze, *Cumulative Advantage and Inequality in Science*, 47 Am. Soc. Rev. 615 (1982). A humbler example is Barry Schwartz's study of behavior in waiting rooms, which finds that the various sorts of accommodative deference (waiting time, escorting, proffering drinks) accorded to higher status clients tend to feed into and subserve one another, so that in the aggregate they unintentionally violate the norm of distributive justice they sought to conform to. "While each server grants a client his proper due, the resulting distribution (effected by two servers) allows some clients somewhat more than their due." Barry Schwartz, Queuing and Waiting: Studies in the Social Organization of Access and Delay 152 (1975). Schwartz finds this same kind of "multiplication of social profits implicit in the strain toward status congruence" in the distribution of unproductive and costly waiting time in courts, where "some persons and groups are relatively exempt from waiting. . . . [In] the courtroom . . . the powerful are most likely to enjoy such advantage." *Id.* at 29.

shapes the judicial agenda. Organized parties can undertake sustained campaigns of litigation. The classic example is the NAACP's campaign against school segregation.[75] A more recent example is the continuing corporate campaign to curtail punitive damage awards.[76] The scale of these "party effects" is displayed in Charles Epp's comparative study of the rights agenda of courts of last resort in the U.S., Canada, England, and India.[77] He found that an enlarged rights agenda was best explained not by "top-down" theories of judicial ideology but by a "bottom-up" theory focused on the organizational and financial resources of the groups advocating such cases. So organizations fare better in court not only in terms of results, but in terms of setting the courts' agenda.

IV. THE CORPORATIZATION OF THE LAW

At the same time that APs are becoming more dominant in the legal world they are themselves changing. Although it is difficult to generalize about such a large and diverse population, it appears that overall APs are moving away from their origins as instruments devoted to supplying specific goods or services to NPs and are increasingly guided by concerns with their own power, longevity, and reputation. According to an eminent organization-watcher, "virtually every development associated with industrialization and the establishment of the corporate form of organization . . . [has] caused mission to be displaced as an organizational goal in favor of the systems goals, notably profit and especially growth . . . ."[78] The famous example of the March of Dimes re-inventing itself after the conquest of polio is a convenient symbol of this tendency within corporate organizations. Now corporations change their names to efface any connection with particular functions.

And the relations among the various sorts of APs are changing as well. In the past thirty years the business corporation has achieved an ascendancy over government entities and non-profit associations. Business corporations have for a long time enjoyed a privileged position in American government, enjoying subsidies, solicitude, and deference.[79] Since the 1970s, this has been accentuated by a precipitous decline in confidence in governmental institutions[80] and a great augmentation of the political activity of business entities and their satellite foundations and think-tanks.[81] There has been a major increase in business lobbying, in the political activity of CEOs, in electoral activity, and in the formation of orga-

---

[75] MARK V. TUSHNET, THE NAACP'S LEGAL STRATEGY AGAINST SEGREGATED EDUCATION, 1925-1950 (1987).

[76] *See, e.g.*, STEPHEN DANIELS & JOANNE MARTIN, CIVIL JURIES AND THE POLITICS OF REFORM (1995).

[77] CHARLES EPP, THE RIGHTS REVOLUTION: LAWYERS, ACTIVISTS AND SUPREME COURTS IN COMPARATIVE PERSPECTIVE (1998).

[78] HENRY MINTZBERG, POWER IN AND AROUND ORGANIZATIONS 286 (1983).

[79] *See* CHARLES E. LINDBLOM, POLITICS AND MARKETS: THE WORLD'S POLITICAL ECONOMIC SYSTEMS (1977).

[80] *See* SEYMOUR MARTIN LIPSET & WILLIAM SCHNEIDER, THE CONFIDENCE GAP: BUSINESS, LABOR, AND GOVERNMENT IN THE PUBLIC MIND (1987).

[81] On the rise of think tanks, see THOMAS BYRNE EDSALL, THE NEW POLITICS OF INEQUALITY 117-20 (1984). *See also* DAVID M. RICCI, THE TRANSFORMATION OF AMERICAN POLITICS: THE NEW WASHINGTON AND THE RISE OF THINK TANKS (1993).

nizations and coalitions to carry these out.[82] The thrust of much of this has been to reduce or soften governmental regulation of corporate activity. Governmental functions—prisons, police, even military operations—have been farmed out to the private sector. At the same time business corporations have penetrated and patronized other institutions—schools, universities, arts, healthcare, sports. Their presence has been naturalized—they are not seen as inhabitants of the specialized realm of production, but as institutions of civic life. They have discarded their old names based on their work (e.g., AT&T, Standard Oil) to become Verizon or Exxon, sonorous invocations of institutional dynamism. Formerly, public spaces might be named after heroic figures or public benefactors; now it has come to seem natural for stadiums and parks to be named after corporations. As civic actors, corporations occupy some of the space left by the contraction of civic participation by individuals through voluntary associations, at the same time as those associations become more corporate and less participatory.[83]

Corporate parties are not merely part of the clientele of unchanging adjudicative institutions. In important ways, the increasing presence of APs transforms the institutions of adjudication. Meir Dan-Cohen argues that as courts encounter more organizational parties, their decision-making shifts from an arbitral model focusing on retrospective examination of "a self-contained private [dispute] . . . involving exclusively the rights and interests of the contending parties" to a regulation model that seeks prospectively to "shape the form of future transactions and interactions" among a whole category of parties.[84] The shift that Dan-Cohen describes has impressed other observers as well.[85] "Since organizations augment the social ramifications of judicial decisions, they incline the judge toward the regulatory mode."[86] As the ratio of general-to-specific effects increases, courts shift from an arbitral to a regulatory style.[87] The presence of organizations makes courts more future-oriented, more managerial, more utilitarian, and generally more "legislative." But this in turn raises the stakes in any given litigation and confers additional advantage on those parties that can plan and invest accordingly.[88]

---

[82] See DAVID VOGEL, FLUCTUATING FORTUNES: THE POLITICAL POWER OF BUSINESS IN AMERICA (1989); see also Edsall, supra note 81, at 107-41; KEVIN PHILLIPS, WEALTH AND DEMOCRACY: A POLITICAL HISTORY OF THE AMERICAN RICH (2003).

[83] See ROBERT D. PUTNAM, BOWLING ALONE: THE COLLAPSE AND REVIVAL OF AMERICAN COMMUNITY (2000).

[84] MEIR DAN-COHEN, RIGHTS, PERSONS, AND ORGANIZATIONS: A LEGAL THEORY FOR BUREAUCRATIC SOCIETY 128 (1986).

[85] See Abram Chayes, The Role of the Judge in Public Law Litigation, 89 HARV. L. REV. 1281 (1976); see also Horwitz, supra note 3.

[86] DAN-COHEN, supra note 84, at 128. If we distinguish the outcomes of judicial action as either special effects (i.e., on the parties involved) or general effects (i.e., on wider audiences, including potential parties), we can translate the shift from arbitral to regulatory style as an increase in the ratio of general to special effects. Marc Galanter, The Radiating Effects of Courts, in EMPIRICAL THEORIES ABOUT COURTS 117 (K. Boyum & L. Mather eds., 1983).

[87] On the distinction between special effects (i.e., impacts on the parties before the court) and general effects (i.e., impacts on others), see Galanter, supra note 86, at 117, 124-27.

[88] For a classic discussion, see Stewart Macaulay's description of litigation between the automobile manufacturers and their dealers. Macaulay, supra note 20, at 99-101.

The regulatory shift is evidenced in a set of interlinked changes that are pervasive in American courts. There are fewer trials—not just fewer as a percentage of all terminations—but fewer absolutely. For example, although the number of civil filings in the federal district courts has increased by a factor of five since 1962, the number of civil trials has decreased by thirty-two percent.[89] Comparable declines are found in state courts and in criminal as well as civil trials. The decline in trials is accompanied by the rise of managerial judging, with intensive pre-trial supervision of cases, more terminations by pre-trial adjudication (e.g., summary judgment, motions to dismiss), judicial promotion of settlements, and the embrace of Alternative Dispute Resolution.[90] Legislators and judges, beguiled by tales of a litigation explosion and overuse of the courts, incline to restricting access to the courts. But these restrictions are not broadside; they target the claims of NPs, not those of organizations.[91] A recent and poignant example is the September 11th Victim Compensation Fund which removed the claims of natural persons from the legal system. Individuals were given (generous) scheduled compensation but were deprived of any forum for their potentially embarrassing non-monetary claims, while the APs—airlines, airport authorities, security firms, insurance companies, and governmental units—were protected from any legal accountability to NPs. But the act made "no effort to divert property damage, business disruption, or insurance subrogation claims out of the legal system."[92]

---

[89] In 1962, some 5802 cases in the Federal District Courts terminated "during or after trial" making up 11.5% of dispositions. In 2004, the corresponding figure was 3951 (just 1.7% of all dispositions). *See* ADMINISTRATIVE OFFICE OF THE U.S. COURTS, FEDERAL JUDICIAL CASELOAD STATISTICS: MARCH 31, 2004, tbl. C-4 (2004), http://www.uscourts.gov/caseload2004/tables/C04Mar04. pdf. The Administrative Office (AO) counts as a trial "a contested proceeding before a jury or court at which evidence is introduced." Federal Judicial Center, 2003-2004 District Court Case-Weighing Study app. F (2004), http://www.fjc.gov/public/pdf.nsf/lookup/CaseWtsF.pdf/$file/ CaseWtsF.pdf (Form JS-10). The definition of trial varies in the state courts. *See* Marc Galanter, *The Vanishing Trial: An Examination of Trials and Related Matters in Federal and State Courts*, 1 J. EMPIRICAL LEGAL STUD. 459, 533-34 tbl.A-2 (2004). In sorting out terminations, the AO's record-keeping category is cases terminated "during or after trial," so the number of trials counted includes cases that settle during trial and some evidentiary proceedings that do not lead to judgments. So, the count here is not a count of completed trials but of cases that reach the trial stage. These figures provide an inexact but useful indicator of both the magnitude and year-to-year trends in trial activity. For a full discussion of the counting of trials problems, see Galanter, *supra*, at 475-76.

[90] *See* Galanter, *supra* note 89; Judith Resnik, *Migrating, Morphing and Vanishing: The Empirical and Normative Puzzles of Declining Trial Rates in Courts*, 1 J. EMPIRICAL LEGAL STUD. 783 (2004).

[91] Current examples include restrictions on class actions (Class Action Fairness Act of 2005, Pub. L. 109-2, 119 Stat. 4 (2005); John F. Harris, *Victory For Bush On Suits; New Law to Limit Class-Action Cases*, WASH. POST, Feb. 18, 2005, at A1) and proposed limits on medical malpractice claims. Steve Lohr, *Bush's Next Target: Malpractice Lawyers*, N.Y. TIMES, Feb. 27, 2005, § 3, at 1 (describing Bush administration legislation that would cap non-economic damages in malpractice suits at $250,000 and limit attorneys' fees). Also in 2005, the Department of Health and Human Services proposed to restrict trials of Medicare claims: hearings will be shifted from 140 Social Security offices around the country to just four sites; most hearings will be held by teleconference or telephone and those beneficiaries who insist on a face-to-face hearing will waive their right to receive a decision within ninety days. Robert Pear, *Medicare Change Will Limit Access to Claim Hearing*, N.Y. TIMES, Apr. 24, 2005, at 1.

[92] Gillian K. Hadfield, *The September 11th Victim Compensation Fund: An Unprecedented Experiment in American Democracy*, in THE FUTURE OF TERRORISM RISK INSURANCE (Defense Re-

NPs may depart the courts along various paths—by judicial outsourcing to auxiliaries or ADR forums, by conscription into captive tribunals by mandatory arbitration clauses,[93] by contractual confinement to "internal" tribunals within APs.[94] Bryant Garth describes the evolution of a "segmented and hierarchical" system in which "high stakes business disputes" enjoy "a full array of alternatives" including courts and elite ADR providers, while ordinary litigants are pushed into "settlement-oriented ADR processes dominated by quick-and-dirty arbitration and by mediation conducted by private individuals accountable neither through review processes nor appeal."[95]

Individuals with their passions and their occasional appetite for vindication,[96] for establishing truth, and for challenging authority, are eased out of the courts, which become more focused on economic claims. Policies designed to pressure parties to settle (like F.R.C.P. Rule 68) "delegitimatize all noneconomic motives associated with litigation."[97] In such an environment, repeat-players can use settlement strategy to vitiate the production of precedent favorable to claimants, who are reasonably equivalent to NPs. As full-blown contest over non-economic principles is squeezed out, law is "de-moralized"—as signified by the invariable qualifier in all settlements that the defendant does not admit any wrongdoing. This feature of our legal system is neatly displayed in a New Yorker cartoon by Lee Lorenz, who anticipated by fifteen years the Global Tobacco Settlement which said in effect, we'll give you $300 billion but there is no admission of any wrongdoing.

V. CULTURAL INDULGENCE

In addition to these structural advantages, APs enjoy "cultural" advantages in the legal forum. For more than a century American courts have been receptive to the notion that corporate actors are persons or entities with rights of their own rather than merely creatures of the state or instruments of NPs.[98] Corporations are

---

search Institute, 2005).

[93] On the increasing prevalence of adhesive mandatory pre-dispute arbitration clauses, see Jean R. Sternlight, *Creeping Mandatory Arbitration: Is It Just?*, 57 STAN. L. REV. 1631 (2005); David S. Schwartz, *Enforcing Small Print to Protect Big Business: Employee and Consumer Rights Claims in an Age of Compelled Arbitration*, 1997 WIS. L. REV. 33.

[94] Lauren B. Edelman & Mark C. Suchman, *When the "Haves" Hold Court: Speculations on the Organizational Internalization of Law*, 33 LAW & SOC'Y REV. 941 (1999).

[95] Bryant G. Garth, *Tilting the Justice System: From ADR as Idealistic Movement to a Segmented Market in Dispute Resolution*, 18 GA. ST. U.L. REV. 930, 932 (2002).

[96] Individual litigants vary in the extent to which they seek justice or moral vindication instead of, or in addition to, a satisfactory solution to their immediate discomforts. A survey of Detroit residents found that the proportion of respondents reporting serious problems who sought justice or vindication was tiny in all areas other than discrimination. Leon Mayhew, *Institutions of Representation*, 9 LAW & SOC'Y REV. 401, 413 (1975). A study of the Illinois Attorney General's Consumer Fraud Bureau found that the desire for "public-oriented" remedies as opposed to private relief varied directly with income level. Only 4% of those with incomes of less than $12,000 requested a public remedy, in contrast to 28% of those with incomes over $17,000. Eric Steele, *Fraud, Dispute and the Consumer: Responding to Consumer Complaints*, 123 U. PA. L. REV. 1107, 1140 (1975).

[97] Frank B. Cross, *In Praise of Irrational Plaintiffs*, 86 CORNELL L. REV. 1, 29 (2000).

[98] *See* Mayer, *supra* note 3; Schane, *supra* note 3; DONALD L. HOROWITZ, THE COURTS AND SOCIAL POLICY (1977).

"persons" for purposes of enjoying the protection of the Fourteenth Amendment's Due Process and Equal Protection Clauses.[99] Commercial corporations enjoy the same freedom of the press as do individuals under the First Amendment.[100]

"I accept the four thousand years in Limbo with the understanding that it in no way constitutes an admission of wrongdoing."

In a string of decisions since the mid-1970s, the Supreme Court has conferred on corporations significant Bill of Rights protections involving double jeopardy,[101] search and seizure,[102] and, most importantly, free speech protection for corporate political spending and advertising.[103] One commentator characterized these opinions as symbolic of "the transformation of our constitutional system from one of individual freedoms to one of organizational prerogatives."[104]

---

[99] *See, e.g.*, Santa Clara County v. S. Pac. R.R., 118 U.S. 394 (1886); Minneapolis & St. Louis Ry. Co. v. Beckwith, 129 U.S. 26 (1889); Smyth v. Ames, 169 U.S. 466 (1898). These late nineteenth-century decisions displaced earlier jurisprudence that denied that corporations were "persons" or "citizens" and viewed them as groups or partnerships. *See also* Mayer, *supra* note 3; Schane, *supra* note 3; HOROWITZ, *supra* note 98.

[100] *See* Grosjean v. American Press Co., 297 U.S. 233, 244 (1936).

[101] *See* U.S. v. Martin Linen Supply Co., 430 U.S. 564 (1976).

[102] *See* Marshall v. Barlow's Inc., 436 U.S. 307 (1977).

[103] *See* First Nat'l Bank v. Bellotti, 435 U.S. 765 (1976).

[104] Mayer, *supra* note 3, at 578.

Within the legal profession, the greatest prestige is enjoyed by those who represent large corporations.[105] Mirroring the prestige structure of the bar, many judges think that big-dollar commercial cases are what properly deserve the attention of courts and the routine matters of individuals are "junk cases" that should be addressed elsewhere. As noted earlier, appellate judges are inclined to think that they must protect corporate defendants against misguided claimants and prejudiced juries.[106]

But the warm feelings of judges for the corporate world are not reciprocated. Although corporations have in recent years increasingly used litigation as a strategic tool in managing business relationships, they have not embraced the courts. John Lande, who interviewed senior executives of publicly-held firms about their views, found that

> [m]ost said they were dissatisfied with the results in their experience with litigation and even more were dissatisfied with the process. Most believe that the courts are not sensitive to the needs of business. Many had doubts about the process of finding the facts, especially when juries make the decisions, and questioned the fairness of court outcomes. They were virtually unanimous that there has been a litigation explosion, and the vast majority believed that most suits by individuals against businesses are frivolous.[107]

Although they enjoy an array of rights, corporations are largely immune from criminal punishment.[108] They can't be imprisoned, and it is difficult to use fines effectively to deter corporate wrongdoing, for most corporate crimes are difficult to recognize and easy to conceal. The high stakes mean that adequate deterrence would require that fines be astronomical to achieve deterrence.[109] And fines have the disadvantage in that the effects are likely to fall on innocent parties—low level workers, customers, stockholders.[110] So, except in the glare of scandal, corporate organizations tend to be regulated in a sort of "restorative" mode that has gone out of fashion in dealing with individual offenders. On the other hand, corporate actors are frequent and successful users of the criminal justice system to punish offenses against themselves.[111]

---

[105] *See infra* text accompanying notes 121-23.

[106] *See supra* text accompanying note 65.

[107] John Lande, *Failing Faith in Litigation? A Survey of Business Lawyers and Executives' Opinions*, 3 HARV. NEGOT. L. REV. 1, 51 (1998). The thrust of Lande's findings is confirmed in other survey evidence. For example, a 1992 survey of business executives by Business Week found that 62% felt that "the U.S. civil justice system significantly hampers the ability of U.S. companies to compete with Japanese and European companies." Mark N. Vaumus, *The Verdict From the Corner Office*, BUS. WK., Apr. 13, 1992, at 66.

[108] *See* Coffee, *supra* note 18.

[109] Corporations can be punished by punitive damage awards, but such awards are hedged with protections that are not available to bar harsh criminal sentences for recidivist NPs. States may "freely consider extraterritorial misconduct when sentencing criminal recidivists, [but] such freedom is absent in the imposition of punitive damage awards." Wayne A. Logan, *Civil and Criminal Recidivists: Extraterritoriality in Tort and Crime*, 73 U. CIN. L. REV. 1609, 1626 (2005).

[110] *See* Coffee, *supra* note 18, at 390.

[111] See John Hagan, *The Corporate Advantage: A Study of the Involvement of Corporate and Individual Victims in a Criminal Justice System*, 60 SOC. FORCES 993-94 (1982).

Rather than chastening, many of the follies and blunders of corporations are deemed worthy of solace in the form of tax deductions.[112] Corporations enjoy a relative impunity to moral condemnation for single-minded pursuit of advantage that would be condemned as unworthy if done by NPs. (For example, changes in residence or status to secure tax advantages, or relocating assets to avoid liability.) While individuals who invoke the legal system arouse suspicion and reproach,[113] corporate actors are rarely condemned for aggressively using litigation in pursuit of their interests.[114] (Compare the outrage at the McDonald's coffee spill case with the sanguine response to the Texaco-Pennzoil award.)[115]

Being seen as a "tool" of corporations was once stigmatizing to lawyers. Back in 1910, Woodrow Wilson noted that "the country . . . distrusts every 'corporation lawyer' [and] supposes him in league with persons whom it has learned to dread, to whom it ascribes a degree of selfishness which in effect makes them public enemies . . . [The lawyer] stands stoutly on the defensive.[116] Theron G. Strong, a lawyer contemporary of Wilson, who kept a wonderful journal through the years when modern corporate practice emerged, disdainfully described the subservience of lawyers to their corporate masters. Lawyers on annual retainers to corporations, Strong thought,

> become little more than a paid employee[s] bound hand and foot to the service of [the corporation] . . . [the lawyer] is almost completely deprived of free moral agency and is open to at least the inference that he is virtually owned and controlled by the client he serves.[117]

Throughout much of the twentieth century, the large firm that serves corporate clients was portrayed as the exemplary site of legal professionalism, where lawyers exercise their autonomy to restrain the unreasonable or anti-social demands of clients. But research suggests that large corporate firm lawyers may have less autonomy vis-à-vis their clients than lawyers in smaller practices. Robert Nelson concluded that

> the notion that lawyers struggle with clients over fundamental questions about the common good is simply wrong . . . in general large firm lawyers strive to maximize the substantive interest of their clients within the boundaries of legal ethics.[118]

---

[112] *See* Reed Abelson, *Tax Reformers, Take Your Mark*, N.Y. TIMES, Feb. 11, 1996, § 3, at 12.

[113] See David Engel, *The Oven Bird's Song: Insiders, Outsiders, and Personal Injuries in an American Community*, 18 LAW & SOC'Y REV. 551, 553-54 (1984); Valerie P. Hans, *The Jury's Response to Business and Corporate Wrongdoing*, 52 LAW & CONTEMP. PROBS. 177 (1989); HANS, *supra* note 10, at 22-49.

[114] *See* Ross E. Cheit, *Corporate Ambulance Chasers: The Charmed Life of Business Litigation*, in STUDIES IN LAW, POLITICS, AND SOCIETY 119-20 (Austin Sarat & Susan S. Silbey eds., 1991).

[115] See Edward O. Laumann & John P. Heinz, *Specialization and Prestige in the Legal Profession: The Structure of Deference*, 1977 AM.B. FOUND. RES. J. 155.

[116] Woodrow Wilson, *The Lawyer and the Community*, 192 N. AM. REV. 604, 620 (1910).

[117] THERON G. STRONG, LANDMARKS OF A LAWYER'S LIFETIME 353-54 (1914).

[118] ROBERT L. NELSON, PARTNERS WITH POWER: THE SOCIAL TRANSFORMATION OF THE LARGE LAW FIRM 258-59 (1988). A review of recent literature reports a decline in the autonomy of large firm lawyers. John M. Conley and Scott Baker, *Fall from Grace or Business as Usual? A Retrospective Look at Lawyers on Wall Street and Main Street*, 30 LAW & SOC. INQUIRY 783, 814-15 (2005).

Many believe that the large firm sector was once populated by lawyer statesmen who induced corporate clients to refrain from acting against the public interest.[119] Stuart Speiser, who tested these claims by examining the biographies and collected papers of reputed lawyer statesmen and the published histories of leading law firms, found that they contained no evidence of any instance or policy of such counseling. Such "client purification," he concluded, was "a pure myth" and "merely wishful thinking . . . there never was such an operating tradition."[120] Lawyering by leading firms in deals giving rise to the corporate scandals of recent years has not allayed concern about lawyer independence of powerful clients.

Lawyers are more comfortable with corporations than is the public at-large. As more of their work and income comes from corporate sources, the disparity has widened. In 1975, Heinz and Laumann found, Chicago lawyers were "considerably more supportive of big business than . . . the general population." By 1995 the difference was accentuated. "Three-quarters of [a sample of the national population] adopted the position that large companies had too much power—the same percentage as in 1975." But only 31% of Chicago lawyers held this view in 1995, down from 52% in 1975.

Table 4. Portion who believe large companies have too much power

	National population	Chicago lawyers
1975	78%	52%
1995	75%	31%

Source: JOHN P. HEINZ ET AL., URBAN LAWYERS: THE NEW SOCIAL STRUCTURE OF THE BAR 199-200 (2005)

Those who are best served by lawyers and the legal system hold them in low esteem. Their lawyers, however, are rewarded not only by higher incomes, but by standing within the legal profession. Heinz and Laumann reported that the prestige ranking of legal fields mirrors the structural division of the profession, "with fields serving big business clients at the top and those serving individual clients (especially clients from lower socioeconomic groups) at the bottom."[121] "The higher a specialty stands in its reputation for being motivated by altruistic (as opposed to profitable) considerations, the lower it is likely to be in the prestige order."[122] This was in 1975. Twenty years later they observed that the prestige order had "undergone a crystallization." From 1975 to 1995 the disparity between the highly prestigious corporate fields and the less prestigious individual-service fields increased. Prestige was located in "fields serving large and powerful organizations."

---

[119] *See, e.g.*, ANTHONY KRONMAN, THE LOST LAWYER: FAILING IDEALS OF THE LEGAL PROFESSION (1993).

[120] Stuart M. Speiser, *Trial Balloon: Sarbanes-Oxley and the Myth of the Lawyer-Statesman*, 32(1) LITIGATION 5, 67, 69 (2005).

[121] HEINZ & LAUMANN, *supra* note 30, at 127.

[122] Laumann & Heinz, *supra* note 115, at 202.

Contrariwise, "the more a field is oriented toward public service, rather than profit, the lower its prestige."[123] The accentuation of hierarchy in professional prestige reflects more general changes in the representation of status hierarchies, in the spread of "winner-take-all" reward structures,[124] and the displacement of indistinct strata by avowedly precise ordinal rankings (like *U.S. News & World Report's* law school rankings and the *American Lawyer's* ranking of law firms)—a development in virtually every field of endeavor.

VI. PUBLIC AMBIVALENCE ABOUT THE DISTRIBUTIVE TILT OF THE LAW

Wider publics have a different take on the legal preeminence of corporate actors. That those with superior fiscal and organizational resources enjoy advantages in litigation has been appreciated by most observers (not just on the left) for a long time.[125] Although survey researchers seem to avoid asking questions about organizational potency per se, the responses to their questions about treatment of rich and poor reveal a sanguine public estimation that the legal system is biased in favor of the "haves." Thirty years ago, 59% of a national sample agreed that "the legal system favors the rich and powerful over everyone else."[126] Twenty years ago, when asked whether "[t]he justice system in the United States mainly favors the rich" or "treats all Americans as equally as possible," 57% of respondents chose the "favored the rich" response and only 39% the "equally" response.[127] In a 1995 survey conducted by *U.S. News & World Report*, fully three-quarters of the respondents thought that the American legal system affords less access to justice to "aver-

---

[123] All of the above from JOHN P. HEINZ ET AL., URBAN LAWYERS: THE NEW SOCIAL STRUCTURE OF THE BAR 81-89 (2005).

[124] See ROBERT H. FRANK & PHILIP J. COOK, THE WINNER TAKE ALL SOCIETY (1995).

[125] From then-ex-President William Howard Taft's 1908 talk to the Virginia Bar Association:

> [E]verything which tends to prolong or delay litigation . . . is a great advantage for that litigant who has the longer purse. The man whose all is involved in the decision of the lawsuit is much prejudiced in a fight through the courts, if his opponent is able, by reason of his means, to prolong the litigation and keep him for years out of what really belongs to him. The wealthy defendant can almost always secure a compromise or yielding of lawful rights because of the necessities of the poor plaintiff.

William Howard Taft, *The Delays of the Law*, 18 YALE L.J. 28, 33 (1908). Taft stresses that it is not judicial bias but institutional structure that confers advantages on the rich:

> The complaints that the courts are made for the rich and not for the poor have no foundation in fact in the attitude of the courts upon the merits of any controversy which may come before them, for the judges of this country are as free from prejudice in this respect as it is possible to be. But the inevitable effect of the delays incident to the machinery now required in the settlement of controversies in judicial tribunals is to oppress and put at a disadvantage the poor litigant and give great advantage to his wealthy opponent.

Id. at 35. In contemporary work Taft's notion of "rich" parties has been elaborated by what some have called "party capability theory," which analyzes the systemic advantages enjoyed by parties that have greater resources, are recurrent players, and are organizations. *See, e.g.,* McCormick, *Party Capability Theory, supra* note 69; Atkins, *Party Capability Theory, supra* note 69.

[126] BARBARA A. CURRAN, THE LEGAL NEEDS OF THE PUBLIC 234 (1977). The survey interviews were conducted in March, 1974. *Id.* at 10.

[127] ABC News/Washington Post Survey 1985 (USACWP.196.R24) (on file with author).

age Americans" than to rich people—and four out of five of these thought "much less."[128] In August 1998, only 33% of respondents to a national survey thought "[c]ourts try to treat poor people and wealthy people alike." But 90% agreed that "[w]ealthy people or companies often wear down their opponents by dragging out the legal proceedings."[129] Half-a-year later in another national survey, 80% of respondents thought that the "wealthy" receive better treatment from the courts than do other people and two-thirds agreed that "[w]hen a person sues a corporation, the courts generally favor the corporation over the person."[130] I think it is fair to conclude that wide sections of the American public share an enduring sense that legal institutions, whether intentionally or inadvertently, operate to amplify the advantages of "haves" in general, including corporations.[131]

Yet this awareness is only part of the legal culture of the American public. Large sections of the public subscribe to a complex of beliefs about law, lawyers, and lawsuits that I have elsewhere called the "jaundiced view." By this I refer to the familiar beliefs that the U.S. is overflowing with frivolous litigation, brought by self-styled victims and inspired by greedy lawyers, and encouraged by irresponsible juries and activist judges. In this "litigation lottery," claimants walk away with immense and undeserved sums. Useful business and civil activities are inhibited. The system is out of control and causes immense damage, undermining the country's economic strength and unraveling the fabric of trust that underlies civic life. Space permits only a single example, whose authorship (by a lawyer who subsequently was elevated to Solicitor General of the United States) testifies to the respectability as well as the audacity of such fulminations.

---

[128] Stephen Budiansky et al., *How Lawyers Abuse the Law*, U.S. NEWS & WORLD REP., Jan. 30, 1995, at 50. The same poll shows the public placing responsibility for this imbalance squarely on lawyers. Respondents were asked:

> *Here are some things that people say about lawyers. Which one of the following comes closest to your views?*
>
> *Lawyers have in important role to play in holding wrongdoers accountable and helping the injured.*
>
> *Lawyers use the legal system to protect the powerful and get rich.*

Press Release, U.S. News & World Report, Americans Have Mixed Feelings About the Legal Reforms Contained in the House Republicans' Contract with America (Jan. 21, 1995) (on file with author). Fifty-six percent affirmed the "protect the powerful and get rich" response; only 35% the "helping" response. *Id.*

[129] AMERICAN BAR ASSOCIATION, PERCEPTIONS OF THE U.S. JUSTICE SYSTEM 65, 114 tbl.4 (1999), available at http://www.abanet.org/media/perception/ perceptions.pdf. This 90% response, quite uniform across demographic groups, is the closest to unanimity of any response to any item in a lengthy survey, outranking complaints about delay, expense, and leniency toward criminals.

[130] National Center for State Courts, How the Public Views the State Courts: A 1999 National Survey, Presented at the National Conference on Public Trust and Confidence in the Justice System (May 14, 1999), www.ncsconline.org/wc/publicationsires_amtptc_publicviewcrtspub.pdf.

[131] A 1995 survey of Iowans (n=803) slices things a bit finer than the national surveys cited above. Respondents were asked which groups are treated better or worse than others in the courts. 82.8% thought wealthy people were treated better and 80.1% thought "big business" was treated better. The only other groups that were thought to be so favored were politicians (77.5%) and celebrities (83.7%). About 2% of respondents thought each of these groups was treated worse than others. Iowa Supreme Court Survey Questions and Responses, in DAVID ROTTMAN, NATIONAL CENTER FOR STATE COURTS, STATE COURT SURVEYS ON PUBLIC TRUST AND CONFIDENCE 59 (1998).

> Our mechanism for the peaceable resolution of civil disputes has transmogrified into an insatiable organism that is devouring a segment of our society and culture from the inside-out. Like the giant underground fungus discovered several years ago in Michigan, which manifests itself above the ground only in the form of an occasional mushroom, our civil justice system parasite is barely perceptible to the average person on a day-to-day basis, except for the occasional but increasingly frequent news reports of a freakish lawsuit or outlandish jury verdict. But the destructive process is nevertheless continuously at work, growing and relentlessly consuming vital resources and disabling our productive capacity.[132]

The jaundiced view flourishes most luxuriantly among corporate and governmental elites, but many elements of it have been embraced by wider publics. It is supported by a web of stories about abusive lawsuits, frivolous claims, and outrageous awards.[133] One of the salient features of this discourse is that it depicts upstanding, beneficent corporations and governments being exploited by rapacious individuals and their lawyers. The master narrative is that opportunistic plaintiffs who harm themselves by acting irresponsibly and then attempt to fasten responsibility on beneficent organizations and secure undeserved compensation are "the source and carriers of [a] devastating social disease."[134] These stories and the discourse in which they are embedded are disseminated by a massive campaign to impugn the legal system[135] and delegitimize claimants and their lawyers who use the system against APs. This propaganda campaign is promoted by corporations and their political allies, supported by right-wing foundations and think tanks, and has enjoyed great success in resisting debunking. William Haltom and Michael McCann propose that the jaundiced view is so resilient because it is constantly confirmed and reinforced by the conventions of news reportage in the mass media. Corporate propaganda and media reportage combine to project the "reigning common sense" about the legal system.[136] The APs' success on the legal front in the culture wars has succeeded in neutralizing the public's great fund of cynical knowledge about the tilt of the legal system and its appreciation of the legal dominance of APs.

---

[132] Theodore B. Olson, *The Parasitic Destruction of America's Civil Justice System*, 47 SMU L. REV. 359 (1994). Further examples may be found in Marc Galanter, *An Oil Strike in Hell: Contemporary Legends About the Civil Justice System*, 40 ARIZ. L. REV. 717 (1998). *See also* WILLIAM HALTOM & MICHAEL MCCANN, DISTORTING THE LAW: POLITICS, MEDIA, AND THE LITIGATION CRISIS (2004).

[133] *See* Galanter, *supra* note 132, at 720, 726-33; *see also* HALTOM & MCCANN, *supra* note 132, at 155-56. All or virtually all of these stories have long been exposed as fabrications or, at best, misrepresentations. *See* Robert M. Hayden, *The Cultural Logic of a Political Crisis: Common Sense, Hegemony, and the Great American Liability Insurance Famine of 1986*, in STUDIES IN LAW, POLITICS AND SOCIETY 104, 104-08 (1991); Stephen Daniels, *The Question of Jury Competence and the Politics of Civil Justice Reform: Symbols, Rhetoric and Agenda-Building*, 52 LAW & CONTEMP. PROBS. 269 (1989); Steven Brill & James Lyons, *The Not-So-Simple Crisis*, AM. LAW., May 1986, at 1; Gail Diane Cox, *Tort Tales Lash Back*, NAT'L L.J., Aug. 3, 1992, at 1; Fred Strasser, *Tort Tales: Old Stories Never Die*, NAT'L L.J., Feb. 16, 1987, at 39.

[134] HALTOM & MCCANN, *supra* note 132, at 59.

[135] *Id.* at 223. *See generally* DANIELS & MARTIN, *supra* note 76, at 43-51.

[136] HALTOM & MCCANN, *supra* note 132, at 177, 297.

VII. CONCLUSION

In describing the ascendancy of the APs in the legal arena, I don't mean to portray the judicial system as one in which individuals never prevail or obtain vindication. What I have tried to describe is a structural and cultural setting that seems to be growing over time. Thanks to growth-inducing supplements, the seven-footers are becoming eight-footers. For almost half a century, starting in the days of the New Deal, the enactment of new rights, the development of more favorable judicial doctrine, the emergence of a more proficient plaintiffs' bar, and increasing awareness of the possibility of legal redress enabled individuals to be more successful in using the courts to secure remedies against corporate actors than they were earlier.[137] We moved away from the pre-World War Two world of infrequent and inadequate compensation described by Friedman, Russell, and Bergstrom, and displayed in the response to the Triangle Fire or the Hawk's Nest Disaster,[138] to a world in which liability is regularly if unevenly imposed on APs at the instance of NP claimants. NPs were able to exert control over APs through enactment of new rights, imposition of liability by courts, and responsive administrative regulation, reinforced by mounting cultural expectations of remedy and protection. But about thirty years ago the legal world underwent a climate change, The cultural supports for enhanced accountability were weakened by distrust of government and the exaltation of the market. Regulation is enfeebled and liability in particular is threatened by a massive recoil against enhanced accountability ("tort reform" to curtail remedies by caps, to restrict access by regulating contingency fees and class actions) and a sustained public campaign to disparage and weaken the civil justice system while demonizing lawyers, especially those who represent individuals in their battles with APs—"tort lawyers," "contingency fee lawyers," "class action lawyers." But the onus tends to rub off on all lawyers, who are regarded as undermining prosperity and unraveling the fabric of social life.[139] In a historic reversal from the time that lawyers were viewed as pillars of the establishment, such anti-lawyer attitudes are particularly prevalent among "top people"—those with more education, higher incomes, and more prestigious occupations.[140]

---

[137] On the broadening of remedy in the preceding period, see Marc Galanter, *The Turn Against Law: the Recoil Against Expanding Accountability*, 81 TEX. L. REV. 285 (2002). *See also* LAWRENCE M. FRIEDMAN, TOTAL JUSTICE 5367 (1985).

[138] RANDOLPH E. BERGSTROM, COURTING DANGER: INJURY AND LAW IN NEW YORK CITY, 1870-1910 (1992); Lawrence M. Friedman, *Civil Wrongs: Personal Injury Law in the Late 19th Century*, 1987 AM.B. FOUND. RES. J. 351; Lawrence M. Friedman & Thomas D. Russell, *More Civil Wrongs: Personal Injury Litigation, 1901-1910*, 34 AM. J. LEGAL HIST. 295 (1990). For an overview of the treatment of disasters before and after World War II, see Marc Galanter, *Bhopals, Past and Present: The Changing Legal Response to Mass Disaster*, 10 WINDSOR Y.B. ACCESS TO JUSTICE 151 (1990).

[139] On the public animus against lawyers, see MARC GALANTER, LOWERING THE BAR: LAWYER JOKES AND LEGAL CULTURE (2005); Marc Galanter, *Predators and Parasites: Lawyer-Bashing and Civil Justice*, 28 GA. L. REV. 633 (1994); Marc Galanter, *The Faces of Mistrust: The Image of Lawyers in Public Opinion, Jokes, and Political Discourse*, 66 U. CIN. L. REV. 805 (1998).

[140] On the distribution of public estimation of lawyers, see PETER D. HART RESEARCH ASSOCIATES, A SURVEY OF ATTITUDES NATIONWIDE TOWARD LAWYERS AND THE LEGAL SYSTEM (1993).

The legal forum, increasingly dominated by APs, becomes more amenable to economic policing and less hospitable to dramas of moral vindication. The role of moral outrage and human solidarity and empathy are undercut by campaigns to limit remedies for NPs. The stakes in these struggles are escalating, because the potential for remedy and protection is expanding, driven by advances in science, technology, and social management. As more things are capable of being done by human institutions, the line between unavoidable misfortune and imposed injustice shifts. Bioethicists Allen Buchanan, Dan W. Brock, Norman Daniels, and Dan Wickler observe that

> [t]he boundary between the natural and the social, and between the realm of fortune and that of justice, is not static. What we have taken to be moral progress has often consisted in pushing back the frontiers of the natural, in bringing within the sphere of social control, and thereby within the domain of justice, what was previously regarded as the natural, and as merely a matter of good or ill fortune.[141]

Once, having an incurable disease was an inalterable misfortune; now a perception of insufficient vigor in pursuing a cure or refusal to authorize an experimental treatment can give rise to a claim of injustice. As the scope of possible interventions broadens, more and more the presence of avoidable bad things or the absence of achievable good things are evaluated in terms of that intervention. Thus famine or social subordination or a flawed appearance is not inalterable fate, but a matter of appropriate interventions. What was seen as fate may now be seen as inappropriate policy. Advances in medical care and biotechnology have creased a whole new realm of justice issues concerning death, transplants, reproductive technologies, stem cells, DNA, and so forth. Like medicine and technology, law and policy enlarge both the supply of answers and the supply of unanswered questions.

For the most part the advances in human capability and control that drive the justice frontier are located in or managed by APs, either corporations or governmental bodies. By creating new capacities for intervention, they produce new potential for regulation and remedy. But they can use their agility as legal players to resist having their responsibilities measured by heightened expectations that reflect new technical possibilities. The capacity of legal institutions to project and enforce norms that weigh and balance the new possibilities of control will depend primarily on the course of democratic politics. Widespread public gullibility about representations of the civil justice system induces pessimism. But the new possibilities for intervention and control will impinge on and be appreciated by the more educated and affluent, the very sectors of the population most distracted by current misreadings of the system.

James Coleman reminds us that "[t]he modern corporate actor will not be the last social invention to be made. . . . It will eventually be displaced."[142] Much the same might be said of the present forms of courts and the legal profession. At the

---

[141] ALLEN BUCHANAN, DAN W. BROCK, NORMAN DANIELS, & DAN WICKLER, FROM CHANCE TO CHOICE: GENETICS AND JUSTICE 83 (2000); *see also* JUDITH N. SHKLAR, THE FACES OF INJUSTICE 5, 51-82 (1990).

[142] JAMES S. COLEMAN, FOUNDATIONS OF SOCIAL THEORY 552 (1990).

moment it appears that APs are well on their way to capturing the legal profession and overwhelming or circumventing the courts. Whether the APs can be tamed by the courts depends on the emergence of a democratic politics that is informed by the public's basic insight into dominance of APs and the distributive tilt of the legal system. It will also depend on the inventiveness of lawyers in coming up with new formats and devices for making public policy and effectively controlling APs.

AFTERWORD

How the Haves Stay Ahead

Robert W. Gordon

Marc Galanter's classic article (Galanter 1974: hereafter "*Haves*") was written in the early 1970s. We can now see that time as when the high tide of progressive liberalism was beginning to ebb. Much of the legislation and case law of the forty years between 1932 and 1972 added up to a vast expansion of governmental action and capacity. Much of this expansion benefited wealthy and powerful interests, perhaps especially the construction of an enormous military and national-security-intelligence apparatus, built with a massive flow of tax dollars to defense contractors. But it delivered benefits to Have-Littles as well. By the accretion of incremental patchwork measures, the new American state, staffed by a career bureaucracy and financed through a progressive tax system, committed itself to manage the business cycle so as to reduce unemployment as well as to control inflation; to regulate some of the more egregious forms of market failure and of discrimination against minorities, women and the disabled; and to provide social insurance against the common misfortunes of life.

Most of these policies were initiated by the federal executive and Congress; others by federal and state courts motivated to make real and effective the formal promises of equality before the law. All had been inspired and lobbied for by aroused social movements. There had been a surprising run of victories for groups other than large business interests—Social Security, the Wagner Act, The Fair Labor Standards Act, the progressive tax code of 1939, subsidies for home ownership through the Federal Housing Authority, the GI Bill opening higher education to people on the lower rungs of the class ladder, Medicare (1965), the Civil Rights (1964) and Voting Rights (1965) Acts, the Immigration and Nationality Act that ended the old quotas favoring [western and northern] European immigrants (1965), the National Environmental Policy (1969) and Endangered Species Acts (1973), the Occupational Health and Safety (1970), Consumer Product (1972) and National Traffic and Highway (1966) Safety Acts, and the War on Poverty (1964); and the proposed Equal Rights [for women] Amendment, which passed the Senate by a vote of 84-8 in 1972.

Galanter's article was, among many other things, an effort to explain why so many of the progressive-liberal initiatives for social change had apparently reached the limits of their potential or had stalled out altogether. (Note his subtitle: "Speculations on the Limits of Legal Change.") The great contribution of the article was that it went well beyond local and contingent political explanations to locate obstacles to social reform and redistributive policies in the institutional structure of the legal system itself. The article is probably best known and most cited for its analysis of the advantages enjoyed by repeat players (RPs) against one-shot (OS) adversaries in litigation. But it is just as valuable if not more so for its analysis of structural asymmetries outside the courts—in both RP and RP, and in RP/OS relations. The courts are mostly routine enforcers of RP interests against OS parties (e.g. routine debt-collection.) But because courts place parties on a footing of formal equality, OS parties look to them for redress against more powerful RPs. RPs maintain many advantages even in this forum—higher-priced lawyers and expensive expertise, staying power, ability to plan strategically and lose a few battles to win a longer war. They are also far better placed than OS claimants to win the wars of attrition in the trenches of implementation—capturing administrative agencies and raising the costs of enforcement. In short Haves retained many advantages even through—what turned out to be—an anomalous and fleeting historical moment in which the legal system was stacked with judges and aligned with political forces committed to overcoming substantive disadvantages of weaker parties.

RISE IN ECONOMIC INEQUALITY

Since Marc Galanter wrote *Haves*, American society has become significantly more unequal, to the point where observers routinely call our time a new Gilded Age. Profits from productivity gains, the share of gains from economic growth, have accrued in the last 30 years almost entirely to the already rich—the top 1 per cent of wealth holders—and most of that share in turn to the *very* rich, the top .01 per cent. In the wake of the Great Depression of the 1930s, public policies prevented the very wealthy from regaining all their prior relative share of wealth, with the result that in the period from 1945 to 1975 wealth and income differences were less extreme than at any previous period in American history. But from 1975 onwards wealth and income differentials began to increase; and that general trend was only briefly arrested by the financial collapse of 2008. In the gradual recovery from the ensuing depression, the top wealth-holders' share has not only recovered but increased.

Meanwhile the incomes of the middle class have stagnated; their retirement savings have collapsed; and the poor are even worse off than before the depression (Saez 2003, Piketty & Saez 2006, Atkinson, Piketty & Saez 2011, Saez 2013). Public policies like the erosion of progressive taxation through tax cuts, tax expenditures and lax enforcement of tax laws against proliferating avoidance schemes; policies disfavoring union organization; financial deregulation of consumer and mortgage credit; bankruptcy "reform" making it much harder to discharge consumer debt; trade policies putting American labor in direct competition with that of developing economies while protecting professionals like doctors and lawyers; large subsidies of public funds to defense contractors, agribusiness, health providers, fossil fuel industries and charter schools; the guarantee of monopoly rents to pharmaceutical and entertainment industries; cuts in funding for public colleges and in student loans and grants while college costs rise steeply—are among the major factors producing increases in inequality (see, among a flood of books and articles documenting these trends: Stiglitz 2012, Jacobs & Skocpol 2005, Baker 2011, Noah 2012). Even welfare policies designed to cushion against economic failure contribute to growing inequality:

The United States today provides economic security for workers in old age (via Social Security and Medicare) but very little to children, young adults, and anyone who spends their time caring for others rather than working for a market wage. The current recession has left young people, for instance, disproportionately unemployed, but the safety net often denies them unemployment insurance—because they lack a work history—and even public assistance if they have no children. (Alstott 2012.)

Some of the policies that have contributed to growing inequality, clearly, are policies weakening the redistributive effects of tax and transfer programs, such as tax cuts for the top income brackets; lower tax rates on capital gains; the near-elimination of the federal estate tax; a variety of credits and deductions handed out through the tax code, such as the mortgage interest deduction that is most valuable to affluent homeowners; toleration for tax avoidance; and cuts in welfare benefits for the poor. But most of the sources of growing inequality are in policies that contribute to inequality in *pre-tax* income and wealth. How do those come about? Some schools of thought like to attribute pre-tax differentials to talent, education, enterprise, hard work and value added to society (see, e.g., Mankiw 2013); but these are not very convincing as adequate explanations.[1]

Galanter's classic article identified some of the sources of the success of the Haves in the structural advantages conferred on them by the ordinary workings of the legal system. My project in this essay is to speculate on what we might find if we were to extend Galanter's inquiry into structural advantages beyond the litigation context that lies at the center of his work to the broader law-making and law-implementing processes of our society. If we do that, I believe, we'll find more examples of how decision-making and dispute-processing institutions tend to reinforce and augment the privileges and power of the already-privileged and powerful. This effort here is preliminary, sketchy, and suggestive, and not in the least exhaustive. I'm quite confident that even a small amount of further work would uncover *many* more examples of such structural advantages—as well, I would like to hope, as some counter-examples of fora or processes that help level the playing field for the benefit of Have-Nots.

Let's start with:

Advantages Conferred by Dominant Political Ideology

Despite all the innovations of progressive liberalism and state expansion in the 20th century, mainstream American ideology retains a persistent libertarian bias. What's popularly assumed to be the benchmark norm is the classical-liberal state under the rule of law. Such a state's principal functions are to protect private property and enforce contracts; to supply a limited number of public goods—law-and-order (civil peace), a common defense, and some infrastructure; and to tax citizens (just) enough to pay for these. This basic rule-framework may be altered

---

[1] Just to mention a few objections: people at the bottom of the income ladder work quite as hard as (or harder than) people at the top; returns to education don't explain why the top .01 per cent is so very much wealthier than their fellow highly educated in the top 1-to-20 per cent; and many in the very top brackets are not creative entrepreneurs but successful monopolists or real estate or stock speculators, rent-seekers of government subsidies and contracts, or executives skilled at stacking compensation committees with cronies who will inflate their pay regardless of how well or badly their companies perform.

by democratic legislatures—but only within strict limits enforced by constitutional courts preventing undue encroachments on liberty, property, and the operations of capitalist free markets: the courts' special mission is to put a brake on populist attempts to use the government to redistribute wealth and power from those who have them to those who have less. The classical-liberal state came closest of course to being articulated in the formal legal system as the default constitutional order of the U.S. in the late 19th and early 20th centuries. Even then it was never really that close, since the constitutional courts of that time actually approved a very wide range of legislative departures from the norm in the form of aggressive regulatory and repressive legislation; and in fact the volume and range of state activity grew steadily throughout the entire period (Novak 2008).

Though this classical-liberal state never existed, the *idea* of the minimal state and "small government" still exert an ideological pull on many Americans as a kind of natural order, the default system of political economy. Deviations from the ideal are suspect, bear a burden of justification, and are perpetual targets for political attack and subject to erosion and rollback. The point that matters for this essay is that this imaginary order is one in which—before any new policy can load the scales in favor of the rich and well-organized—the "Haves" already come out way ahead. The ideal is formally equal legal treatment for every *sui juris* legal person coupled with abhorrence for "redistributive" "class legislation." At its high point classical liberalism excluded women altogether from eligibility for full formally-equal treatment, and included blacks only notionally, but did include as it still does artificial persons such as corporations (the subject of Galanter 2006, "Planet of the APs: Reflections on the Scale of Law and its Users," reprinted in the preceding chapter and hereafter *APs*). The law, which forbids the rich as well as the poor to beg for bread and sleep under bridges, alike protects their property and liberty. As a practical matter then it protects the power of the propertied Haves to control, subject only to such limits as market competition can provide, the lives and fates of the Have-Nots or Have-Littles, who need access to the Haves' property to survive. The law that mechanically enforces contracts according to their terms automatically reinforces the advantages of those who have the power to draft such terms and impose them on the other party. Theoretically the Have-Littles can enforce their formally equal juridical rights in courts as equals, but their livelihoods and status in civil society may depend on their not giving offense to the rich and powerful; and in any case their access to rights is effectively conditioned on access to lawyers, an expensive private resource. The great benefit for the propertied of the Rule of Law is that they need not recruit private militias (or, as in contemporary Russia, mafiosi and ex-KGB thugs) to defend their holdings against redistribution by trespass and theft and to enforce their one-sided contracts but can count on the legal system to do it for them.

Advantages of Wealthier and Better-Organized Parties in the Political Arena

The economic and organizational advantages of the Haves are easily translated into political advantages that in turn make it easier for them hold on to what they have, to acquire a larger relative share, and defeat the claims of Have-Littles. These are very well developed in the literatures on political economy, so I'll just quickly summarize them here.

Agenda-control. Probably the most important exercise of power is the power to keep issues off the political action agenda—even issues that have robust popular support. Single-payer national health care never made it into the Congressional debates over reforming health care. Neither did nationalizing banks after the financial crisis; or even breaking up the biggest banks. Cutting Social Security benefits is routinely on the table for legislative action; expanding such benefits (until very recently) has not been. As Steven Lukes argued in his classic study of power (Lukes 2005) the most effective forms of power keep issues from ever being raised as action items for political decisionmakers.

Financial support for parties. The two major parties' supporters are polarized by income: lower-income people are more likely to support Democrats; higher-income to support Republicans. But both parties draw significant financial support from the wealthy, especially the financial industry. The Democratic Leadership Council emerged to promote a more business-friendly party. Its policy fruits were a bipartisan deregulatory agenda, tax cuts, and protection of high executive pay. (See generally Hacker & Pierson 2010, ch. 6.)

The main way in which Have-Littles can amplify political voice is simply by voting for Democrats. But most Democrats cannot stray too far from corporate sponsors, which limits their ability to recruit voters on economic grounds.

Money buys political access and responsiveness. Larry Bartels' study (2008: 257-65) of the U.S. Senate in the 1980s and 90s finds that senators are "vastly more responsive to affluent constituents than to constituents of modest means." The preferences of the richest top third are given 50% more weight than those of the middle third; those of the bottom third given no weight at all. Senators don't just respond to financial interests, they are also more responsive to ideological views of middle and high-income constituents (even to point of overriding their own partisan inclinations). Again, the lowest third's ideological preferences are given *no weight at all.* Republicans are twice as likely as Democrats likely to respond to high-income constituencies. Senators generally remain unresponsive even to politically active—informed, voting, contacting—low-income constituents. A partial but not full explanation for these differences between responsiveness to top and middle is in the size of campaign contributions.

The organizational edge. Galanter points out that organizations are best suited to realize RP advantages: they have experience, expertise, are adaptable, and are strategic; they can and do plan for the long term. To expand on this last point: they may lose a legislative battle, but are back the next day, getting amendments with loopholes and exemptions, gutting funding for enforcement, getting their staff picks, placing their lobbyists in the anteroom to rule-making, or in the agency itself. The tax code, for example, undergoes periodic moments of reform, sometimes to make it more progressive and eliminate loopholes for corporations and wealthy individuals, like the reforms of 1986. These were followed by a barrage of special preferences and exemptions; and calculated war on IRS enforcement efforts. Funds for enforcement staff and audits were cut; for a while enforcement was turned over to inefficient and expensive private collection agents; and the agency put more resources into auditing low-income recipients of the Earned

Income Tax Credit than finding major tax evaders (Johnston 2003). The Dodd-Frank legislation designed to strengthen financial industry regulation after the 2008 financial collapse has suffered much the same fate, as an army of lawyers and lobbyists infiltrated the administrative process to defang the administrative rules necessary to put the legislation into effect (Edwards 2013).

In the 1960s and early 70s legislation to protect consumers, workers and the environment was procured by newly mobilized social movements. Since then organizational advantages have mostly shifted toward conservatives. Businesses revitalized umbrella associations such as the Chamber of Commerce, the Business Roundtable and the National Federation of Independent Businesses, gave them an aggressive anti-regulatory, anti-labor and anti-tax agenda, and financed political candidates who supported them (see, e.g., Phillips-Fein 2009, Martin 2008). Even around non-economic "social" issues conservatives proved superior organizers of ordinary voters. Many evangelical churches, galvanized by the removal of tax exemptions for (segregated) Christian academies and the Supreme Court's church-state decisions, created formidable new voting blocs; as did suburban families resisting school and housing integration and increasing tax rates. Such movements focused as intensely on purging moderate Republican incumbents as liberals. Some of these movements, of course, were not movements of Haves at all, but rather grass-roots revolts of people who one might predict would vote Democratic out of their economic interests, but are hostile to liberals on cultural issues. These rapidly attracted the attention and support of conservative funders, who helped build them into national networks of "values voters" and incorporated them into Have-dominated party coalitions (Critchlow 2011, Martin 1996, Skocpol & Williamson 2012).

One of these funders' most successful under-the-radar innovations has been the development of ALEC (American Legislative Exchange Council) into a vehicle for drafting pre-fabricated model legislation that can be introduced in Republican-controlled state houses. ALEC does not lobby, in the usual sense of the word: it simply finds friendly legislators to introduce its bills. The same group of funders also underwrites a new cluster of conservative public-interest law firms to bring and intervene in lawsuits supporting their causes; and a very effective ideological apparatus of think-tanks like Cato, Heritage, and the American Enterprise Institute, ready to deploy quasi-academic studies, position papers, and press releases justifying conservative initiatives (Teles 2008, Southworth 2008).

These groups aren't just looking for legislative victories; they are looking to use organizational advantages and incumbency to reinforce strategic advantages, by changing rules of the political game. Probably the important of these changes are in redrawing of electoral districts, enactment of new voting requirements that suppress minority voting; and legislation weakening the few organizations that reliably support Democrats and liberal policies—labor unions and the plaintiffs' bar. Conservative state legislators act to abolish collective-bargaining rights for public sector unions and enact right-to-work laws. Even when Democrats regained control of the federal executive and Congress in 2008, labor law reforms (such as the Employee Free Choice Act or EFCA, a bill to make voting for a union easier by having workers simply check off a preference on a card) were repeatedly blunted—reflecting both the strength of corporate opposition and New Democrats' ambivalence towards labor unions. They (alongside, it must be said, groups with more public-spirited motivations) promote "school reform," meaning diversion of taxpayer funds to charter and private schools, in part with the objective of weakening teachers' unions. Galanter himself has described at length the massive corporate propaganda and lobbying campaigns for "tort reform" (e.g. Galanter 1993, 2002). These have a double purpose, to delegitimate the claims of people who seek compensation for harms inflicted by corporate conduct, and the lawyers who help them, as greedy opportunists; and, with initiatives such as regulation of contingent fees, limiting punitive damages, and imposing damage caps on recoveries, to cut into the profits of another group of reliably Democratic contributors, the plaintiffs' bar.

It is still not entirely clear why conservatives have been so much more successful than liberals in building political organizations. Successful political organization requires both money and passion. Factions favored by business groups always have more money. Much of the passion on the left of the political spectrum has been devoted to furthering particular groups and causes—racial and ethnic minorities, gender equality, LGBT rights, and the environment, rather than in building broad coalitions. The one faction capable of exercising significant countervailing power on economic issues is organized labor, which even at its peak was only a fitful advocate of social-democratic policies; and in any case is now much weaker.

Is the best explanation for why the Haves prevail in legislative influence simply that they have more money—to influence official conduct, prevail against adversaries, and dig for buried treasure (like tax expenditures)? Or is it Galanter's explanation, that Haves stay ahead because of RP advantages conferred by superior organization? Surely it is some combination of both. Groups like the major environmental and civil liberties/civil rights organizations, and organized labor, are well-organized and well-informed; they have plenty of expertise and are certainly RPs in state and national politics. Yet without ability to match major campaign contributions of the wealthy they can't approach the kind of access well-financed organized interests have.

MONEY BUYS PROFESSIONAL WEALTH AND INCOME DEFENSE

In modern state systems, as theorists of oligarchy (e.g. Winters 2011: 24) have pointed out:

> [W]ealth defense no longer involves oligarchs arming themselves and fighting to defend property claims, or deploying material resources to hire the coercive capabilities of others.... The struggle for oligarchs shifts to deploying material resources to specialized professionals (lawyers, accountants, tax avoidance consultants, lobbyists) to keep as much of their wealth and income as possible out of state hands, thus shifting the costs of the state and even of property defense for oligarchic fortunes to poorer actors in the system. Thus burden falls particularly hard on the middle and upper-middle classes, whose material resources are large enough to fund the state (including welfare provision) but not large enough individually to purchase the armies of professionals to shift the financial burdens upwards to oligarchs.

The wealthy also have the organizational advantage in that their interests are relatively uniform and thus require relatively little coordination to aggregate. Unlike most Have-Not groups, they can contribute to lobbying representatives without much fear that their interests will be betrayed or traded off against those of others in their coalition.

Rent-Seeking Generally

The expanded state creates its own clienteles, new classes of Haves: recipients of government largesse, tax expenditures, subsidies, and contracts, licenses and monopolies. These in turn use that largesse to organize effectively to attract yet more largesse and privilege, and to repel attempts to cut it. This dynamic produces the familiar line-ups of public choice and collective action theory—structurally very similar to Galanter's RPs and OSs—of concentrated versus diffuse interests (Wilson 1974, Olson 1965). The defense industry; the National Rifle Association; the banking and financial services, oil and gas, pharmaceutical, telecom and movie industries; health insurance companies and medical providers; Cuban exiles; agribusiness; and the American Association of Retired People all hire lobbyists and target campaign contributions to keep their advantages even against occasional (as for example in the case of gun control) substantial public opposition.

Not all successful rent-seekers are perfectly co-extensive with the rich: elderly voters and gun owners for example are not rich but are numerous, politically savvy, and well-organized. The benefits of poor and weak clients, however, like recipients of food stamps or welfare or Medicaid are politically easy to cut and always the first to be sacrificed in times of austerity.

Privatization of Public Functions Generally

Ironically, one way that Haves use their power in the public sphere is to remove state functions to the private sphere. At the beginning of the 19th century, many governmental functions were farmed out to private agents charging fees or collecting a percentage of recoveries for their services. Such systems proved in many instances to lead to unacceptable levels of inefficiency, corruption and perverse incentives, and by the end of the century most of these functions were reassigned to salaried public officials (Parrillo 2013). In the last thirty years state policies have swung back to favor privatization of many public functions, like managing prisons or collecting delinquent taxes or even fighting or providing support for military actions. In some cases privatization seems to have realized the efficiencies hoped for it, but in many others has led to serious problems: insufficient oversight, illegal and abusive conduct by private actors not subject to public sanctions, undermining democratic norms of transparency, rationality and accountability, and indifference to public values (Verkuil 2007, Freeman & Minow 2009).

Outsourcing, in short, reduces accountability to people subject to or injured by the regime. Privatization also often means that distribution of social benefits happens through markets where users are consumers rather than citizens, so that those who pay more can get more. And of course a primary motive is often to avoid unions, which reduces employee voice.

Advantages of Maneuverability in a Landscape of Ignorance

The Haves also possess huge advantages of stealth. The media are mostly incurious and inexpert, bored by policy details, and inclined to report debates about policy as clashing partisan assertions with no attempt to sort out which are true and which distortions or lies. The general public is often more interested in policy than the media, but also ignorant of details. Special preferences in the tax code—tax expenditures and exemptions, for example, tend to fly under the radar, unnoticed. The important battles for influence are often post-legislation, in the trenches of implementation by administrative agencies and enforcement. After a big crisis—financial meltdown, food safety scare, mine explosion, oil spill, corporate scandal—entrenched interests will allow reformers their splashy substantive victory in legislation, but reserve real efforts to sabotaging or blocking enforcement.

Advantages of Inertia

Most proposals with majority policy support don't become law. More specifically, as Bartels explains, if middle-class opinion deviates from well-off, it doesn't become law (Bartels 2008). Mobilizing for change is hard work: whereas opponents need to control only one of our governmental system's many choke points to stop it. In the U.S. Senate, the filibuster has recently become routine, so that 60 votes are needed to pass legislation. (In November, 2013, the Senate majority abolished the filibuster for Presidential nominations, but not for legislation.) Since conservatives achieved dominance on federal and state courts, judges have become another veto point against liberal legislation, agency action, or litigation (more on this below).

Advantages Conferred by Legal Complexity

As Galanter and Gillian Hadfield (2000) have pointed out, legal complexity favors the Haves, because it takes expensive legal and other expertise to understand and manipulate. It also often confers practical immunity from civil and criminal actions against well-resourced offenders, since enforcers know that just a few actions can eat up most of their enforcement budgets. This helps for example to explain why the SEC and Justice Department have undertaken so few enforcement actions against the large financial institutions responsible for the financial crisis of 2008, or criminal prosecutions of their managers, even when it is clear that some of those institutions perpetrated frauds on homeowners and investors and laundered money for organized crime (Rakoff 2013).

Insulation and Class Identification of Haves

As inequality grows, the life-experiences of elites become ever more distant from those of most other people. They live in different neighborhoods; their children go to different schools; they work and vacation in milieux filled with people like themselves, with others present only in subordinate or menial roles that render them partly invisible. Such isolation helps to account for the elites' delusion that their positions are entirely owed to their superior talents, efforts and virtue and those of lesser mortals to laziness or incapacity; for their instinctive sympathy and willingness to extend immunity and lenient treatment to powerful actors like corporate executives or high government officials who stray into wrongdoing ; for the indifference or active contempt many of them feel for the poor and unsuccessful; and for their general cluelessness about how ordinary people live and the problems they face. As elite control over politics tightens, potential democratic controls on plutocratic excess weaken, and channels of mobility (like affordable education) become harder to navigate.

RETURNING TO GALANTER'S ORIGINAL TERRAIN: RULE-CHANGE THROUGH COURTS

So far we've been discussing general advantages enjoyed by the Haves in the contest for strategic advantages in the lawmaking process generally. Let's now return to Galanter's initial puzzle: why, despite the fact that relative Have-Nots had seemingly gained new rights and rule-changes through the courts, which, because parties to litigation are formally equal and so "judicial outcomes are more likely to be at variance with the existing constellation of political forces" (*Haves* at 138 [p. 53 as reprinted here]), they had not been able to consolidate their gains. Rule-change secured by Have-Nots through courts may not have much impact because courts can't devise regulatory or administrative machinery and can't tax and spend; and conservatives can use lobbying quite effectively to qualify or roll back prior Have-Not rule changes and enforcement regimes. Moreover the formal legal system sits on top of many layers of "unreformed" discretionary legal subsystems. "Structurally (by cost and institutional overload) and culturally (by ambiguity and normative overload) the unreformed system effects a massive covert delegation from the most authoritative rule-makers to field-level officials and their constituencies responsive to other norms and priorities than are contained in the 'higher law'" (*Haves* at 147-8 [p. 60 here]). The effect is similar to that of privatizing public functions: shift of discretion to less accountable actors.

Nowhere has such delegation had such dramatic effects as in criminal prosecution. In 1984 Congress (following the example for several states) authorized a commission to establish guidelines for sentencing defendants convicted of federal crimes. Congress was worried that sentencing judges were too lenient and that sentences varied too widely from judge to judge. In the same period, Congress created many new federal crimes, lengthened statutory sentences, and enacted mandatory minimum sentences for many offenses.

Because over 95% of criminal offenses are disposed of by plea-bargain rather than trial, the new regime effectively shifted the responsibility for determining appropriate levels of punishment from judges to prosecutors, who fix the penalty by deciding what charges to bring. The Supreme Court has belatedly tried to restore some discretion to judges by making the guidelines advisory rather than mandatory (*U.S. v. Booker* 2005), but prosecutors can neutralize judges suspected of excessive leniency by upping the charges. A scheme designed to minimize discretion through rules has increased discretion in officers who are almost completely unaccountable (Stith & Cabranes 1998, Stuntz 2011). Unlike other administrative agencies who are constrained to separate investigating, policymaking, and adversary-advocacy functions, prosecutors combine these functions (Lynch 1998). They are legally immune from civil suits for abuses (see, e.g., *Connick v. Thompson* 2011). They are also effectively immune from professional discipline: even prosecutors whom courts have found helped convict the innocent by fabricating evidence, colluding in police perjury, or suppressing exculpatory evidence are rarely fired or demoted, and almost never sanctioned by bar associations (Keenan et al. 2011). Courts can control prosecutorial abuse only indirectly by excluding evidence obtained by unconstitutional means. Courts could serve a valuable function by reviewing sentences that are excessive, cruel, and disproportionate to offenses under the Eighth Amendment; but have understandably declined to take on such a monumental and politically unpopular supervisory role. There is no general political support for adequate funding of criminal defense lawyers, but courts could put some teeth into the constitutional requirement that criminal defendants have competent publicly funded lawyers (*Gideon v. Wainwright* 1963) by raising standards for lawyers' fees and caseloads, and by reversing convictions for ineffective assistance of counsel (currently, *Strickland v. Washington* 1984 sets a very high bar for reversal): the courts have declined this role as well.

The discretion of prosecutors is nowhere more important, and more insulated from public scrutiny, than in the decision to decline prosecution. Such decisions often seem to confer a decided advantage on Haves. Many have commented, for example, on the refusal of the Justice Department to prosecute high-level officials for ordering or engaging in torture in the "Global War on Terror" while coming down hard on whistleblowers like Thomas Drake, John Kiriakou, and Bradley Manning who exposed government abuses; and its failure to prosecute high-level executives of the banks responsible for the financial crisis, including those who engaged in massive fraudulent lending practices, while pursuing small-time cases of mortgage fraud by individuals who made misleading statements on loan applications (see, e.g., Greenwald 2011).

Haves Repopulate the Judiciary

Since Galanter wrote *Haves*, of course, the top level of judicial lawmaking itself has been fundamentally transformed through strategic appointments. When in control of the federal executive, conservatives in President Reagan's, G.W.H. Bush's, and G.W. Bush's Administrations centralized judicial selection in the Justice Department. Instead of choosing moderate corporate attorneys (as Eisenhower did) they chose young and reliably ideological judges (Goldman 1997). When in opposition, they used the filibuster and other delaying tactics to block appointments from the other side.[2] At the state level, where most judges are elected, judicial selection has become a shockingly corrupt process, a contest between the Chamber of Commerce and the plaintiffs' bar to see who can buy more favorable judgments with campaign contributions. Money spent in state judicial elections

---

[2] The Senate majority has changed the rules to abolish the filibuster for judicial appointments, but other tactics of delay and obstruction persist. Moreover, appointments are not ideologically symmetrical: Republicans are more likely to nominate radicals of their own party, Democrats moderates. Federal judges of either party are almost always former corporate lawyers or prosecutors; plaintiffs' lawyers, labor lawyers, progressive public-interest, and criminal defense lawyers almost never reach the federal bench.

often pays off in immediate and direct results (see Lessig 2012 at 230-1 for data on state court decisions favoring contributors). Captured courts sometimes favor plaintiffs; more often, they become instruments for rolling back or hindering enforcement of Have-Not gains secured in prior legislation or court decisions.

Substantive Rule-Changes Pushed by Haves in Courts

Conservative capture of the upper courts was never complete, conservative ideologies have many conflicting strands (libertarians and promoters of business versus cultural authoritarians, for example), and conservative judges like liberal judges often feel compelled by precedent or principle or statutory text to decide against their ideological convictions; so the direction of change has not been uniform across all fields. Nonetheless one can observe several broad trends in judicial policymaking since the 1980s. There is a general tendency to reinforce discretion of those in authority, and to confer practical immunity on abusers: of prosecutors and police over criminal defendants; of prison administrators and guards over the imprisoned; of employers over employees and labor organizations; of creditors over consumer debtors; of manufacturers accused of producing harmful externalities over those claiming to be victims. When government authorities target businesses, on the other hand, business usually wins. In other words, the tendency of decisions is to reinforce rather than diminish already existing inequalities in civil society. Haves-biased judges have asymmetric advantages over Have-Not-sympathizers if they can capture courts because it's much easier for judges to *raise barriers* to equalization than to *enforce* equalizing rules.

Here is a short list of examples of such decisions:

Contracting for privatized dispute-settlement. I mentioned earlier the Haves strategy of privatizing public functions to diminish or avoid responsibility for abuses. As Galanter himself notes (*APs* at 1402-03 [p. 100 as reprinted here]), in recent years employers and sellers of financial services like consumer credit and securities brokerage have pursued a strategy of privatization by contract: the inclusion in their standard form contracts with consumers or employees of clauses mandating that disputes be settled by arbitration. These typically exclude class actions in arbitration as well as litigation, which put the victims of sharp practice at the mercy of arbitration panels chosen by the corporate party, and unable to get any structural or collective remedies of abusive practices. Such procedural clauses amplify the pre-existing advantage that contract partners with more market power have over their counterparts, that of drafting one-sided contracts and imposing them on the weaker party: the new clauses minimize the risk that weaker parties might persuade equalizing courts (such as those of California) to strike the terms as unconscionable. The U.S. Supreme Court has essentially demolished the power of state courts to regulate mandatory arbitration clauses by holding that most such regulations are preempted by the Federal Arbitration Act of 1935 (see, e.g., *AT&T Mobility v. Concepcion* 2011; *American Express Co. v. Italian Colors Restaurant* 2013).

Hostility to anti-discrimination claims. Federal courts, again with the Supreme Court in the lead, have been making a series of incremental decisions that chip away at the ability of plaintiffs to litigate anti-discrimination claims.

One of the most important cases limits the ability of plaintiffs to bring class action claims trying to show that the employer systematically practices discrimination. The Supreme Court has handed discriminating employers what is essentially an instruction manual for employers who wish to discriminate but avoid class actions: publish a centralized non-discrimination policy but delegate to small subunits the responsibility for hiring and promotion (see *Wal-Mart v. Dukes* 2011). In suits claiming age discrimination, plaintiffs must now prove that employers' sole motive for firing or not hiring or promoting was the victim's age; if there was any other plausible motive, the suit fails (*Gross v. FBL Financial Services* 2009). A woman suing because her company paid her less than men for the same work lost her case because the Court held that the Statute of Limitations on her claim began to run with the first unequal paycheck, not years later when she first learned about the practice, and had expired (*Ledbetter v. Goodyear Tire & Rubber* 2007; this one was reversed by Congress). In June 2013 the Court imposed higher proof burdens for employees claiming employers fired them in retaliation for complaining about discrimination, and narrowed the class of supervisors whose discriminatory practices could be imputed to employers. In a series of careful empirical studies, Clermont and Schwab (2004, 2009) conclude that over time, employment discrimination plaintiffs have been winning a lower proportion of cases during pretrial and at trial; have more of their successful cases appealed; and are more likely to lose on appeal.

Hostility to private rights of action. When in control of Congress, liberals enacting progressive legislation such as the civil rights laws sometimes took care to provide for enforcement by "private attorneys general": injured parties who could bring civil suits to enforce the laws, both as a supplementary means of enforcement and as insurance against future Administrations' unwillingness to enforce (see Farhang 2010). Even if Congress had not specifically provided for private enforcement, liberal courts often read statutes to "imply" private rights of enforcement. Conservative judges have used their dominance of federal courts to try to cut back on private rights of action in three ways. One is to refuse to find implied rights unless Congress has expressly created them (Karlan 2003). A second is to apply strict rules of standing to sue to private plaintiffs, requiring that, for example, environmental plaintiffs prove concrete and direct injury from actions affecting the environment (see *Lujan v. Defenders of Wildlife* 1992). And a third is to hold that federal regulation "preempts" all state regulation in the field, so that injured parties are prevented from seeking remedies in state courts for harms that the federal government regulates (see McGarity 2008).[3] The Court has also effectively shut out another class of plaintiffs, foreigners who have suffered injury from American corporations' actions overseas, by ruling that U.S. courts have no jurisdiction to try such claims under the Alien Tort Claims Act (*Kiobel v. Royal Dutch Petroleum Co.* 2013).

Raising procedural barriers. A pair of Supreme Court decisions has greatly magnified the difficulties that plaintiffs face getting their claims past sum-

---

[3] These efforts to cut back private enforcement of public law have been only intermittently and occasionally successful. Statutes continue to grant express private rights of action, and RP litigators of such actions have themselves become an entrenched set of interest groups preventing more cutbacks. See David Engstrom, *Public Regulation of Private Enforcement*, 107 N.W.U. L. Rev. 1689 (2013).

mary dismissal in federal courts (*Bell Atlantic v. Twombly* 2007; *Ashcroft v. Iqbal* 2009). It is no longer enough for a plaintiff to plead facts which, if proved true, would support a legal claim for relief. Now the plaintiff's recital of facts must appear plausibly enough true on their face to justify having the case go forward. What this means in practical effect is that when, as is usually the case, the defendant possesses most of the evidence of relevant facts, the plaintiff has to guess what those facts are before she can get discovery; and if her guess is deemed too speculative, she loses the case at the pleading stage. Once again, this new pleading doctrine has been particularly hard on plaintiffs alleging employment discrimination (Schneider 2010); but it raises a significant barrier to access to all federal civil plaintiffs.

Amplification of corporate political voice; constriction of labor voice. The Court's decisions striking down Congress's attempts to limit corporate spending and advertising on political campaigns (*First National Bank v. Bellotti* 1978; *Citizens United v. Federal Election Commission* 2008), on the ground that such restrictions violate corporate "persons" their rights of free speech under the First Amendment, are well-known. As Galanter pointed out in *APs*, these cases are part of a series endowing artificial persons with the constitutional rights of real ones (*APs* at 1405 [p. 101 here]). In fact First Amendment doctrine is increasingly invoked as a shield against any kind of regulation, including laws requiring that companies disclose product contents and post signs notifying workers of their rights under law. When facing criminal charges, corporate persons often fare much better than real ones: as Galanter points out, under deferred prosecution agreements corporations are often given restorative/rehabilitative treatment that individual criminals don't get any more.

At the same time, a series of decisions diminish organized labor's political voice by prohibiting unions from using non-members' or dissenting members' union dues for political purposes (see, e.g., *Communications Workers v. Beck* 1988; *Knox v. Service Employees International Union* 2012; see also *Harris v. Quinn* 2014). The courts have further disempowered a whole class of workers, undocumented immigrants, by removing them altogether from the protection of labor law's remedies against firing union organizers (*Hoffman Plastic Compounds, Inc. v. National Labor Relations Board* 2002).

STRUCTURAL CHANGES IN LEGAL PROFESSION

Distribution of Legal Services Follows General Trends in Economic Inequality

I need not elaborate on these trends, since Galanter discusses them at length in *APs*. Since he wrote, the differences in the proportion of legal services going to corporate as contrasted with individual clients has only increased. Meanwhile, the combination of public policies and the depression has further reduced legal resources for Have-Not parties in both civil and criminal matters.

Doctrines and Policies Designed to Hamper Have-Not Advocacy

David Luban has aptly described this cluster of policies as "silencing doctrines . . . statutes, rules, and judicial decisions that allow opponents to attack the funding or restrict the activity of their adversaries' advocates." He points out that "in recent years, a pattern of silencing doctrines has begun to emerge challenging-to greater or lesser extent-virtually every principal source of support for low-income public-interest lawyering: the LSC [Legal Services Corporation], IOLTA [Interest on Lawyers' Trust Accounts] programs, law school clinics, and fee awards in civil rights cases" (Luban 2003: 220). Some of the main examples:

The principal source of funding for lawyers for low-income people is the Federal Legal Services Corporation. Conservatives beginning with Ronald Reagan have always disliked the LSC and have repeatedly tried to zero out its funding; it has only been saved largely by aggressive pushback by the organized bar. The enemies of the LSC have however crippled its efforts by forbidding the lawyers it funds from taking on several classes of cases and from engaging in structural reform activities. They may not represent "ineligible" aliens, any types of incarcerated persons, or public housing residents facing eviction because charged with drug offenses. They may not lobby, or engage in political organizing or voting drives or redistricting initiatives, help people form unions or "associations," or seek to influence legislation or rulemaking. They may not bring class actions or request awards of attorneys' fees in civil rights cases (LSC Regulations, 45 CFR §§1600-1640: http://www.lsc.gov/about/regulations-rules/lsc-regulations-cfr-45-part-1600-et-seq). The obvious purpose of the restrictions is not only to prevent lawyers for poor people from taking on unpopular clients, but from allowing those clients to approximate some of the principal advantages available to Haves—of going beyond winning in individual cases to bring about structural changes in institutions and rules.

The Supreme Court has piled on Congress's efforts to cripple public-interest advocacy through a series of decisions making it harder even for non-LSC lawyers for successful plaintiffs to recover attorneys' fees. The most damaging of these cases (*Buckhannon v. W. Va. Dept. of Health & Human Services* 2001) denies attorneys' fees to lawyers whose adversaries settle on terms favorable to plaintiffs instead of litigating and losing. The case promotes strategic capitulation to avoid paying fees; and deprives plaintiff-side law firms of recoveries needed to finance litigation for other clients. As already mentioned, several states have severely restricted the clients and cases that tort personal-injury lawyers can afford to take on by enacting caps on damages—which among other consequences limit recoveries of the people who have been most severely injured (Daniels & Martin 2005).

SOME FAIRLY BLEAK CONCLUSIONS

This catalogue of evolving trends and policies favoring the reinforcement of existing advantages of Haves in the legal system and the accumulation of even more advantages is distinctly discouraging to anyone who favors progressive policies or just even-handed justice. Are there countervailing policies or trends which would tend to redress the balance of legal-political advantages in favor of Have-Not and Have-Little interests?

An honest answer would have to be: Not many. Historically, growing economic inequality gradually allows governments to fall under the control of oligarchs—

"extractive" interests who can use it to extract subsidies, privileges and concessions from the labor and taxes of ordinary citizens, to entrench and protect their interests, and prevent organized challenges from others. (See generally Acemoglu & Robinson 2012, ch. 12.) It may be that the period 1932-1975 was something of an anomaly in our politics, one in which a catastrophic failure of economic elites, followed by a mass mobilization of sacrifice in wartime, followed then by an extraordinary period of economic growth, created political majorities favoring sharing of productivity gains, generous social provision, and movements to bring excluded and subordinated groups into full citizenship. In an era of slow growth and shrinking opportunities for all but a tiny superelite, those majorities are tending to splinter, as Have-Littles come to see the gains of Have-Nots coming at their expense. The one association of the post-war period capable of pursuing a general political strategy aggregating the interests of relative Have-Nots, and funneling them into demands for government policies to promote employment and social democracy, was the labor movement. Unions were always of course an unstable progressive ally; at their worst racist and socially reactionary; and prone to forget about other groups if their local demands were met; but in any case their power has waned and no comparable organizations are in prospect to replace them.

On the other hand, the relative success of some conservative groups in organizing and mobilizing their constituencies, such as church-going evangelicals and "suburban warriors" fired up by racial integration and property taxes, does show that effective bottom-up political organization is still possible—even though these groups' considerable political successes may owe as much to their adoption by national political organizations and elite funding support as to their organizing prowess. On Galanter's terrain of the legal system, it's clear that successful organization can reap the advantages of his RPs. The tort plaintiffs' bar organized through what became the Association of Trial Lawyers of America (ATLA; since 2006 renamed the American Association for Justice): it shared litigation strategies and expert witnesses, lobbied state legislatures, and elected sympathetic state court judges; and won many strategic advantages until the corporate defense and insurance bar forcefully—and very effectively—countermobilized in the 1980s. Like the labor movement, the plaintiffs' bar generally speaks in a populist key as representative of powerless little guys against business interests, but in a crunch puts its guild interests first. Its preferred method of dispute settlement, jury trial, is incredibly expensive; it can only afford to take on clients whose case is strong enough and injuries severe enough to generate contingent fees; and at worst, as in some mass-tort class actions, it colludes with corporate adversaries and a compliant judiciary to settle cases to maximize its fees at the expense of its clients (Weinstein 1995, Coffee 1995). For all its expense and faults, however, it remains, like unions, one of the few forces organized enough to challenge the power of corporate interests in courts and in politics; which is why, as with unions, its power is always under assault.

On specific issues, liberal groups have proven abilities to mobilize. The environmental movements have become regular institutionalized RPs in politics and litigation, in part from having installed at the heart of administrative decision-making requirements like that for Environmental Impact Statements, mandating that large engineering or development projects take account of environmental interests and creating public and private bureaucracies to enforce the mandate. Movements for recognition and equal treatment of marginalized groups—racial and ethnic minorities, women, immigrants, the disabled, and most recently and spectacularly, gays and lesbians, have been able to score notable gains in courts and legislatures. More ad hoc organizations responding to what they perceive as important government assaults on their interests—such as the wildfire protests in 2012 against SOPA (Stop Online Piracy) and PIPA (PROTECT IP) Acts, which many techies and internet users believed to be draconian invasions of rights to fair use of copyrighted materials—can succeed in changing legislators' minds. These are however all quite specialized movements: none of them has a broad-based political agenda—even though Martin Luther King's civil rights movement in its later phases certainly expanded its focus on racial equality to embrace a general politics of equality.

The one recent movement of recent times that seemed to have such a broad-based agenda is the Occupy Wall Street movement and its many local offshoots of 2011-2012, whose slogan was "We are the 99%!" Many people plausibly give the Occupy movements credit for shifting the national political conversation away from deficits to income and wealth inequality. It probably deserves such credit, but its participants refused, as a matter of principle, to form any institutional structures or mechanisms for aggregating and channeling its demands into an effective political organization. The Have-Littles and Have-Nots have yet to find a regular and reliable set of platforms to advance their interests. One can only hope that expanding inequality, bringing with it visible public anger at the realization that the game is rigged and the deck is stacked against economic security and opportunity for the great majority of people in society, may eventually provoke them into effective challenges to the Haves. In the meantime, the Haves continue to increase their edge, and to stay ahead.

ROBERT W. GORDON
Professor of Law, Stanford University; and
Chancellor Kent Professor of Law and Legal History, Emeritus,
Yale University

Stanford, California
May, 2014

REFERENCES

ACEMOGLU, Daron & James A. ROBINSON (2012). *Why Nations Fail: The Origins of Power, Prosperity and Poverty.* New York: Crown Publishers.

ALSTOTT, Anne L. (2012). "Going Beyond Market Correction," *Boston Review,* Sunday, March 4, 2012. https://www.bostonreview.net/alstott-beyond-market-correction

ATKINSON, Anthony B., Thomas PIKETTY and Emmanuel SAEZ (2011). "Top Incomes in the Long Run of History," 49 *J. Econ. Lit.* 3.

BARTELS, Larry M. (2008). *Unequal Democracy: The Political Economy of the New Gilded Age.* New York and Princeton: Russell Sage Foundation and Princeton University Press.

BAKER, Dean (2011). *The End of Loser Liberalism.* Washington, DC: Center for Economic and Policy Research.

CLERMONT, Kevin M. and Stewart J. SCHWAB (2004). "How Employment Discrimination Plaintiffs Fare in Federal Court," 1 *J. Empirical Legal Stud.* 429.

——— (2009). "Employment Discrimination Plaintiffs in Federal Court: From Bad to Worse?" 3 *Harvard Law & Policy Rev.* 103.

COFFEE, John C. (1995) "Class Wars: The Dilemma of the Mass Tort Class Action," 95 *Colum. L. Rev.* 1343.

CRITCHLOW, Donald T. (2011). *The Conservative Ascendancy: How the Republican Right Rose to Power in Modern America.* Lawrence: Kansas University Press.

DANIELS, Stephen and Joanne MARTIN (2005). "The Texas Two-Step: Evidence on the Link Between Damage Caps and Access to the Civil Justice System," 55 *DePaul L. Rev.* 635.

EDWARDS, Haley Sweetland (2013). "He Who Makes the Rules," *Washington Monthly* (March/April 2013).

FARHANG, Sean (2010). *The Litigation State: Public Regulation and Private Lawsuits in the U.S.* Princeton: Princeton Univ. Press.

FREEMAN, Jody and Martha MINOW (eds.) (2009). *Government by Contract: Outsourcing and American Democracy.* Cambridge: Harvard University Press.

GALANTER, Marc (1974). "Why the 'Haves' Come Out Ahead: Speculations on the Limits of Legal Change," 9 *Law & Society Rev.* 95.

——— (1993). "News from Nowhere: The Debased Debate on Civil Justice," 71 *Denver U. L. Rev.* 77.

——— (2002). "The Turn Against Law: The Recoil Against Expanding Accountability," 81 *Texas L. Rev.* 285.

——— (2006). "Planet of the APs: Reflections on the Scale of Law and its Users," 53 *Buff. L. Rev.* 1369.

GOLDMAN, Sheldon (1997). *Picking Federal Judges from Roosevelt Through Reagan.* New Haven: Yale University Press.

GREENWALD, Glenn (2011). *With Liberty and Justice for Some: How the Law is Used to Destroy Equality and Protect the Powerful.* New York: Metropolitan Books.

HACKER, Jacob S. and Paul PIERSON (2010). *Winner Take-All Politics.* New York: Simon & Schuster.

HADFIELD, Gillian K. (2000). "The Price of Law: How the Market for Lawyers Distorts the Justice System," 98 *Mich. L. Rev.* 953.

HUBBARD, F. Patrick (2006). "The Nature and Impact of the 'Tort Reform' Movement, 35 *Hofstra L. Rev.* 437.

JACOBS, Lawrence R. and Theda SKOCPOL (eds.) (2005). *Inequality and American Democracy: What We Know and What We Need to Learn.* New York: Russell Sage Foundation.

JOHNSTON, David Cay (2003). *Perfectly Legal: The Covert Campaign to Rig Our Tax System to Benefit the Super-Rich and Cheat Everybody Else*. New York: Penguin.

KARLAN, Pamela S. (2003). "Disarming the Private Attorney General," 2003 *U. Ill. L. Rev.* 183.

KEENAN, David, Deborah Jane COOPER, David LEBOWITZ and Tamar LERER (2011). "The Myth of Prosecutorial Accountability under *Connick v. Thompson*: Why Existing Prosecutorial Measures Cannot Protect Against Prosecutorial Misconduct," *Yale L.J. Online*, October 25, 2011, viewed at http://www.yalelawjournal.org/the-yale-law-journal-pocket-part/supreme-court/the-myth-of-prosecutorial-accountability-after-connick-v.-thompson:-why-existing-professional-responsibility-measures-cannot-protect-against-prosecutorial-misconduct/

LESSIG, Larry (2011). *Republic, Lost: How Money Corrupts Congress, and a Plan to Stop it*. New York: Hachette.

LUBAN, David (2003). "'Taking Out the Adversary': The Assault on Progressive Public-Interest Lawyers," 91 *Calif. L. Rev.* 209.

LYNCH, Gerald (1998). "Our Administrative System of Criminal Justice," 66 *Fordham L. Rev.* 2117.

LUKES, Steven (2005). *Power: A Radical View* (2d ed.). London: Palgrave Macmillan.

MANKIW, N. Gregory (2013). "Defending the One Per Cent," 27 *J. Ec. Perspectives* 21.

MARTIN, Isaac William (2008). *Tax Revolt: How the Property Tax Transformed American Politics*. Stanford: Stanford University Press.

MARTIN, William Curtis (1996). *With God on our Side: The Rise of the Religious Right in America*. New York: Broadway Books.

McGARITY, Thomas (2008). *The Preemption War: When Federal Bureaucracies Trump Local Juries*. New Haven: Yale University Press.

NOAH, Timothy (2012). *The Great Divergence: America's Growing Inequality Crisis and What We Can Do About It*. New York: Bloomsbury Press.

NOVAK, William J. (2008). "The Myth of the Weak American State," 113 *Am. Hist. Rev.* 752.

OLSON, Mancur (1965). *The Logic of Collective Action*. Cambridge: Harvard University Press.

PARRILLO, Nicholas R. (2013). *Against the Profit Motive: The Salary Revolution in American Government, 1780-1940*. New Haven: Yale University Press.

PHILLIPS-FEIN, Kimberly (2009). *Invisible Hands: The Making of the Conservative Movement from the New Deal to Reagan*. New York: W.W. Norton.

PIKETTY, Thomas and Emmanuel A. SAEZ (2003). "Income Inequality in the United States, 1913-1998," 118 *Q. J. Econ.* 1.

— — — (2006). "The Evolution of Top Incomes: A Historical and International Perspective," NBER Working Paper 11955, National Bureau of Economic Research.

RAKOFF, Jed (2014). "The Financial Crisis: Why Have No High-Level Executives Been Prosecuted?" *N.Y. Rev. of Books*, January 9, 2014.

SAEZ, Emmanuel (2013). "Striking it Richer: The Evolution of Top Incomes in the United States." http://elsa.berkeley.edu/~saez/saez-UStopincomes-2012.pdf

SCHNEIDER, Elizabeth M. (2010). "The Changing Shape of Federal Civil Pretrial Practice: The Disparate Impact on Civil Rights and Employment Discrimination Cases," 158 *U. Pa. L. Rev.* 517.

SKOCPOL, Theda and Vanessa WILLIAMSON (2012). *The Tea Party and the Remaking of American Conservatism.* New York: Oxford University Press.

SOUTHWORTH, Ann (2008). *Lawyers of the Right: Professionalizing the Conservative Coalition.* Chicago: University of Chicago Press.

STITH, Kate and José CABRANES (1998). *Fear of Judging: Sentencing Guidelines in the Federal Courts.* Chicago: University of Chicago Press.

STIGLITZ, Joseph (2012). *The Price of Inequality: How Today's Divided Society Endangers our Future.* New York: W.W. Norton.

STUNTZ, William (2011). *The Collapse of American Criminal Justice.* Cambridge: Harvard University Press.

TELES, Steven (2008). *The Rise of the Conservative Legal Movement.* Princeton: Princeton University Press.

VERKUIL, Paul R. (2007). *Outsourcing Sovereignty: Why Privatization of Government Functions Threatens Democracy and What We Can Do About It.* Cambridge: Cambridge University Press.

WEINSTEIN, Jack (1995). *Individual Justice in Mass Tort Litigation.* Evanston: Northwestern University Press.

WILSON, James Q. (1974). "The Politics of Regulation," in *Social Responsibility and the Business Predicament*, 135 (James W. McKie, ed.). Washington, DC: Brookings Institution.

WINTERS, Jeffrey A. (2011). *Oligarchy.* Cambridge: Cambridge University Press.

CASES

American Express Co. v. Italian Colors Restaurant, 133 S. Ct. 2304 (2013)

Ashcroft v. Iqbal, 556 U.S. 662 (2009)

AT&T Mobility v. Concepcion, 563 U.S. 321 (2011)

Bell Atlantic Corp. v. Twombly, 550 U.S. 544 (2007)

Booker, United States v., 543 U.S. 220 (2005)

Buckhannon Board & Care Home, Inc. v. West Virginia Dept. of Health & Human Services, 532 U.S. 598 (2001)

Citizens United v. Federal Election Commission, 558 U.S. 310 (2010)

Communications Workers v. Beck, 487 U.S. 735 (1988)

Connick v. Thompson, 131 S. Ct. 1350 (2011)

First National Bank of Boston v. Bellotti, 435 U.S. 765 (1978)

Gideon v. Wainwright, 372 U.S. 335 (1963)

Gross v. FBL Financial Services, 557 U.S. 167 (2009)

Harris v. Quinn, 134 S. Ct. 896 (2014)

Hoffman Plastic Compounds, Inc. v. NLRB, 535 U.S. 137 (2002)

Kiobel v. Royal Dutch Petroleum Co., 133 S. Ct. 1659 (2013)

Knox v. Service Employees International Union, Local 1000, 132 S. Ct. 2277 (2012)

Ledbetter v. Goodyear Tire & Rubber Co., 550 U.S. 618 (2007)

Lujan v. Defenders of Wildlife, 504 U.S. 555 (1992)

Strickland v. Washington, 466 U.S. 668 (1984)

Wal-Mart Stores, Inc. v. Dukes, 131 S. Ct. 2541 (2011)

INDEX

Abel, Richard L., 2, 49; with Felstiner *et al.*, 94

Abel-Smith, Brian, 32

Acemoglu, Daron, 126

Access to Justice movement, 6

aggregation of OS claims, 55

adjudication defined, 15

Agnew, Spiro, 63

Albiston, Catherine, v

Allison, Paul D., 96

alternative dispute resolution (ADR)
    generally, iii, iv, 1, 6, 54, 99-100
    court-appended ADR, v, 100
    private mandatory, v
    private voluntary, v

American Association of Justice (AAJ), 6, 126; *see also* Association of Trial Lawyers of America (ATLA)

American Express Co. v. Italian Colors Restaurant, 122

American Legislative Exchange Council (ALEC), 116

"American rule" on attorneys' fees, 6, 125

"appended" settlement systems, v, 42-45, 48-49, 58-59

APs, *see* artificial persons

arbitration
    generally, vii, 30, 31,44, 56, 100, 122
    Supreme Court embrace of, 6, 122

Arnold, Thurman, 60

artificial persons (APs)
    advantages in litigation, 89-90
    capacity to litigate, 96
    criminal punishment, 102, 124
    definition, 7, 77
    cultural advantages, 8, 100-105
    endowed with constitutional rights, 124
    enlarged presence of, 98
    impact on courts, 98
    infirmities of, 79-80
    interaction with natural persons, 81
    population of, 81
    relation to repeat-players, 14

    shift in character, 97
    success rate of, 90-93

Ashcroft v. Iqbal, 123

Aspin, Leslie, 29, 31

Association of Trial Lawyers of America (ATLA), 6, 126; *see also* American Association of Justice (AAJ)

Atkins, Burton M., v, 94

Atkinson, Anthony B., 112

Atleson, James, 56

attacks on civil justice system, 5, 106-107

AT&T Mobility v. Concepcion, 122

attorneys' fees, recovery of, 6, 125

Aubert, Vilhelm, 29

Australia, High Court, v

Babcock, Richard, 3, 28, 60

Baker, Dean, 112

Baker, Scott, 103

Bartels, Larry, 115, 119

Bates, Alan, 26

Battle, Jackson B., 35

Begue, Laurent, 12

Bell Atlantic v. Twombley, 123

Bellow, Gary, 62

Bernstein, Marver, 54

Bergstrom, Randolph E., 108

Bill of Rights, 8, 78, 101

Bingham, Lisa, v, vi

Black, Donald J., 36, 42, 48, 52, 60

Blackstone, William, 77

Blumberg, Abraham S., 32, 34-35

Bogart, William A. (with Kritzer *et al.*), 95

Bohannan, Paul J., 47

Bonn, Robert L., 28, 31

Brill, Harry, 36, 57

Brill, Steven, 107

Brock, Dan W., 109

Buchanan, Allen, 109

About the Author

Marc Galanter, John and Rylla Bosshard Professor Emeritus of Law and South Asian Studies at the University of Wisconsin–Madison and formerly LSE Centennial Professor at the London School of Economics, studies litigation, lawyers and legal culture. He has written extensively on these topics, including *Tournament of Lawyers: The Transformation of the Big Law Firm* (1991) and *Lowering the Bar: Lawyer Jokes and Legal Culture* (2005). He has been editor of the *Law & Society Review*, President of the Law and Society Association, Chair of the International Commission on Folk Law and Legal Pluralism, a member of the Council on the Role of Courts, a Guggenheim Fellow, and a Fellow of the Center for Advanced Study in the Behavioral Sciences. He is a member of the American Law Institute and a Fellow of the American Academy of Arts and Sciences.

Galanter is recognized as a leading American student of Indian law. He is the author of *Competing Equalities: Law and the Backward Classes in India* (1984, 1991) and *Law and Society in Modern India* (1989, 1992) and many articles on the legal system and legal culture of India. He is an Honorary Professor of the National Law School of India and of the National Law University Delhi, served as advisor to the Ford Foundation on legal services and human rights programs in India, and was retained as an expert by the Government of India in the litigation arising from the Bhopal disaster. He is currently engaged in research on access to justice in India and in the United States.

Visit us at *www.quidprobooks.com.*

38187902R00094

Made in the USA
Lexington, KY
28 December 2014